# MODERN TIMES
## —— 1970-99 ——

## MODERN TIMES

# FOREWORD

To celebrate the turn of the century and the new millennium, **THE EVENTFUL CENTURY** series presents the vast panorama of the last hundred years—a century which has witnessed the transition from horse-drawn transport to space travel, and from the first telephones to the information superhighway.

**THE EVENTFUL CENTURY** chronicles epoch-making events like the outbreak of the two world wars, the Russian Revolution and the rise and fall of communism. But major events are only part of this glittering kaleidoscope. It also describes the everyday background—the way people lived, how they worked, what they ate and drank, how much they earned, the way they spent their leisure time, the books they read, and the crimes, scandals and unsolved mysteries that set them talking. Here are fads and crazes like the Hula-Hoop and Rubik's Cube . . . fashions like the New Look and the miniskirt . . . breakthroughs in entertainment, such as the birth of the movies . . . medical milestones such as the discovery of penicillin . . . and marvels of modern architecture and engineering.

**MODERN TIMES** describes the final three decades of the 20th century, from 1970, the year after the first Moon landing, to the beginning of a new millennium. In the 1970s, students in the United States were protesting the Vietnam War; the Cold War rivalry between the U.S. and the U.S.S.R. created tension in Europe, the Middle East, Latin America and Africa; and apartheid was still in place in South Africa. The Watergate Scandal brought down the Nixon Presidency, and the world was plunged into a recession by the oil crisis. Meanwhile, the pocket calculator was invented and feminism was popularized by the publication of Germaine Greer's *The Female Eunuch*. By the 1990s, communism had collapsed, South Africa had its first black president in Nelson Mandela, and Vietnam had become one of Southeast Asia's fastest growing economies. Financial markets operated on a global scale, tiny microchips controlled machines as diverse as personal computers, washing machines and missiles; satellites brought together international TV audiences for live sports and news events, and the Internet had emerged into the public domain, providing instant communication around the world.

# MODERN TIMES
## —1970-99—

Reader's
Digest

The Reader's Digest Association, Inc.
Pleasantville, New York/Montreal

**MODERN TIMES**
Edited and designed by Toucan Books Limited
Written by Antony Mason
Edited by Helen Douglas-Cooper,
Andrew Kerr-Jarrett, Jane MacAndrew
Designed by Bradbury and Williams
Picture research by Wendy Brown

**AMERICAN EDITION**
Edited and Produced by The Reference Works
Executive Editor Harold Rabinowitz
Editor Lorraine Martindale
Production Bob Antler, Antler Designworks

**READER'S DIGEST PROJECT STAFF**
Group Editorial Director  Fred Dubose
Senior Editor Susan Randol
Senior Designers Judith Carmel, Carol Nehring
Production Technology Manager Douglas A. Croll
Art Production Coordinator Jennifer R. Tokarski

**READER'S DIGEST ILLUSTRATED REFERENCE BOOKS**
Editor-in-Chief Christopher Cavanaugh
Art Director Joan Mazzeo

Printed in the United States of America.
Library of Congress Cataloging in Publication Data:

Modern times, 1970-99.
      p. cm—(The eventful 20th century)
      ISBN 0-7621-0272-1
      1. History, Modern—1945- I. Reader's Digest
         Association. II. Series.

      D848 .M63 2000
      909.82—dc21
                                    99-088341

FRONT COVER
From Top: Bill Gates of Microsoft; Washington Post
headline announcing Nixon's resignation; Earvin
"Magic" Johnson.

BACK COVER
From Top: Nelson Mandela; The destruction of the
Berlin Wall; Madonna.

Page 3 (from left to right): Madonna; *Blade Runner*
poster; terrorist; Margaret Thatcher and Ronald
Reagan.

Background pictures:
Page 15: An airplane blown up by terrorists, 1970.
Page 43: France's world-cup winning football team,
1998.
Page 83: Tokyo stock exchange, 1998.

# CONTENTS

# THE MODERN LABYRINTH

## AS THE WORLD STOOD ON THE THRESHOLD OF THE 1970S, A CONFUSION OF CHOICES LAY AHEAD

On March 4, 1970, newspapers around the world carried the obituary of a retired geologist who had spent most of his life in the Carribean testing soil samples for petroleum. In some cities, the obituary was carried on the front page. It was for John T. Scopes, a mild-mannered man who, as a school teacher in Dayton, Tennessee in the early 1920s, found himself at the center of one of the most celebrated trials of the twentieth century—the Scopes "monkey trial." Scopes had taught his class the rudiments of the theory of evolution, which at that time was a crime in Tennessee. The trial was the first one broadcast to the nation over radio and the first to become a "media circus," as the world listened to two celebrated orators, Clarence Darrow and William Jennings Bryan, go at it in the steamy courtroom.

Scopes was found guilty, but the verdict was overturned and the $100 fine ignored. It was not until 1967 that the law he had violated was repealed. Scopes had lived through odd and confusing times. Humankind had made great technological strides, but a World War had been fought in which millions died. At his death the world was in a state of more serious turmoil, facing the threat of total annihilation from the vicissitudes of the cold war. Would the next twenty years bring disaster, or would humankind triumph over its obstacles in the end?

In 1970, the United States was still deeply entrenched in Vietnam. President Nixon had promised troop withdrawals, and indeed American troops were being pulled out. But this gesture was accompanied by a broadening of the war through incursions into Cambodia and Laos, and more aerial bombing. That March, the B-52s of the U.S. Air Force were flying 200 bombing sorties a day over the Ho Chi Minh Trail, the Vietcong supply route through Laos. America seemed mired in a war it could not win, serving as little more than a costly and painful tourniquet to prevent the flow of communism through Southeast Asia. Daily news reports of napalm bombing, Vietcong ambushes and civilian casualties brutalized the whole world; the loss of thousands of young American men in this flawed cause deeply wounded the soul of the United States.

In 1970, the My Lai massacre of 1968 still seared the conscience of many Americans. Reports of the massacre—in which over 100 Vietnamese villagers, including women and babies, were mown down in a frenzy of savagery—had been revealed piecemeal. The instigator, Lieutenant William Calley, was arrested in November 1969; the court martial completed its work in March 1971, and Calley received a life sentence (later reduced to 20 years). "I would be extremely proud," declared Calley, "if My Lai shows the world what war is."

The Vietnam War had profound repercussions. "Make Love Not War" went the flower-power slogan of the hippies in the late 1960s, and Vietnam was the war they were thinking of. Anti-

**RIVAL LOYALTIES**
Badges for and against the Vietnam War.

**HELL NO, WE WON'T GO!**

**SUPPORT OUR BOYS IN VIET-NAM**

## KENT STATE

One of the focal points of the youth movement of the late 1960s was criticism of the war in Vietnam. In his 1968 presidential campaign Richard Nixon had promised to extract his nation from the war, and troop withdrawals began shortly after his election. It came as a deep shock when, in 1970, he authorized massive United States and South Vietnamese incursions into neutral Cambodia, under the pretext of destroying North Vietnamese bases there. This looked like escalation, not withdrawal.

Students on campuses around America reacted with protests, some of which turned violent. "Bums blowing up campuses" was how Nixon dismissed

**THE WAR COMES HOME** Disbelief was the first reaction to the shooting of four students during protests against the Vietnam War at Kent State University on May 4, 1970.

them in an unguarded moment. At Kent State University in Ohio, fire bombs and bottles were thrown, provoking the Ohio governor to call out the National Guard, the state militia. On the third day of rioting, some 300 protesters confronted the guardsmen, who responded to a barrage of stones with tear gas. When the guardsmen appeared to come under attack, they returned fire with live ammunition. Within minutes four students—two men and two women—lay dead; ten others were wounded.

Photographs of the incident were released on May 6, inspiring demonstrations at 115 American colleges. On May 9, Nixon was besieged at the White House by 100,000 protesters. Middle America began to deeply oppose the war. Something was very wrong with America's involvement in Vietnam if the war resulted in the deaths of young Americans on college campuses.

Vietnam demonstrations around the world became more vociferous and confrontational, and the extent of the rift within American society became clear when four student protesters were killed at Kent State University in Ohio in May 1970.

Left-wing and nationalist revolutionary groups saw America's involvement in Vietnam as a symbol of capitalist aggression; it set a standard for violence that was used to excuse the violence of terrorist action. Terrorism was rife in the 1970s in Israel, Argentina, Uruguay, the Basque country of Spain, Northern Ireland, and in Germany and Italy, where urban guerrillas such as the Baader-Meinhof group and the Red Brigades presented a lethal and unpredictable threat to the authorities. Hijackers and bombers readily exported their terrorism abroad. Any city dweller in Western Europe lived with the threat of being blown up by a terrorist bomb, or witnessing the aftermath of such an attack.

Nuclear Armageddon seemed a more remote possibility in the 1970s than during the 1960s, yet far from impossible. Each age has its vision of the apocalypse that seems absolutely real at the time, and nuclear war was that vision in the 1970s. For this reason the Campaign for Nuclear Disarmament (CND) drew large crowds of supporters to its regular demonstrations.

## A new broom

Vietnam and nuclear war, however, remained little more than a backdrop to most people's lives. "Make Love Not War" also referred to the sexual revolution that was sweeping across the Western world. One major change underpinning this was the increasing availability of the contraceptive pill, which freed women from the fear of pregnancy, while the legalization of abortion permitted

**BREAKING FREE** In 1969, braless demonstrators in Chicago still ran the risk of arrest for indecency. In the 1970s, many influential magazines such as *Ms.*, founded in 1972, began promoting the feminist cause. Gloria Steinem, the editor of *Ms.* magazine, is shown speaking at a news conference at the National Press Club in 1977.

women to deal with an unwanted pregnancy if contraception did not work. This meant that women could explore their sexuality with a freedom that had no precedent. The fashion for "hot pants"—short shorts for women that appeared in 1971—would not have been possible without this context.

With this sexual revolution came a new age of tolerance, the so-called "permissive society." Both men and women now expected to have more than one partner before settling down. And as many did not settle down, around the late 1970s single-parent families were becoming increasingly familiar. Homosexuals were encouraged to be more open. American gay activists began the process in New York in 1969; the first public demonstration by the Gay Liberation Front in London took place in November 1970.

Contraception and sexual liberation freed women from the pressure of conforming to a stereotypical life of marriage and babies; in feminist terms,

women could now "take control of their fertility." Feminism had taken a new and more strident tone in the late 1960s: the concept of "bra burning" had arisen from a demonstration against the Miss America Beauty

**DIRECT ACTION** Greenpeace took ecological protest to sea in *Rainbow Warrior*, confronting those involved in the dumping of toxic or nuclear waste and the slaughter of marine animals.

Contest in 1967. There was now a new, younger generation of feminist activists, who wanted to rewrite the book of gender behavior. There was also the older generation of women, who were often outraged by the lack of traditional feminine grace in such outspokenness, but who nonetheless resented the sexual inequalities against which ardent feminists railed. They found common ground in what became known as "Women's Lib."

The "generation gap" became a much-discussed phenomenon in the 1970s. Young people, it seemed, were almost duty-bound to distance themselves from their parents and all they stood for. Parents had to watch in dismay as their offspring grew their hair long, donned Afghan coats and flared pants, criticized the bourgeois aspirations of their elders, lived with members of the opposite sex without any long-term commitment, and disappeared to the other side of the world in search of adventure or a new religion. Some also indulged in mind-altering drugs that were illegal, little understood and potentially lethal. The deaths of rock stars Janis Joplin and Jimi Hendrix in 1970 and Jim Morrison in 1971 seemed to warn of the perils of the drug culture, while the film *The French Connection* (1971) gave a graphic account of the murky criminal world upon which youthful dabbling in drugs depended.

This clash of generations could, however, be interpreted as an effort by the young to rectify the ills of their world—a world that had produced urban terrorism and nuclear warheads. Some found the solution in religion. Eastern religions were in vogue, or at least derivative versions tailor-made for Westerners, such as the Hare Krishna movement and Transcendental Meditation. Others experimented in communal living, or retreated to the

**HERBAL REMEDIES** The age-old wisdom of Chinese medicine became popular, as dissatisfaction grew over the increasing dependency of Western medicine on drug-based cures controlled by the pharmaceutical industry.

countryside to become "self-sufficient" by growing their own food—often in a world colored by a quaint ruralist nostalgia. They explored health foods, vegetarianism, macrobiotics. They took drugs, but deplored the drug dependency of modern medicine, preferring instead to experiment with herbal treatments, acupuncture, homeopathy and other "alternative therapies." It added up to a gentle revolution, which over time left its mark on the lives of the older generation, as young and old learned a cautious mutual respect.

Many shared a common concern for the environment: terms such as conservation, ecology, acid rain and ozone layer entered common language. Greenpeace was founded in Canada in 1971. By the 1980s, for many the apocalyptic vision was not so much impending nuclear holocaust as catastrophic environmental destruction. Awareness of and care for the environment also started to become a commercial consideration: in 1976 Anita Roddick opened her Body Shop in England, the first in a multimillion-dollar chain selling ecofriendly soaps and cosmetics that had not been tested on animals.

**WOMAN AT THE TOP** Britain elected Margaret Thatcher as its first woman prime minister in May 1979. Here, she celebrates her second victory in 1983; a third came in 1987.

## THE MIGHTY MICROCHIP

> The single most influential innovation of the last three decades of the century could well be the silicon chip or microchip. It was first developed in 1970 by the Intel Corporation of California, whose Intel 8080 in 1974 became the first commercially successful microprocessor. The applications seemed limitless: microchip control systems could be introduced in cars, cash registers, washing machines, heating systems, toasters, as well as computers. By 1982, the potential of the microchip had begun to dawn, and *National Geographic* devoted a lead article by Allen A Boraiko to it:
>
> "It seems trifling, barely the size of a newborn's thumbnail and little thicker. The puff of air that extinguishes a candle would send it flying. In bright light it shimmers, but only with the fleeting iridescence of a soap bubble. It has a backbone of silicon, an ingredient of common beach sand, yet is less durable than a fragile glass sea sponge, largely made of the same material.
>
> "Still, less tangible things have given their names to an age, and the silver-gray fleck of silicon called the chip has ample power to create a new one. At its simplest the chip is electronic circuitry: Patterned in and on its silicon base are minuscule switches, joined by 'wires' etched from exquisitely thin films of metal. Under a microscope the chip's intricate terrain often looks uncannily like the streets, plazas, and buildings of a great metropolis, viewed from miles up.
>
> "Even more incongruous, a silicon flake a quarter of an inch on a side can hold a million electronic components, ten times more than 30-ton ENIAC, the world's first electronic digital computer. ENIAC was dedicated in 1946, the ancestor of today's computers that calculate and store information, using memory and logic chips. But ENIAC's most spectacular successor is the microprocessor—a 'computer on a chip.' This prodigy is 30,000 times as cheap as ENIAC, draws the power of a night-light instead of a hundred lighthouses, and in some versions performs a million calculations a second, 200 times as many as ENIAC ever could.
>
> "The chip would be extraordinary enough if it were only low-cost, compact electronics, but its ability to embody logic and memory gives it the essence of human intellect. So, like the mind, the chip has virtually infinite application—and the same potential to alter life fundamentally."

However, the next generation had no patience for this afterglow of the hippie culture. There had long been a violent, anarchic undercurrent in industrialized cities, seen in the skinhead culture that emerged in the late 1960s, and explored in Stanley Kubrick's film *A Clockwork Orange* (1971). In 1975 its new manifestation, punk rock, burst onto stage and screen, hard-edged, foul-mouthed and anti-social. At its heart was anarchic, raucous music that celebrated energy and venom more than musicianship. Indeed, as some punk rockers have explained, musicianship could be a positive disadvantage. But punk's heyday was comparatively short-lived: the negativity of punk quickly ran its course.

### Technology gathers pace

A more significant lifestyle revolution was taking place off-camera, and mainly in California, home of the hippies. But now the focus had shifted from Haight-Ashbury to San Jose, Santa Clara, and Palo Alto—an area to the south of San Francisco that would soon become known as "Silicon Valley." During the early 1970s, companies such as the Intel Corporation at Santa Clara, founded in 1968 by Robert Noyce and Gordon Moore, were finding ways to pile thousands of transistors and electrical circuits onto tiny pieces of silicon to create microchips and microprocessors. The result was to miniaturize computing technology, make it infinitely more powerful, and also make it far cheaper to buy and to run. A wave of inventions followed, starting with the pocket calculator, and moving rapidly to the Personal Computer (PC). The trajectory was phenomenal: the second-generation transistor-based computers of the 1960s could execute 100,000 instructions a second; the Intel 8088 microprocessor of 1981, with 29,000 electrical components, could perform 400,000 instructions a second, while Intel's Pentium processor of 1993, containing 3.2 million transistors, could execute 100 million instructions a second.

The first PC was produced by Apple in 1977. It seemed helpful as a business tool, but few people thought it had any real application for the home. Who needed a computer to calculate the gas bill? But this was before the potential of the computer for wordprocessing had been fully understood. By the 1980s, it had become clear that the typewriter was doomed. Small "desktop" computers were beginning to invade offices, banks, insurance companies and hospitals. The information revolution was under way.

A totally new branch of science developed called Information Technology (IT), as com-

**STANLEY KUBRICK'S CLOCKWORK ORANGE**

**URBAN NIGHTMARE** Stanley Kubrick's *A Clockwork Orange* (1971), based on a novel by Anthony Burgess, was a bleak vision of a near future in which a sadistic gang pursues a course of mayhem, violence and rape.

puters became linked to the expanding web of telecommunications. But this all lay some way in the future. In 1970, most people still had telephones with dials on them, based on the Siemens Neophone introduced in 1929.

To the public at large the real cutting edge of technology still seemed to be space exploration. *Apollo 13*, launched in April 1970, turned out to be a dramatic failure, redeemed by the extraordinary resourcefulness of NASA scientists and the fortitude of the three astronauts. There had been an air of complacency about this third visit to the Moon, before an explosion in the Service Module revealed just how risky these Apollo

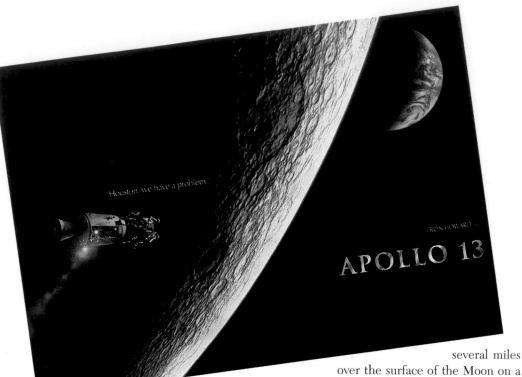

"Houston, we have a problem."

RON HOWARD

APOLLO 13

**A LONG WAY FROM HOME** The 1995 film *Apollo 13* was based largely on transcripts from the real flight in 1970. Apollo represented the cutting-edge technology of space exploration, but it was belt-and-braces improvisation that brought the stricken craft back to Earth.

missions had always been. "Houston, we have a problem," was astronaut Jim Lovell's famous understatement. Through three and a half days of high tension, NASA managed to guide the crippled spacecraft around the Moon so that it could be flung back to Earth, and the three astronauts returned safely. In 1971, the *Apollo 14* astronauts trundled for

### THE BEATLES SPLIT

One of the most successful and influential pop groups in all history, the Beatles split up on April 10, 1970, due to business, personal, and artistic differences. Paul McCartney, who marked the end of an era by deciding to leave the group, stated that he wanted to spend more time with his family. The Beatles—who rose from the streets of Liverpool, England—turned American rock and roll into one of the most vital art forms of the last few decades of the century. The four Beatles—John Lennon, Paul McCartney, Ringo Starr and George Harrison—are known for albums such as *Sgt. Pepper's Lonely Hearts Club Band* and *The White Album*, which demonstrate their innovative and experimental style.

several miles over the surface of the Moon on a "Moon Rover." That same year, three Soviet cosmonauts returning from a 23 day stay on the Salyut space station died when their spacecraft depressurized. The inadequate technology of the Soviet space program was revealed. *Apollo 17* in 1972 was the last manned Moon landing of the century. The Apollo series represented an extraordinary leap forward since the first man in space in 1961.

Back on Earth, a new age of technology could be detected in architecture. The Sydney Opera House was completed in 1973, and its striking shell-like composition soon made it an international landmark on a par with the Taj Mahal and the Eiffel Tower. Arguably, however, this was more the product of the 1950s: Jørn Utzon's design had won the competition way back in 1957. More controversial were the "inside-out" designs by the British architects Richard Rogers and Norman Foster—a trend that resulted in the controversial Pompidou Center, designed by Rogers and Renzo Piano and completed in 1977.

### Intregration in Europe

Less innovative was the Berlaymont Building in Brussels. A curved, cross-shaped tower-block, the building was completed in 1970 as the new home for the Commission of the European Community (EC); with its line of multinational flags outside, it became a familiar symbol for the EC.

At the beginning of the decade the EC

still consisted of the six founder-members that had signed the 1957 Treaty of Rome. Throughout the 1960s, General de Gaulle of France had stood in the way of British entry; he remained president until 1969, and died in November 1970. By this time, Britain was negotiating entry, and in 1972 it signed the Treaty of Rome, along with Denmark and Ireland. These nine, then ten, then twelve and then fifteen countries embarked on a long and much disputed path of European integration—attempting to bury historical and economic differences to form a cohesive trading and political unit. In 1970, however, the European Community was primarily a trading consortium, designed to promote,

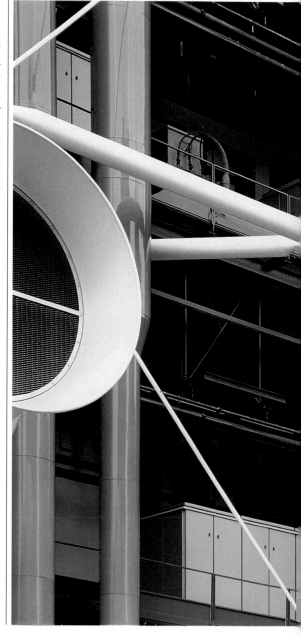

protect and standardize internal trade.

At the same time, Greece remained under the iron fist of the colonels, whose cruel and repressive regime had led to international ostracism; Spain was still ruled by General Franco. Both nations had failed to partake in the prosperity that much of Western Europe was enjoying.

In Britain, the royal family, which would come to occupy so much of the world's media attention in the coming decades, was still young and optimistic. In 1970, Prince Charles was 22 and about to join the Royal Naval College, Dartmouth. The future Diana, Princess of Wales, was nine. Princess Anne was the first of the Queen's children to marry, in 1973. The Queen's sister Princess Margaret was the first to divorce, in 1978.

The Conservative leader Edward Heath was the victor of the election in June 1970, defeating the Labor government of Harold Wilson. It was the first election in which 18-year-old individuals could vote: the voting age, and the age of majority, had been reduced from 21 to 18 in January. The Conservative government inherited persis-

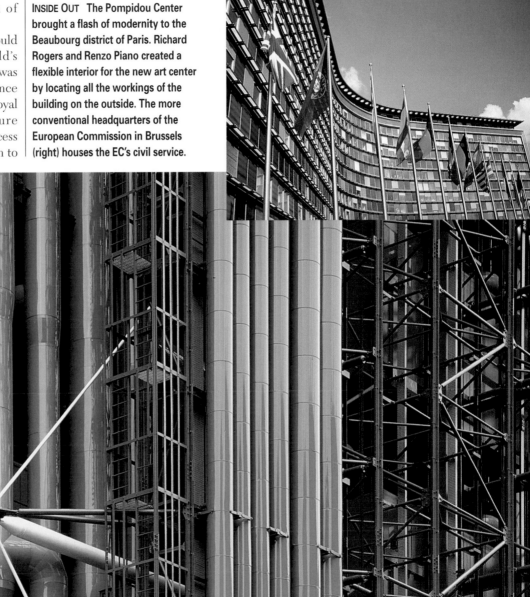

**INSIDE OUT** The Pompidou Center brought a flash of modernity to the Beaubourg district of Paris. Richard Rogers and Renzo Piano created a flexible interior for the new art center by locating all the workings of the building on the outside. The more conventional headquarters of the European Commission in Brussels (right) houses the EC's civil service.

## THE OIL CRISIS

**OIL SHEIK** Saudi Arabia's oil minister, Sheik Ahmed Zaki Yamani, was a key figure in OPEC's oil strategy following the 1973 Arab-Israeli War.

The Western world enjoyed an unprecedented boom in the postwar years until the early 1970s. Then came a sudden economic catastrophe. In sympathy with the Arab nations engaged in the Yom Kippur War with Israel, on October 17, 1973, the Organization of Petroleum Exporting Countries (OPEC) raised the price of crude oil by 70 percent, and imposed an oil embargo on the U.S. and selected allies.

During the boom years the Western industrial nations had become increasingly dependent on OPEC oil, nearly all of which came from Saudi Arabia and the Gulf states. OPEC nonetheless was a cartel, and in 1973, as the U.S. and Western powers showed support for Israel, OPEC decided to use its power for political ends. Not only was the price increased, but OPEC also reduced production, creating a scarcity that boosted the price still further. Saudi Arabia, with 30 percent of the world's reserves, played a key role in this policy, led by its oil minister Sheik Yamani. Equating him with a highway robber, the British press quipped: "Yamani or your life." The Western nations were plunged into crisis. Preparations were made for possible gas rationing, speed limits were lowered to save fuel, factories were put on short weeks, prices rose. OPEC found that the high price of oil was sustainable, and prices rose even after the war had been settled. In 1972, crude oil cost $3 a barrel; by the end of 1973, the price had reached $18 a barrel.

The oil-producing nations became exceptionally wealthy, giving them the means to diversify their industries, and to buy businesses and properties abroad. In the meantime, the Western nations developed their own oil resources, such as North Sea oil and the Alaska fields, reduced oil consumption and looked for alternatives. But this took time, and the recession caused by the 1973-4 oil crisis lasted a decade.

tent labor troubles, as the powerful unions flexed their muscles: 6 million working days were lost in the first six months of 1970 alone. Postal workers went on strike in 1971, for the first time ever. In February 1972, industry was forced to work a three-day week because of power shortages induced by a miners' strike.

There was also the growing problem of Northern Ireland. Troops had been dispatched to Ulster in 1969 to protect the Catholic minority from intercommunal violence. By 1970, these same troops were resented by both the Protestants and the Catholics, and so began three long and bloody decades of "peacekeeping." In August 1970, British soldiers used rubber bullets for the first time in an attempt to quell rioters. In February 1971, the first British soldiers were killed; under emergency powers, internment without trial was reintroduced, sparking off four days of rioting in August. A campaign of Christmas bombing in Belfast included a pub bomb that killed 15. During a demonstration the following January, 13 Catholics were killed by British paratroopers, on the so-called "Bloody Sunday." A new corner had been turned, and from that day on the violence, bombing, resentment, and tragedy escalated.

### Troubled world

In January 1970, the Biafran War came to a close. The attempt by the Igbo-dominated region of Biafra to secede from Nigeria had taken a huge toll, not just in war casualties, but through starvation and disease caused by the blockade. Estimates of deaths range from 500,000 to several million, many of them children. The tragedy pricked the conscience of the world, and resolutions were made to prevent such a humanitarian catastrophe occurring again. But old sores of historic conflict, the legacy of colonial rule, and natural disasters meant that large-scale human tragedy was constantly in the news.

In November 1970, East Pakistan was devastated by a typhoon, which was estimated to have killed 150,000. The following year the two halves of Pakistan went to war, out of which East Pakistan emerged as independent Bangladesh, but at the cost of at least a million deaths and a refugee crisis that brought starvation to 2 million.

There were repressive military dictatorships across Latin America—in Brazil,

Ecuador, Bolivia, Paraguay, Guatemala and Panama. In Haiti, the reviled dictator and self-acclaimed "president-for-life," Dr. François Papa Doc Duvalier, died in April 1971, to be succeeded by his son Jean-Claude (Baby Doc), aged 19, who continued in the style of his father.

For those trying to escape turmoil and poverty in their own countries, emigration remained an option, but this became increasingly difficult. The British Conservative MP Enoch Powell, who had made his notorious "Rivers of Blood" speech in 1968, campaigned against immigration and demanded repatriation of immigrants, always hinting at the dangers of a racial backlash. His attitudes caused deep controversy, and were largely rejected by the young, but he appeared to voice a fundamental racism in British society, which

**BABY DOC** Jean-Claude Duvalier became ruler of Haiti in 1971. At the mere age of 19, he was the world's youngest president.

inspired a series of race relations initiatives in the mid 1970s, as well as immigration controls.

The United States continued to witness regular outbursts of racial hatred: in 1970, white mobs attacked school buses carrying black children, and six people died in race riots in Georgia. The continuing iniquities of apartheid had rendered South Africa a pariah state. In 1970, South African cricketers were prevented from travelling to England by a successful anti-apartheid campaign, adding to South Africa's isolation.

The United States and the Soviet Union fought for control over the troubled countries in the Third World, using foreign aid as a lever. In 1971, the Aswan High Dam in southern Egypt was inaugurated. The mammoth project had taken 11 years to build, with technical and financial aid from the Soviet Union, and it required the

removal of the ancient Abu Simbel Temple, funded by UNESCO. Upon its completion, relations with neighboring Israel were so poor that the dam was a major strategic liability, and the surrounding hills bristled with armaments to defend it from attack.

Considerable change was taking place in the Arab world around 1970. In September 1969, the left-wing Islamic revolutionary Colonel Moammar al-Gaddafi had led the

**REJECTIONIST FRONT** Combining revolutionary zeal and Islamic piety, President Gaddafi has taken an uncompromising line with Israel, rejecting any negotiations. He has also given active support to terrorism, and tried to intervene in Egypt, Sudan and Chad.

VOTE HERE

**THE END OF APARTHEID** In 1994, democratic elections were held in South Africa for the first time. Four years earlier, Nelson Mandela had been released from prison, and was given a rapturous reception on his return to Soweto (right).

coup that brought him to power in Libya. President Nasser of Egypt, a major figurehead and inspiration to many Arabs, died in September 1970, to be succeeded by Anwar al-Sadat. In November, the military wing of the Ba'ath Party took power in Syria, and Hafez al-Assad became president. Both Gaddafi and Assad proved to be radical and somewhat unpredictable players in the politics of the Middle East, but managed to retain power until the end of the century.

The Arab-Israeli conflict and the dispute over Palestine remained an ongoing sore of world politics. This dispute, in 1973, resulted in a world crisis, defining the end of the postwar boom. After the Yom Kippur War that year, the Organization of Petroleum Exporting Countries (OPEC) imposed a five-month embargo on oil exports to the United States and other Western nations that had supported Israel, and tripled the price of crude oil.

It was a lesson in one of the major themes of the final decades of the century: the world, and pivotal world events, were becoming increasingly interconnected. "Globalization" became one of the buzzwords of the era. This provided a useful system of checks and balances. On the other hand, what at one time might look like pillars of support could at others appear to be dominoes lined up and ready to fall.

In the early 1970s, the world appeared to be a dangerous, complex and volatile place, filled with risky choices and potential pitfalls—a modern labyrinth. In the ceaseless tension of the Cold War, a slip-up in foreign policy could possibly lead to nuclear holocaust. The newspapers were filled with the horrors of the Vietnam War; the Arabs and the Israelis were caught in the deadlock of mutually irreconcilable ambition; South America was straddled between revolutionary socialist armed struggle and right-wing dictatorship; South Africa's apartheid regime was the ill-fitting lid on a tinderbox; the problems in Northern Ireland seemed to be spiralling into the abyss. But in the ensuing decades came the United States' withdrawal from Vietnam; the Camp David Peace Accords; the arrival of democracy in South America; the collapse of communism and the Soviet bloc; the release of Nelson Mandela and the end of apartheid; the Good Friday Agreement bringing hope to Northern Ireland. The world was just as complex and complicated, but it perhaps seemed a little less threatening.

**T**HE 1970S OPENED TO A WORLD IN CONFLICT, AS THE SUPERPOWERS EYED EACH OTHER SUSPICIOUSLY OVER DEFENSES BRISTLING WITH NUCLEAR WEAPONS. AS THEY EDGED FALTERINGLY TOWARD DÉTENTE, THE TENSIONS WERE PLAYED OUT BY PROXY IN VIETNAM, CAMBODIA, ANGOLA, CHILE, AND ELSEWHERE. THIS VOLATILE WORLD ALSO PROVED FERTILE GROUND FOR FANATICAL IDEALISTS WHO TOOK UP ARMS AS TERRORISTS, AND WHO HAD A DISPROPORTIONATE IMPACT ON THE ERA.

# A DIVIDED WORLD

## DESPITE NEGOTIATIONS TO LIMIT NUCLEAR ARMS, THE COMMUNIST COUNTRIES AND THE WEST STILL REMAINED WORLDS APART

In 1970 the dark cloud that hung over world politics went by the apt acronym MAD—Mutual Assured Destruction. Facing each other across the Iron Curtain were enough nuclear warheads to annihilate the world several times over—the product of the Cold War, the arms race of the 1960s, and the intense distrust between the superpowers.

For the Soviet Union, this was something of a triumph: the U.S.S.R. had achieved parity in weaponry with America. Marxist theory saw this position as the threshold of a new world. With nuclear weapons effectively neutralized, popular uprisings and liberation movements using conventional weapons could flourish. Capitalism would be on the defensive and communism would prevail.

To the United States it represented an untenable position: the arms race was an economic and political black hole that threatened postwar prosperity and international stability. In the nervous atmosphere of international relations, any minor incident could potentially escalate into a catastrophic nuclear war. For President Richard Nixon, who took office in 1969, addressing the inherent dangers of superpower confrontation was a key issue in his policy. The buzzword was détente (French for relaxation), aimed at reducing tension for the sake of stability, without loss of face. His more conciliatory approach represented a radical break from the confrontational bravado of the Cold War that had dominated the 1960s.

### Common interests

Broadly speaking, the United States and the Western world remained deeply distrustful of the communist powers. Outright opposition to communism had been diluted by the horror of the Vietnam War, the excesses of right-wing military dictatorships, and the revolutionary romanticism of the Western youth movement, but there was enough evidence of the domestic abuses of communist regimes to keep the battle lines drawn clearly enough. The Czechoslovak bid for reform and democratization had been brutally crushed by the Soviet invasion in 1968; dissidents within the Soviet Union were still being persecuted and condemned to labor camps; East Germans were being shot as they tried to flee across the Berlin Wall to escape the limitations of their regime. In China, ordinary people were still suffering the bitter consequences of the Cultural Revolution's deliberate state of turmoil. Communist society had promised fairness for all, but equality was being achieved only by levelling the masses beneath the weight of bureaucratic and often unintelligible oppression.

By 1970, it was clear that the Soviet economy really was groaning beneath the weight of the Cold War. The inscrutable gray faces of the Soviet leadership, as they lined the

**DIVIDED CITY** The Brandenburg Gate symbolized the division of Berlin. Formerly the setting for national celebrations, it lay behind the Wall, just inside the Soviet sector.

---

### THE BERLIN WALL

In *The Spectator* of August 18, 1979, the historian Alistair Horne described crossing the Berlin Wall from the capitalist West to the communist East:

"First of all, four pages of bossy instructions dictate what you may not import: 'Calendars, almanacs and diaries, stamps and stamp catalogues'; records ('unless works of the cultural heritage,' whatever that might mean); newspapers ('unless on the postal list of the DDR'); books 'whose content is aimed against the preservation of peace'; children's toys 'of a military character'; films 'whose content is hostile to the Socialist State' (by some amazing attempt at augury, this also includes unexposed film). Meanwhile, the copious list of banned exports revealingly covered most foodstuffs and textiles.

"So much for the Spirit of Helsinki and Ostpolitik. Subserviently we left our Vogues and Country Lifes in a locker in West Berlin airport. At the frontier we waited an hour (apparently, a very good day), submitting to various checks and form-filling, while a disembodied hand (possibly female) grabbed our passports through a slot in a wooden box. A perfect Le Carré setting, I was thinking when—as we sat in that grim No-Man's-Land—my traveling companion inquired sweetly and with superlative timing: 'Tell me, were you ever a spy?' The question being, strangely, not on the declaration form, I expected the alarms to ring and robot guns to start firing at us through that wooden slot. But, mysteriously we were waved through, and into the Socialist paradise."

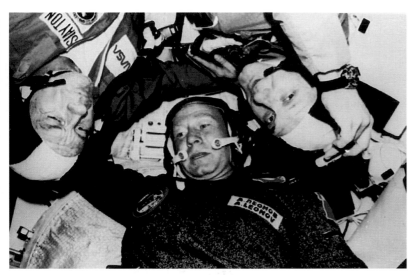

**DÉTENTE IN SPACE**  In July 1975 the Soyuz and Apollo missions met in space. Soviet cosmonaut Aleksey Leonov (center) greets U.S. astronaut Donald Slayton (left).

Kremlin walls for the traditional May Day parade of military might, masked deep worries. Leonid Brezhnev had taken power as Communist Party leader in 1964, determined to enforce a hard-line agenda to redress the liberal tendencies of Khrushchev. His economic strategy was designed to bolster the military and heavy industry, at the expense of agriculture, social welfare and the consumer goods that would have offered some comfort to the Soviet people for their toil. The result was that the Soviet economy had stagnated, and the people were locked into a grim and impoverished world of empty shops and the corruption of black markets. By now, even their leaders were looking for new routes toward progress.

## SALT

In November 1969 the U.S.S.R. and America initiated talks to try to find a way of controlling arms development and military spending. Both sides acknowledged that Mutual Assured Destruction carried with it—almost by inverse logic—a kind of stability: it would be suicidal for one country to initiate war, knowing that it would also be destroyed. A real threat to this stability would emerge, however, if one state had the means to survive the first nuclear attack, or could neutralize any counterattack. This scenario looked feasible with the development of anti-ballistic missiles (ABMs), designed to take out incoming missiles. The bilateral Strategic Arms Limitation Talks (SALT) were set up to address this problem, as well

as to look at limiting the number of long-range or intercontinental ballistic missiles (ICBMs). The negotiations were finally concluded in May 1972, when Richard Nixon and Leonid Brezhnev signed the first SALT agreement in Moscow. Both sides were restricted to two ABM launch sites and, under an interim agreement, the number of ICBMs were limited to current levels for five years, during which negotiations would continue.

The United States reinforced the deals with packages of civilian assistance, such as grain sales and the exchange of technical know-how, all of which helped to bind the U.S.S.R. into the new relationship. This car-

rot-and-stick policy, known as "linkage," built a degree of flexibility into superpower relations, and created a buffer zone for negotiations that helped to shore up stability. For Nixon it was a constructive and realistic reinterpretation of the United State's old anticommunist policy of "containment."

There were other more symbolic gestures, such as an agreement in 1972 to begin cooperating in space exploration. In 1975 three American and three Soviet astronauts brought their orbiting Apollo and Soyuz missions together, and spent four days working together on joint projects. The space race, a toy of the old Cold War mentality, had become a thing of the past.

Europe, meanwhile, was also anxious to defuse tensions. Western European countries stood at the front line before the Iron Curtain, and they feared becoming the main theater of battle in a nuclear confrontation. West Germany's chancellor, Willy Brandt, attempted a rapprochement with Soviet-dominated East Germany and the Warsaw

## THE TERRACOTTA ARMY

In March 1974 farmers drilling a well near the ancient city of Xi'an, central China, struck a life-size terracotta model of a soldier. It was the start of one of the greatest archaeological discoveries of all time. In three huge pits stood rank upon rank of clay soldiers, about 8,000 in all, both infantry and cavalry. They were portrayed wearing the clothes and armor of the Chinese army of over 2,000 years ago, and bore authentic weapons of the time— bows and swords with blades still sharp. The bodies of the figures were cast from molds, but each of the faces had been individually modeled.

These were the guardians in the afterlife of Emperor Qin Shi Huang Di (221-210 BC), who unified China and founded the Qin or Ch'in dynasty. At the center of the 500 acre site is his tomb beneath a pyramid-shaped tumulus, yet to be excavated. The complex is reputed to have taken 700,000 workmen 36 years to construct.

Excavations are set to continue for decades, accompanied by meticulous restoration of the broken fragments. Meanwhile the site has become one of China's key tourist attractions.

**HOLDING THE LINE**  The restored clay soldiers stand as they were 2,000 years ago. Only their layers of bright paint have disappeared.

**SPREADING THE WORD** An impressionable younger generation in China responded enthusiastically to the call of the Cultural Revolution, spreading its message by propaganda, militaristic discipline and terror.

Pact—the Soviet bloc's answer to NATO, founded in 1955—under what he termed Ostpolitik (east policy); but it was hard going, yielding little more than brief openings of the Berlin Wall to allow divided families to see their relatives. Then, in 1974, one of his close aides was revealed as an East German spy, and Brandt was left with no option but to resign—a victim of the Cold War.

On a broader front, the Conference on Security and Cooperation in Europe (CSCE)

**DIPLOMATIC FEAST** President Nixon's visit to China in 1972 marked a turning point in Cold War relations. Once a fervent anti-communist, Nixon was greeted cautiously but cordially by Mao (right) and Zhou Enlai (below left).

was set up in 1972, and reached agreement in a document signed in Helsinki in 1975 by all the European countries from both sides of the Iron Curtain (with the exception of Albania under its hardline Stalinist leader Enver Hoxha), plus the United States and Canada. The "Helsinki Accords" committed the signatories to respecting the existing frontiers of Europe (thereby accepting the borders drawn up after the Second World War), and reaffirmed the principle of non-interference in the internal affairs of other nations. This was the part of the agreement for which the U.S.S.R. and the Warsaw Pact countries had been pushing since the 1960s.

The West's quid pro quo was to demand closer cooperation with the Soviet bloc in areas such as trade, science, technology and the environment, and a commitment to respect basic human rights and liberties. The accords were not binding and lacked teeth: whenever the West criticized the Soviet bloc countries for human rights abuses, they would vehemently protest that these were internal affairs. But Helsinki provided an important benchmark.

### The China card

Nixon had been able to put pressure on the U.S.S.R. by bringing China into the superpower equation. This move had an unlikely origin in ping-pong. In early 1971, China invited Western international table tennis teams to take part in an informal tournament. It included the first Americans to visit China officially in nearly 25 years. The pragmatic veteran leader Zhou Enlai, premier since 1949, called the event "a new page in the relations between the Chinese and American people." Nixon saw an opening to this vital but politically isolated country, and in July 1971 he dispatched his assistant for national security, Henry Kissinger, on a secret mission to China to take the temperature. Then in February 1972 Nixon made an official visit, a turning point in superpower politics. "Ping-pong diplomacy" continued to provide a non-controversial background for a political thaw over several years.

China had distanced itself from the U.S.S.R. in 1959, and relations had deteriorated further in the late 1960s. The U.S.S.R. justified its invasion of Czechoslovakia in 1968 on the grounds that it reserved the right to intervene in any communist country that deviated from the path of the Revolution—a policy that became known as the Brezhnev Doctrine. From 1966 on, Soviet troops had been mass-

ing on the Chinese border, and a series of clashes ensued. The Chinese began to fear that the Brezhnev Doctrine might be applied to them. Hence China saw it as expedient to engage in some bridge-building with the United States.

Nixon had staked much of his early career on his anti-communist campaigns, so for many the image of him smiling on the Great Wall and chatting with Chairman Mao Zedong seemed incongruous; but to his conservative public, Nixon's record as an anti-communist carried reassurances that he was not about to have the wool pulled over his eyes. The strategy paid off: it made the Soviet leaders more circumspect, and sharpened their desire to reach agreement in arms negotiations. Nixon was able to show himself to be even-handed by traveling to Moscow in May 1972 to sign the SALT agreements.

But Chinese politics remained hard to fathom. In the late 1960s the excesses of the "Red Guard" phase of the Cultural Revolution, and the chaos that ensued, threatened to undermine popular support for Mao, and erase all his achievements. Ever the cunning politician, in 1968 he raised the military supremo Lin Biao, a leading figure in the Long March, to a position of power, citing the Soviet military threat. By grooming Lin as his successor, Mao was essentially reinforcing his position with the army. In response to a renewed build-up of Soviet arms along the border and incursions into Xinkiang in northwestern China in 1969, Lin declared martial law. But Lin had overstepped his brief, and the leadership was now split. On the one side were those led by Mao's radical wife Jiang Qing, who was a central figure in the Cultural Revolution; on the other were those who supported Lin. The former prevailed, Lin was sidelined, and he allegedly died in a plane crash in September 1971, while fleeing to the Soviet Union after a failed coup.

As Mao weakened in old age, the Cultural Revolution staggered on, but was now tempered by the moderate voice of Zhou Enlai, whose position had been unaffected by the Jiang-Lin feud. Faced with renewed economic chaos, in 1973 Mao and Zhou brought the moderate Deng Xiao-ping back into the limelight as deputy premier. A supporter of a more liberal form of economy driven by incentives, Deng had been purged by the

## WATERGATE

With the nation divided over Vietnam and the economy faltering, the United States was already suffering a loss of confidence when it was plunged into a crisis reaching the highest level of government—the president himself.

On June 17, 1972, during the run-up to the presidential election in which the Republican Richard Nixon was re-elected, five burglars had been caught in an attempt to raid and bug the Democratic Party's election headquarters in a complex of offices and apartments called Watergate in Washington DC. It transpired that the culprits were veteran CIA operatives working for a Republican organization called the Committee to Re-Elect the President (CREEP). Documents they carried linked them directly to White House staff. The following year two journalists working for the *Washington Post*, Bob Woodward and Carl Bernstein, began to unearth evidence of a massive cover-up within the White House, involving senior Republican aides close to the president. Slowly but surely the journalists, federal judge John Sirica and a Senate committee peeled back the layers of the conspiracy.

One of the burglars revealed that he and his accomplices had been under pressure from the White House to remain silent, and that the former attorney general John N. Mitchell had authorized the break-in. Bit by bit the White House's version of events began to fall apart as the participants spilled the beans. In June 1973 the president's legal adviser, John W. Dean III, told the Senate committee that the White House chief of staff, Bob Haldeman, and the chief domestic affairs adviser, John Ehrlichman, were involved in the cover-up. But was the president himself involved? It was a charge that Nixon denied: "I am not a crook," he famously declared.

In July 1973, investigators discovered that Nixon had taped his conversations in the Oval Office. Faced with unrelenting legal pressure, he was obliged to release transcripts of the tapes in December 1973. When a critical 18-minute section of one tape was missing, supposedly deleted in error by his secretary, Nixon's credibility began to wear thin. In May 1974 moves were made to begin impeaching the president on the grounds of obstruction of justice, abuse of power and defiance of subpoenas. In late July Nixon came under pressure from his own legal staff to release transcripts relating to days after the break-in. On July 27 the House Judiciary Committee voted for impeachment. On August 5 Nixon released three vital transcripts that showed that he had approved pay-offs to the burglars to buy their silence, and that he had been lying ever since. Nixon resigned on August 8, the first president to do so.

**NEWS HOUNDS  Two key players in the Watergate story were *Washington Post* reporters Carl Bernstein (left) and Bob Woodward.**

**THE DECENT THING On August 8, 1974, Nixon resigned rather than face impeachment.**

**ROASTED BEFORE THE COURTS** Mao's radical wife Jiang Qing (left) and the other members of her "Gang of Four" were arrested a month after Mao's death in September 1976. They were tried in 1980-81, found guilty and condemned to long prison sentences.

Cultural Revolution in 1967. In 1975, he sought to promote technological advances via the "Four Modernizations": agriculture, industry, science and technology, and defense. However, his rehabilitation was seen as a challenge by Jiang Qing and her associates, who managed to oust him again when Zhou died in January 1976. But when the public used the traditional Ch'ing-Ming festival in Beijing to express their esteem for the late Zhou, it was clear that the radicals had lost popular support.

## Changing of the guard

Nixon's significant achievements in foreign policy were not matched by his performance at home. Inflation was running high; the economy was beginning to stumble under the effect of the oil crisis; Vietnam remained a sore wound, and his government was tarnished with corruption. Re-elected with a convincing mandate in 1972, within months his vice-president, Spiro Agnew, had been forced to resign over corruption charges. Nixon had long been labeled "Tricky Dick"; as the Watergate bugging scandal began to unravel in 1973, his claim to integrity looked increasingly fragile. After months of clinging to office amid a growing howl of national indignation, he was forced to resign in August 1974. He was replaced by his vice

president, Gerald Ford, who tried to maintain Nixon's foreign policy initiatives over the next two years, and kept Kissinger on as secretary of state. But Ford was decisively swept from office in 1977 by the Democrat Jimmy Carter, a peanut farmer, ex-governor of Georgia and a comparative unknown who scored well for his promises of clean government and a more informal style. But Carter's strong emphasis on human rights in foreign affairs had the effect of spotlighting criticism of the Soviet human rights record, which aggravated tensions. Defense spending once more began to rise.

In China, meanwhile, the death of Chairman Mao at the age of 82 in September 1976 heralded a series of rapid and significant changes. Soon after his death, his widow Jiang Qing attempted to seize power from Mao's chosen successor Hua Guo-feng, but the tide had turned against her. In October she and the other members of her so-called "Gang of Four"

## SOLZHENITSYN EXPELLED

After the publication of *One Day in the Life of Ivan Denisovich* in 1962, Alexandr Solzhenitsyn was hailed in the West as the great literary voice against Soviet oppression. A semi-autobiographical novel recounting the wretched life of a labor camp inmate and the triumph of humanity in adversity, it had slipped through the net of Soviet censorship in the brief post-Stalinist relaxation of the Khrushchev years, and even received the stamp of official approval. Under the more authoritarian Brezhnev regime, Solzhenitsyn was forced to publish privately in the underground format called *samizdat* (self-publishing), and homemade copies of his work passed from hand to hand. His novels *Cancer Ward* and *The First Circle*, both again revolving around the deprivation of prison camps and exile, were smuggled out to the West and published in 1968 to great acclaim. By this time Solzhenitsyn had become a severe embarrassment to the Soviet Union—a great literary figure deeply critical of the communist regime, yet too well known to silence. To add to Soviet discomfort, in 1970 he was awarded the Nobel prize for literature, but he was unwilling to go to Stockholm to collect the award for fear of being prevented from returning to his family.

In 1971, the year that his fictionalized history *August 1915* appeared, Solzhenitsyn was the victim of a failed assassination attempt. He was stabbed by a poisoned needle in a cathedral in southern Russia, but he survived the severe illness that this induced. Two years later the first volume of his *Gulag Archipelago* was published in the West. This blistering exposé of the Soviet labor camp system proved too much for the KGB: on February 12, 1974, he was arrested, condemned for treason and dispatched to West Germany within 24 hours. He was the first Russian citizen to suffer the indignity of summary expulsion since Leon Trotsky. The Soviet reasoning was that his voice would become less strident when it sounded from the West, and it was not far off the mark. Solzhenitsyn led a reclusive life in Vermont concentrating on a series of histories (*October 1916* and others), and works designed to give the West a better understanding of the Soviet perspective. To the dismay of propagandists, he did not prove an unequivocal advocate of democracy and capitalism; nor did he openly welcome the changes after the collapse of the Soviet Union.

He returned to Russia in 1994. He was soon disenchanted and became as fervent a critic of the new regime as he had been of the last one, displaying the same highly independent mind that had first brought him to the world's attention.

**BELATED HONOR**
**Solzhenitsyn receives the Nobel prize for literature from King Karl Gustav of Sweden (above) in October 1974. He had been awarded the prize in 1970.**

were arrested, expelled from the Communist Party, and berated as "filthy and contemptible, like dog's dung," by the official press that they once controlled. Few in the nation, exhausted by the turbulence of the Cultural Revolution, shed any tears for Jiang Qing when in 1981 she was sentenced to death (subsequently commuted to life imprisonment) for what were deemed "counter-revolutionary crimes."

Political tensions now relaxed as millions of victims of the Cultural Revolution were released from detention, and the economy was reinvigorated by "special economic zones" and foreign investment. Hua Guofeng remained in power until 1981, but all the while the moderate Deng Xiao-ping was extending his power base and influence. His faction prevailed when Hua Guo-feng was replaced by Hu Yaobang, Deng's protégé.

The trend toward liberalization in China encouraged some dissidents to call for a fifth modernization: democracy. They expressed their views on posters attached to what became known as the "Democracy Wall" in Beijing. The Chinese authorities, however, were not ready to countenance such liberties. Dissent was stifled in 1979, and Wei Jinsheng, the leader of the Democracy Wall movement, had to serve fifteen years in jail. Nonetheless, the United States felt that closer relations would allow a way forward, and gave the People's Republic of China full diplomatic recognition, although Taiwan remained a sticking point—the United States continued to recognize it as independent, but gave it reduced diplomatic status.

Among the superpowers, only the regime in the U.S.S.R. remained unchanged, with the ageing Brezhnev reinforcing his position by becoming Marshal of the Soviet Union (the chief military officer) in 1976 and Chairman of the Presidium of the Supreme Soviet (effectively president) in 1977. But he was presiding over an economy that looked increasingly moribund, after he had consistently ignored the proposed reforms of his more moderate prime minister, Alexei Kosygin. Dissidents attempted to apply the tenets of the Helsinki Accords, only to find themselves subject to harassment by the

HOSTAGES TO FORTUNE  Soviet physicist Andrei Sakharov and his wife Yelena Bonner (left), both high-profile human rights activists, spent seven years in internal exile. Fellow activist Anatoly Shcharansky (below, center) was exchanged in a prisoner swap in 1986.

notorious Soviet State Security Committee, the KGB. Andrei Sakharov, a highly respected physicist who had helped to develop the U.S.S.R.'s hydrogen bomb, and his wife, the human rights activist Yelena Bonner, spoke out against harassment, only to be subjected to greater persecution. This intensified after Sakharov was awarded the Nobel peace prize in 1975. The Helsinki Accords, enshrining the right to freedom of movement, had been signed two months before the announcement of the award, but Sakharov was not permitted to leave the U.S.S.R. to receive the prize. Another dissident, Anatoly Shcharansky, was arrested for "treason and anti-Soviet agitation"; after failed attempts to leave Russia for Israel, he had become a founder-member of the Soviet Helsinki Group, monitoring Soviet compliance to the Helsinki Accords. In 1978, he was sentenced to 13 years in a labor camp.

This uncompromising treatment of dissidents extended to the U.S.S.R.'s satellites in Eastern Europe, and even beyond their boundaries. In one particularly flagrant inci-

dent in 1978, the Bulgarian defector Georgi Markov, who broadcast for the BBC World Service, was murdered in London by an agent; like a victim in a fanciful spy novel, he was assassinated by a poisoned pellet shot into his thigh from an umbrella. Soviet defections remained a feature of the 1970s.

THE DEAL IS DONE  President Jimmy Carter and Soviet President Leonid Brezhnev meet to sign the SALT II agreement, June 1979.

Touring ballet companies from the U.S.S.R. regularly lost their leading dancers, such as the Bolshoi Ballet's Mikhail Baryshnikov, who fled his KGB minders in Toronto in 1974.

Strategic Arms Limitation Talks continued, this time focusing on "delivery vehicles"— the submarines, land-based missile launchers and airplanes capable of dispatching nuclear warheads. Although missile numbers had been limited, the arrival of the new generation of Multiple Independently targeted Re-entry Vehicles (MIRVs), which could carry up to five separately programmed warheads on a single missile, threatened to upset the balance of arsenals.

In 1979, after seven years of negotiations, agreement was reached on how, and at what level, to maintain parity in nuclear weapons delivery—and how this could be verified. SALT II was signed by Jimmy Carter and Leonid Brezhnev in Vienna in June 1979. It then had to be ratified by the Senate. But before the Senate could do so, events in Central Asia threw cold water on much of the constructive détente that had been achieved over the preceding decade.

## Afghanistan

Afghanistan was a monarchy, but since 1955 its prime minister, Mohammed Daud Khan, had courted the U.S.S.R. During the 1970s the country collapsed into turmoil. In 1973 Daud overthrew the monarchy in a coup, but subsequently attempted to distance himself from foreign influence. After an ill-tempered break with Brezhnev, Daud was killed in 1978 in a bloody coup staged by pro-Soviet army officers. Rival military factions then began to fight among themselves, and simultaneously had to deal with the growing threat of Muslim insurgents.

On December 24, 1979, the Soviet army intervened, on grounds justified by the Brezhnev Doctrine. A crack force of Soviet troops seized the airport in Kabul, making way for the airlift of an invasion force, which was backed by the movement of heavy artillery down the main trunk road to the capital. On December 27 another bloodbath at the presidential palace took place, and the Soviet protégé Babrak Karmal became president, a post he held until 1986. The U.S.S.R. quickly took control of the capital and, with their massive military superiority and complete control of the air, fanned out to tame the rugged hinterland.

As they did so, they displaced 2 million people as refugees, who fled into Pakistan.

Afghanistan proved to be the U.S.S.R.'s Vietnam, drawing them to commit 100,000 troops to an unconquerable war against a committed enemy, comprising the Islamic guerrilla forces known as the Mujaheddin. At home the war caused much resentment and criticism. When the dissident Andrei Sakharov proposed that the world boycott the 1980 Olympic Games in Moscow, he was exiled to the closed city of Gorky.

The Soviet war in Afghanistan threw détente into reverse; the United States and the West did not know the limit of the U.S.S.R.'s ambition, and feared that Moscow might be in search of a warm-water port on the Indian Ocean or the Gulf. Thus, SALT II was never ratified. Brezhnev died in November 1982 to be replaced by the former head of the KGB, Yuri Andropov. America, under the presidency of Ronald Reagan, became more anti-Soviet, and strengthened its military force. The Cold War had received a late frost.

**HEARTS AND MINDS** The Soviet army was destined to spend almost a decade in Afghanistan. Their enemies, the Mujaheddin (below), were technologically outclassed, but determined to the point of fanaticism.

# FLASHPOINTS

**MANY PARTS OF THE WORLD WERE RACKED BY CONFLICT AS NATIONS TOOK UP ARMS TO RESOLVE LOCAL DISPUTES AND GRIEVANCES**

During the term of office of President Jimmy Carter in the late 1970s, his national security adviser Zbigniew Brzezinski produced a dismal forecast: "The factors that make for international instability are gaining the historical upper hand over the forces that work for more organized cooperation. The unavoidable conclusion of any detached analysis of global trends is that social turmoil, political unrest, economic crisis, and international friction are likely to become more widespread during the remainder of this century."

The world had witnessed a difficult decade, and its troubles showed no prospect of relenting. Despite the security afforded by the new era of superpower relations and agreements on arms limitations, this provided no brake to the mass of more localized disputes—and indeed

perhaps invited them to flourish because the danger of nuclear catastrophe had been allayed. This process conformed to Marxist analysis, and the U.S.S.R. continued to encourage left-wing revolution around the world. In response, America often found itself supporting corrupt and brutal regimes.

To try to avoid becoming victims of this superpower game of cat and mouse, some 100 nations joined the "Nonaligned Movement," an idea promoted by leaders such as Jawaharlal Nehru of India in the 1950s and 1960s. But old rivalries often

proved stronger than common interests. One of the first conflagrations of the 1970s arose out of civil war in Pakistan, and threatened to engulf the Indian subcontinent.

The partition of India had created an unwieldy Pakistan, consisting of two blocks of Muslim-dominated territory, East Pakistan and West Pakistan, separated by 1,000 miles of Indian territory. It was not a happy union. East Pakistan deeply resented the way in which West Pakistan—the smaller of the two in terms of population—dominated politically and economically, and especially resented the authoritarian government of General Yahya Khan. When the country held its first full one-man-one-vote elections in December 1970, the Awami (People's) League (AL) of East Pakistan, led by Sheik Mujibur Rahman, won a sweeping victory, but West Pakistan refused to accept this

**A CRUEL WAR   The struggle for Bangladeshi independence took a dreadful toll as the fortunes of war swung back and forth. Bengalis who had collaborated with West Pakistan (below) were rounded up, and many were executed.**

1970 War in Pakistan leads to independence for Bangladesh; Idi Amin takes over in Uganda

1973 The U.S. pulls out of Vietnam; Chile's President Allende overthrown; Yom Kippur War

1975 North Vietnamese take Saigon; Khmer Rouge take over in Cambodia; Lebanese civil war begins

1976 Soweto uprising in South Africa

1977 General Zia deposes President Bhutto in Pakistan

1978 Camp David Agreement formulated

1979 Sandinistas oust President Samoza in Nicaragua

result. The AL then waged a campaign of civil disobedience, which escalated into violence. West Pakistan responded with a military onslaught of brutal efficiency. It launched an attack on East Pakistan's capital, Dhaka, on March 25, 1971, killing 7,000 in two days.

With West Pakistan close to delivering the *coup de grâce* to the newly declared "sovereign independent republic of Bangladesh," 2 million East Pakistani refugees came spilling over the border into India. The situation was intolerable to India and its prime minister, Indira Gandhi. In December 1971, India declared war on West Pakistan and sent an army into East Pakistan in support of independence. Faced with overwhelming logistical difficulties, West Pakistan capitulated after just 17 days. Bangladesh had won its independence, but it was an ominous start to nationhood. The war had cost somewhere between 1 and 3 million lives, and during the rest of the century Bangladesh suffered a litany of devastating floods, violent military coups and chronic poverty.

Back in West Pakistan (now called Pakistan), Zulfikar Ali Bhutto took over power from Yahya Khan, promoting "Islamic Socialism" under the banner of his Pakistan People's Party. But in July 1977, Bhutto was ousted in a military coup led by General Zia ul-Haq. Zia's Islamic version of martial law

remained in force until the end of 1985, while Bhutto, accused of conspiracy to murder a political opponent, languished in prison until he was hanged in 1979.

## The Yom Kippur War

The U.S.S.R. and America both kept a close eye on the conflict over Bangladesh, but they were not drawn into it. This was not the case in the increasingly vexing turmoil of the Middle East. Indeed, in 1973 America put its military forces on full alert to face off threatened intervention by the U.S.S.R.: the world appeared to be approaching the brink of a superpower confrontation.

The death of Egypt's President Gamal Abdul Nasser in 1970 had brought Anwar Sadat to power. The prospects for Egypt looked desperate, with a spiralling population rising by a million a year, and limited resources constricted to the narrow belt of the Nile Valley and Delta. Sadat realized that Egypt needed a new vision—one that mirrored Nixon's policy of détente and flexibility. He expelled 20,000 Soviet advisers and courted America instead. The strategy was inspired in part by the hope that it might result in the recovery—by diplomatic means—of Sinai, one of the territorial gains acquired by Israel through its decisive and humiliating victory over combined Arab forces in the Six-Day War of 1967. When

**ROLE REVERSAL** Israel's forces were caught uncharacteristically off-guard by the Yom Kippur War of October 1973. Moshe Dayan (top), the Israeli minister of defense, was held responsible for Israel's initial setbacks.

this initiative proved fruitless, Sadat formed a coalition with Syria, now under the military rule of President Hafez al-Assad, and they launched a combined attack on Israel on the Jewish holy day and festival of Yom Kippur, October 6, 1973. Although 11 months in the planning, it took the Israelis by surprise, and both Egypt and Syria made rapid advances.

Aided by American arms, the Israelis began pushing the invaders back, recovering lost ground before advancing beyond the territory won in 1967. Within three weeks Israeli forces had reached the Suez Canal and encircled the Egyptian army in Sinai. It was at this point that the United States military went on full alert, as the U.S.S.R. threatened to intervene on behalf of the Arab nations. It was the first real test of the new era of superpower détente. Fevered negotiations ensued as President Nixon's secretary of state, Henry Kissinger, traveled back and forth between Tel Aviv and Cairo to negotiate a settlement. A cease-fire agreement between Israel and Egypt was signed on November 11, and a peace agreement was eventually forged on January 1974.

**THE ULTIMATE PRICE** Anwar Sadat, Menachem Begin and Jimmy Carter in 1979, celebrating the signing of the Camp David Accords (above). Sadat was assassinated three years later by militant Arabs (right).

Meanwhile, the Arab members of the Organization of Petroleum Exporting Countries (OPEC) decided to play the "oil card" with a 70 percent price rise for crude oil, a reduction in oil production and an embargo on sales to the United States. The aim was to put pressure on Israel to renounce its 1967 territorial gains; to punish America for supporting Israel; and to keep the Middle East at the center of the world agenda. The effect, however, was more widespread: it caused a world recession, crippling rich and poor nations alike.

Israel eventually agreed to withdraw from Sinai in several stages between 1974 and 1979. In June 1975 the Suez Canal opened for the first time in eight years. In 1977 Sadat, aware that permanent conflict with Israel was costing his struggling nation too much, began a series of negotiations in a search for lasting peace, and in November he traveled to Jerusalem to meet the new prime minister of Israel, the hawkish former terrorist, Menachem Begin. This was an unprecedented and deeply controversial move for an Arab leader. President Carter played the honest broker between Sadat and Begin, and the result was one of this troubled era's great triumphs of diplomacy: a peace treaty was agreed to at the presidential retreat Camp David, Maryland, in September 1978, and signed in Washington in March the following year. For the first time an Arab nation affirmed Israel's right to exist.

But Sadat was ploughing his own furrow, and the Camp David Peace Accords cost

him his life. They infuriated hard-line Arab states, most notably the mercurial president of Libya, Moammar al-Gaddafi, as well as the new breed of Muslim fundamentalists. Sadat was assassinated by a group of disaffected Egyptians during a military parade in 1981. By this

time, however, the Arab World was beginning to show signs of disunity that would have dismayed the Pan-Arabist supporters of Nasser a decade before. Israel remained the great bone of contention.

## Lebanon in crisis

Some 700,000 Palestinians had been displaced by the creation of Israel. When Israel captured the West Bank, the Gaza Strip and the Arab Old City of Jerusalem during the Six-Day War of 1967, a further exodus occurred: 400,000 fled to Lebanon and 250,000 to Jordan, which had previously ruled the West Bank. In Jordan, Palestinian refugees enjoyed a certain amount of autonomy within their camps; many resisted full integration into Jordan, preferring to hold out for their own state. The camps also proved a hot bed for motivated armed guerrillas of the Palestinian Liberation Organization (PLO), who were determined to reverse Palestine's territorial losses. Jordan's moderate King Hussein soon became exasperated by the activities of the PLO, and in 1970-1, after a brief civil war, Jordan expelled the bulk of the Palestinians, most of whom fled to Lebanon.

Since gaining independence in 1945 Lebanon had managed to maintain a delicate balance of power between its two communities of Maronite Christians and Muslims, and

had flourished into one of the Middle East's most prosperous nations. The presence of large numbers of Muslim Palestinian refugees exacerbated tensions, however: the arrival of thousands more from Jordan in 1970-1 tipped the balance, especially when they began to meddle in Lebanese politics on the side of leftist Muslims and the Druzes (a local Muslim sect). The Christians, a numerical minority, were fearful of losing their power base. As tensions rose, they sought the protection of their heavily armed militias, notably the right-wing Christian Phalangist Party. A mounting exchange of atrocities escalated in 1975 into full-scale civil war.

Lebanon split in two, with Christians essentially to the north, and Muslims and Druze to the south. Once-prosperous Beirut was similarly divided along the so-called Green Line, and raked by machine-gun fire and artillery. This phase of the war lasted until the Syrians, fearing an Israeli invasion, intervened on behalf of the Christians in 1976, and imposed a cease-fire overseen by an Arab League peacekeeping force. But war rumbled on into the 1980s, producing a death toll of over 100,000.

Within this unstable situation, activists of the PLO were able to operate with impunity, carrying out countless raids across the Israeli border. Israel's response was to attack PLO bases in southern Lebanon, and it launched an invasion in March 1978, after which a UN peacekeeping force (UNIFIL) was installed along the border. In June 1982 the Israelis mounted a full-scale invasion to flush out the

### WHERE EAST MET WEST

Before 1975 Beirut was considered a dream city by many. At the crossroads between Asia and Europe, it was a wealthy cosmopolitan financial center and an exotic tourist destination, imbued with the mysteries of the East. Almost overnight Beirut was wrecked by the civil war.

PLO, advancing to the outskirts of Beirut. The PLO leadership was forced to evacuate Beirut in August under the protection of a multinational peacekeeping force, and headed for other Arab countries. The Israelis then withdrew but, as they did so, Christian militias moved into the Sabra and Chatilla refugee camps and massacred between 700 and 3,000 Palestinians, apparently to avenge

**STREETS OF FEAR** By 1978 large strips of the Lebanese capital, Beirut, had become snipers' alleys, where Christian phalangist militiamen (above) fought against Muslim opponents.

**VICTIMS ALL** Palestinians mourn the dead in the Sabra refugee camp, 1982 (right). A bomb wrecks the French barracks in Beirut, 1983.

## THE BOAT PEOPLE

In early 1977 the first Vietnamese refugees were discovered drifting in the South China Sea, packed onto the decks of old fishing junks. They were escaping the repressive regime imposed upon South Vietnam after the victory of the Communist North in 1975. The first waves of "Boat People" elicited great compassion. Camps were set up for them in Thailand, Indonesia, Malaysia, the Philippines and Hong Kong. America, China, Canada, Australia, Britain, France, West Germany and more than 60 other countries took in Vietnamese refugees.

In 1979, boats began leaving in large numbers from North Vietnam: soon 10,000 refugees were fleeing Vietnam every month. As their numbers increased, the response cooled. Most of these Boat People were classified not as political refugees, but as economic migrants. Many headed for Hong Kong, where they were placed in overcrowded detention camps, while their claims to asylum were examined. Most got no further than this, and mandatory repatriation began in 1989. Slowly the message reached Vietnam: the outside world was not a pot of gold. In the 1990s the flow of Boat People dwindled to a trickle, but by this time over a million Vietnamese had fled their homeland in the turmoil that followed the end of the Vietnam War.

**CLIMBING TO A NEW LIFE** One of 29 South Vietnamese refugees on board a boat found by U.S. navy ship *White Plains* in July 1979.

**UNDIGNIFIED EXIT** The last Americans leave Saigon by helicopter in April 1975. The mighty U.S. military had been outsmarted by a guerrilla army, as this Vietnamese poster (below) proudly proclaims.

the assassination of the Christian president-elect, Bashir Gemayel, two days before. These atrocities sent a wave of revulsion around the world.

America resisted the temptation to intervene in this complex hornets' nest, but it did send troops to Beirut in 1982 to join French and Italian soldiers in the multinational force that oversaw the PLO evacuation. Militant Muslims saw this force as pro-Christian and pro-Israeli. On October 23, 1983, Muslim suicide bombers blew up the barracks of the United States' marines, killing 241. In a separate attack 58 French soldiers were killed. For America, these events stirred painful memories of Vietnam.

### Vietnam

At the beginning of the 1970s the United States had over 500,000 personnel in Vietnam. These were largely "draft" soldiers, conscripts from ordinary American homes fighting a lethal war against a wily and determined enemy. For all their superiority in firepower and technology, America's forces were being outwitted by a guerrilla army.

Faced with huge costs, a crescendo of criticism at home and abroad, and daily newspaper and television reports with graphic images of the war's horrors, President Nixon had little option but to extricate the United States, and abandon the attempt to stem the flow of communism through Southeast Asia. As early as his 1968 election campaign, he had pledged to reduce American combat commitment in Vietnam. He adopted a policy known as "Vietnamization," by which the South Vietnamese would take increasing responsibility for the prosecution of the war, albeit assisted with American arms, logistical support and military training. While American ground troops were leaving, however, the United States maintained its overwhelming air superiority. Furthermore, in 1970-71, America and South Vietnamese forces attacked the Ho Chi Minh Trail, the communist supply route that started near Hanoi in North Vietnam and then snaked southward within the borders of Laos and Cambodia before emerging into South Vietnam. These attacks had the effect of spreading the war beyond the bounds of Vietnam and of destabilizing its neighbors.

Peace talks between the United States and North Vietnam, held in Paris, had started in 1968, but they bore little fruit. Nixon held out for "peace with honor and not peace with surrender." In March 1972 the North Vietnamese launched a full attack on the South, reminiscent of the Tet Offensive in 1968. This was repulsed by massive United

## THE KILLING FIELDS OF CAMBODIA

Only after the Vietnamese invasion in 1979 did the world become aware of the depths of horror suffered by the people of Cambodia under the rule of Pol Pot. As more and more mass graves were uncovered, statistics escalated. Somewhere between 1 and 2 million Cambodian citizens had died during the Khmer Rouge's reign of terror. Many had succumbed to disease, malnutrition and exhaustion as a result of Pol Pot's chaotic economic experiment, but many, too, were victims of wholesale genocide.

Pol Pot wanted a peasant country of pure Cambodians, so some 225,000 Chinese, 100,000 ethnic Vietnamese, 12,000 Thais, 100,000 Muslims and 2,600 Buddhist monks were executed. Pol Pot also had an irrational hatred of the educated classes. Doctors, teachers, military officers and any other professionals, university graduates, anyone who spoke French (the old colonial language), any critics of the new regime, and—most absurd of all—anyone who wore glasses, all were systematically liquidated. Because the Khmer Rouge wanted to save ammunition, many were killed with bamboo knives, or beaten to death with farm implements, or suffocated with polythene bags—often by soldiers who were little more than children. Some specific locations were set aside as places of mass execution: these became known as the "killing fields."

At Choeung Ek, 10 miles southwest of Phnom Penh, some 40,000 people were executed and the bodies thrown into 129 mass graves. Many had been brought here from the Tuol Sleng prison in Phnom Penh, where they were photographed, then tortured, before being herded to their deaths. Pyramids of skulls have been assembled as evidence of the madness that killed at least a fifth of the Cambodian population between 1975 and 1979.

**EVIL GRIN** Pol Pot was usually seen smiling, apparently unconcerned that he was responsible for the deaths of over a million Cambodians.

North Vietnamese chose to ignore the Paris Accords, and gradually increased their pressure on the South's demoralized army, now starved of American assistance and funding. In March 1975, the North Vietnamese made a massive push southward, eventually taking Saigon on April 30 and bringing the war to a final close. It had cost the lives of 58,000 Americans and 2 million Vietnamese. The United States remained haunted by the experience for at least two decades; Vietnam will be traumatized by it for generations. As Vietnam was unified under the communist government of Hanoi, and Saigon was renamed Ho Chi Minh City, it was clear that the United States had failed to halt the spread of communism; it had only delayed it.

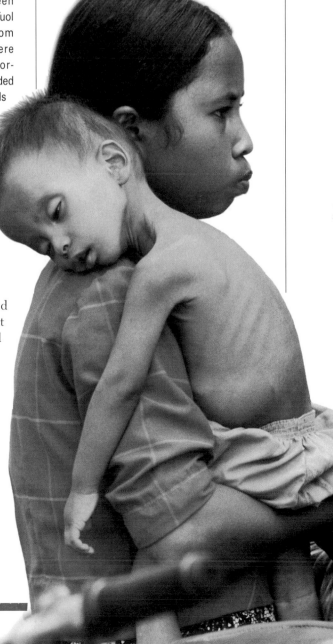

States' air attacks. The last ground combat troops left in August 1972.

On October 20, 1972, secretary of state Henry Kissinger declared that "peace is at hand." This announcement, which was music to so many Americans' ears, came just a few days before the presidential elections, in which Nixon won a resounding victory, but the Republicans vigorously denied that it was a cynical ploy to woo voters. In fact, the peace was still some way off, particularly for the Vietnamese themselves. In order to reinforce North Vietnam's desire to reach a settlement, and to persuade the South that America was not simply giving in and leaving it vulnerable to communist aggression, Nixon ordered 11 days of massive air strikes on Hanoi and the North, commencing on

December 18, 1972. This so-called Christmas Bombing Campaign brought widespread condemnation, but it had its effect. A cease-fire agreement was signed in Paris on January 23, 1973. Under the Paris Peace Accords, America agreed to withdraw all troops and military advisers from Vietnam, prisoners of war would be exchanged, and the 17th parallel would be respected as the dividing line between the two countries.

Over the next two years the

**BEYOND HELP** As Cambodia fell to the advancing Khmer Rouge in 1975, and the noose tightened on Phnom Penh, thousands fell victim to malnutrition.

## IDI AMIN

Few national leaders have acquired a more sinister reputation than President Idi Amin Dada of Uganda. Amin had risen from a humble background to become commander of the army and air force in 1968. In 1971, Amin staged a military coup, with the promise of returning the country to civilian rule. In 1972, he expelled all Asians with British passports. Amin next turned his ferocity on dissenters within his country. Judges who criticized the expulsions were brutally treated; many were killed and others fled the country. The justice system collapsed.

Amin was a complex character. He could be affable and charming, sometimes playing the buffoon. He demonstrated canny diplomatic skills, and became chairman of the Organization of African Unity in 1975-76. But beneath this image lay a streak of vicious ruthlessness. Events came to a head in 1977. In February the Archbishop of Uganda and two former cabinet ministers were bundled away from a protest rally in Kampala, and never seen alive again. Shortly thereafter army officers revolted over the favoritism shown toward Amin's own people, the minority Kakwa, but they were crushed. Members of the Acholi and Lango tribes and Christians were now being persecuted and exterminated. The final death toll of Amin's rule is put at somewhere between 100,000 and 300,000.

It was Amin's plan to annex borderlands belonging to Tanzania that triggered his downfall. His exiled opposition organized the Uganda Liberation Front which, supported by Tanzanian troops, invaded Uganda in 1979. Amin fled, first to Libya and then to Saudi Arabia, which sheltered him as a fellow Muslim. He has lived in Jeddah since 1980.

**RECKLESS TYRANT** After Idi Amin's expulsion of Asians, Uganda's economy collapsed.

### Pol Pot

There were worse repercussions. As the North Vietnamese pushed into South Vietnam, the Chinese-backed Khmer Rouge overran the pro-American military government of General Lon Nol in Cambodia. They took the capital Phnom Penh in April 1975, and started to evacuate its entire population at gunpoint. This was Year Zero of a bizarre and horrific social experiment by the Khmer Rouge, fanatical communists hardened by years of insurgency in the jungles of eastern Cambodia. Inspired by the Chinese Cultural Revolution and a nationalistic interpretation of the ancient Khmer civilization of Cambodia, they wanted to create an egalitarian peasant society devoid of the corrupting influences of the modern world. City dwellers were herded into the countryside to labor on collective farms with primitive tools; money was abolished; schools and temples were closed. Tens of thousands were summarily executed; hundreds of thousands died of disease and starvation.

The Khmer Rouge were led by the shadowy tyrant Pol Pot. Partly educated in France, he had been involved in revolutionary politics since the 1940s. He remained an enigma right up to his death in 1998. "We know that he is a monster," said Prince Norodom Sihanouk, a hereditary leader of Cambodia, "but if you meet him he is nice. He is not ugly, and is a little fat. He is a man who smiles, speaks gently, quite unlike his image as a second Hitler." Yet he was largely responsible for the deaths of at least one-fifth of his nation.

When the Khmer Rouge began to make aggressive incursions into Vietnam in 1978, the Vietnamese responded by invading Cambodia, taking Phnom Penh in January 1979. The Khmer Rouge were pushed into the jungles on the border with Thailand, from where they carried out a destabilizing guerrilla campaign for the next two decades. China, which had supported the Khmer Rouge throughout, then launched a punitive raid on northern Vietnam. However, the Chinese forces proved to be militarily inept, suffered heavy casualties and withdrew after three weeks. The Vietnamese remained in Cambodia (renamed Kampuchea)

**OUT WITH THE OLD** Young Portuguese in Lisbon went on the rampage in April 1974 after the coup by leftist military officers. Pictures of leaders of the *ancien regime* were hurled out of government offices and burned.

until 1989, playing the thankless triple role of traditional enemy, hated occupation force and savior.

### Into the vacuum

The force of arms also came into play in Africa, where the legacy of colonialism was taking longer to resolve than had been forecast during the more optimistic years of the 1960s. Portugal was one of the last colonial powers to relinquish its grip on its African possessions; its rulers in Lisbon had struggled for many years against increasing insurgency by armed liberation movements, particularly in Angola and Mozambique. In 1974, Portugal's right-wing government led by Marcello Caetano was overthrown by left-leaning military officers in the bloodless "Revolution of Flowers." Facing chaos at home, they had little option but to grant independence to Portugal's African possessions: Angola, Mozambique, Guinea-Bissau, Cape Verde, and São Tomé and Príncipe. In the Far East, mean-

**THE FORCE OF ARMS** The FNLA leader Holden Roberto (standing in the car, with sunglasses) rode through the streets of Nova Lisboa (now Huambo) in Angola in December 1975 to celebrate the formation of a coalition government with UNITA.

while, Indonesia took advantage of the power vacuum to seize East Timor.

In Angola a government was formed by a coalition of three guerrilla armies, the MPLA, FNLA and UNITA, but they soon fell out with one another and began a civil war that was to last for the rest of the century. The Marxist MPLA, led by Agostinho Neto, occupied the capital and central region, forming the government; the FNLA, backed by Zaire, controlled the north; and UNITA held the south. UNITA, led by Jonas Savimbi, had ties with China, but was also supported by South Africa. Between 1975 and 1988, the South Africans made numerous military incursions deep into southern Angola on the pretext of securing their borders and attacking bases of SWAPO guerrillas waging a liberation campaign in Namibia.

To bolster the ruling regime in Angola, the Cubans sent 10,000 troops in 1975. This was a new departure: the Soviet Union was effectively intervening by proxy. America was in no mood to retaliate. Some 17,000 Cuban forces were similarly involved in Ethiopia, where they were sent in support of the pro-Soviet military junta that had ousted Emperor Haile Selassie in 1974. Haile Selassie, who had once ruled over a court of

arcane and medieval splendor, died the following year while under house arrest, probably murdered by strangulation. The Marxist military regime of Mengistu Haile Mariam subsequently had to fight growing insurgency in the provinces Eritrea and Tigray, and a border war with Somalia over the Ogaden region in 1977-8, beggaring an already impoverished region.

The excesses of self-aggrandizing African tyrants invited a mixture of scorn, resentment and bewilderment from the outside world. In 1977 President Jean-Bedel Bokassa of the Central African Republic declared himself emperor in an extravagant ceremony costing an estimated $30 million, while his fellow countrymen lived off an average annual income of $250. In Uganda President Idi Amin was leading a regime of increasing cruelty bordering on insanity. Such antics played into the hands of apologists for the white-dominated regimes of Rhodesia and South Africa.

Rhodesia had unilaterally declared itself independent in 1965, but because it was ruled by a self-appointed government of the white minority, led by Ian Smith, it was not recognized internationally. Two Cuban-trained, Soviet-armed guerrilla armies, formed along tribal lines, waged war against the regime: the mainly Shona ZANU led by

the Marxist Robert Mugabe, and the mainly Ndebele ZAPU led by Joshua Nkomo. The war became increasingly ugly as the guerrillas targeted white farmers in remote parts of the country, massacring them, their families and their black staff. Missionaries likewise were shown no mercy: in February 1977, for example, three Jesuits and four Dominican nuns were murdered at a mission station close to Salisbury, adding to a toll of some 800 civilian casualties.

White Rhodesians fought a vigorous and sometimes equally ruthless campaign to suppress the guerrillas. They also crossed over into Mozambique, whose Marxist government, led by the Frelimo Liberation Army chief Samora Machel, was giving support and protection to guerrilla forces fighting in Rhodesia. Responding to this, the Rhodesians built up a counter-revolutionary guerrilla force in Mozambique, called Renamo. Mozambique was already struggling economically: after independence, the Portuguese colonists had stripped it bare, taking with them the proverbial light bulbs. Now its industries, railway lines and power stations were decimated by Renamo sabotage, plunging the nation into long-term poverty. Some 600,000 were killed in the civil war between Mozambique's government and Renamo, and nearly 500,000 children died of malnutrition.

As outcasts in the international community, the white Rhodesians lacked both politi-

**PEACE FOR RHODESIA** Guerrilla leaders Joshua Nkomo (left) and Robert Mugabe presented a united front at talks in London that led to the end of white-minority rule and the birth of Zimbabwe in 1980.

cal and military support, and were now also contending with the effects of world recession. Smith's regime was eventually brought to the negotiating table, and on December 21, 1979, agreed to allow black-majority rule, but with the guarantee of 20 white seats in the 100-seat parliament. In 1980, Robert Mugabe was elected prime minister of the new Zimbabwe. He invited Joshua Nkomo to partake in power-sharing, but this arrangement broke down along tribal lines in 1982.

South Africa, fearing the spread of insurgency from beyond its unreliable postcolonial borders, conquered Renamo in Mozambique after peace came to Zimbabwe. Within its borders, South Africa was facing increasing pressure from its own black population, the victims of the discriminatory laws of apartheid. In an effort to shed responsibility for its black population, the South African government formed a series of "homelands" or Bantustans (Transkei, Bophuthatswana, Venda and Ciskei) between 1976 and 1981, and declared them independent, thus effectively turning a large percentage of black South Africans into immigrants. However, the Bantustans were

**SPREADING VIOLENCE** Following riots and bloodshed in Soweto in June 1976, protests spread to other parts of South Africa. At the University of Western Cape, at Bellville near Cape Town, 27 people were killed in two days' rioting in August.

not recognized by the international community. Ruthless police methods helped to keep the lid on black resentment and the activities of the African National Congress (ANC). Resentment flared up, nonetheless, notably in the black township of Soweto, outside Johannesburg, in 1976. When thousands of schoolchildren and students demonstrated against the imposition of Afrikaans as the language of education, they were fired upon by police and hundreds were killed.

### Military rule

Strong-arm tactics were not the monopoly of the emerging nations. In Greece, a group of generals overthrew the government of Colonel George Papadopoulos in 1973, following weeks of unrest and student protests. This had more widespread repercussions when the generals tried to engineer a takeover in Cyprus in favor of EOKA, a Greek underground organization pursuing the goal of enosis, political union between Cyprus and Greece. It represented a direct threat to the Turkish population of Cyprus who, under the agreement worked out when the island became independent from Britain in 1960, enjoyed power-sharing rights. When the moderate Greek leader Archbishop Makarios fled Cyprus and an EOKA representative was installed as presi-

dent, Turkey invoked its status as guarantor and protector of Turkish Cypriots and invaded. Cyprus became a divided nation, with Greek and Turks confronting each other over the "Attila line," patrolled by the

**END OF AN ERA** The people of Athens came out onto the streets on July 24, 1974, to celebrate the fall of the military government, and the return to civilian rule under Constantine Karamanlis.

United Nations. This debacle was the undoing of the Greek generals back in Athens; they made way for a civilian government after seven years of hard-line military rule.

Similar conflicts were also being played out in Latin America, but here nations were more clearly divided into the haves and have-nots; this was a consequence of the faltering of rapid industrial expansion in the 1960s, along with rising inflation, unemploy-

## SALVADOR ALLENDE

**DEMOCRATIC MARXIST** Salvador Allende was a potent symbol of idealistic aspirations.

In 1970 Salvador Allende became president of Chile, the world's first democratically elected communist leader. He introduced a raft of socialist policies—nationalizing key industrial sectors, expropriating large agricultural estates to create peasant cooperatives, and freezing prices of essential goods. The economy began to stagnate, but this was masked by salary increases for workers, financed by printing more money. Inflation soared, reaching a rate of 162 percent in 1972. Nonetheless, Allende had widespread support, and was re-elected in March 1973.

In the months that followed, the country was hit by food and gas shortages, strikes and riots. Chile was pushed to the verge of civil war. On September 11, 1973, the army mounted a coup and surrounded the presidential palace. Allende and his guards resisted for two hours but, staring defeat in the face, Allende turned his gun on himself. A socialist dream had collapsed, and an era of violent repression began under the dictatorship of General Pinochet.

ment and foreign debt. Correspondingly, the political polarities were more clearly identified as left-wing and right-wing. Many left-wing activists attempted to gain power through legitimate democratic means, and in Chile in 1970 the Marxist Salvador Allende became president. It emerged later that the CIA had covertly attempted to sabotage Allende's election campaign, to protect American business interests in Chile. The United States was not going to allow communism to flourish within what it saw as its legitimate sphere of interest.

Elsewhere, inspired by the revolution in Cuba in 1958, Marxist guerrilla movements sprang up across the region—in Nicaragua, in El Salvador, in Uruguay and in Argentina. If their governments were not already right-wing, militaristic and repressive, they soon became so. Gradually, all Latin American countries fell to military regimes: by 1975 the only countries in the region that still had elected governments were Venezuela, Colombia and Costa Rica.

In Nicaragua, after nearly a decade of guerrilla activities, the left-wing Sandinistas ousted the corrupt government of President Anastasio Somoza in 1979. Meanwhile, violent confrontations between guerrillas and the U.S.-supported right-wing governments of El Salvador increased toward the end

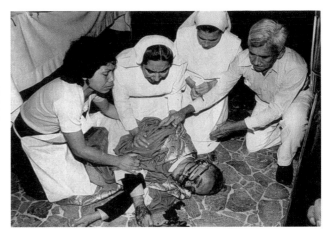

**COLD-BLOODED MURDER** Archbishop Oscar Romero was killed by a right-wing death squad during mass in San Salvador in 1980.

of the 1970s, made all the more lethal by ruthless right-wing militias. In 1980 the Archbishop Oscar Romero was assassinated by a right-wing paramilitary squad as he celebrated mass in San Salvador, and 40 people were killed when the crowds at his funeral were attacked. In 1979-80 over 9,000 Salvadoran civilians perished. In Uruguay and Argentina military governments faced opposition from an elusive enemy—a class of combatants that came to symbolize the violence and uncertainty of the age: terrorists.

**UNDER GUARD** A sports stadium is the improvised jail for thousands of prisoners, brought in for questioning by Chile's military government after the fall of President Allende.

# THE AGE OF TERRORISM

## DETERMINED GROUPS OF ARMED MILITANTS UNLEASHED LETHAL CAMPAIGNS OF VIOLENCE IN PURSUIT OF THEIR AIMS

With hindsight it would appear that terrorism achieves little besides death and mutilation, shock, revulsion and disgust, the reinforcement of old antagonisms, and the renewed determination of governments not to accede to the demands of the perpetrators. In the 1970s, however, there was a widely held belief that terrorism and guerrilla warfare could deliver—or at least contribute to—the toppling of unjust governments or the introduction of radical change, as had been witnessed in a number of countries since the Second World War, notably China, Israel and Cuba.

Essentially terrorism is a strategy of small-scale war adopted by causes that do not have the resources to mount a full-scale military campaign. The terrorists' aim is to cause maximum mayhem, discomfort and fear in order to destabilize the existing order and achieve change that cannot be won by political negotiation and persuasion. Branded criminals and terrorists by their targets, to their sympathizers they are freedom fighters and martyrs.

Throughout the 1970s and much of the succeeding decades newspapers carried daily stories of terrorist attacks: airplane hijacks, kidnaps, random shootings and street assassinations, letter bombs, parcel bombs, bombs in buses, in bars, under cars, on trains, in shops, museums, theaters, cinemas, even bandstands. Governments were determined not to give the impression that terrorists had the upper hand: normal life should continue, but this could only be achieved by increasing public security to minimize risk. Security searches became a fact of life, at airports, at the entrances of museums and shops. Some governments took this further by introducing spot searches and summary arrests, if not the entire apparatus of a repressive police state.

Anyone could be the unwitting victim of terrorism, and its perpetrators, the terrorists, became adept at salving their consciences over the deaths of innocent people. They claimed that this was a regrettable but inevitable by-product of fighting for a just cause; or that blame should be directed at the governments for forcing the terrorists to resort to this action.

The governments of several countries provided practical and moral support for terrorism, offering training facilities, financial assistance and arms. These included Eastern bloc countries, notably East Germany and Cuba, which had a political interest in undermining states that were not already within the communist sphere; the Islamic-socialist republic of Libya, ruled by Moammar al-Gaddafi, fiercely anti-Western, and flushed with money from its oil; Syria and Yemen. Support for terrorism was even to be found in the United States, where the descendants of Catholic Irish immigrants donated funds to NORAID, which paid for terrorist weapons for the IRA.

### The PLO

The 1970s opened with one of the most gruelling crises involving hijacks. Between September 6 and 9, 1970, Palestinian terrorists made a number of hijack attempts and succeeded in seizing three airliners—American, Swiss and British—that they redirected to a military airstrip in Jordan. While more than 300 hostages sweltered inside the aircraft, the hijackers negotiated for the release of six fellow terrorists held in Swiss and German prisons and that of a 24-year-old Palestinian heroine, Leila Khaled, who had been captured in a failed hijack on September 7 and was being held in Britain. After a week during which all but 54 of the hostages were set free, the hijackers evacuated the remaining hostages and blew up the

**THE ANONYMOUS FACE OF TERRORISM**
A girl recruit to the Basque separatist organization, ETA. The masked and armed terrorist became an all-too-familiar sight in the world's media.

1970 Baader-Meinhof gang goes on the run

1972 "Black September" raids Munich Olympics

1973 ETA kills Spanish prime minister

1975 Carlos "The Jackal" holds OPEC ministers hostage in Vienna

1976 Plane hijack victims freed by Israeli commandos at Entebbe

1978 Aldo Moro kidnapped and killed by Red Brigades

1979 IRA kills Lord Mountbatten

1980 Shining Path begins its campaign of terror in Peru

aircraft in a massive blaze. By September 30 the seven imprisoned terrorists had been handed over in exchange for the hostages. Effectively, the Western governments had capitulated to the terrorist demands—an outcome that they became increasingly determined not to repeat.

The hijackers were members of the Popular Front for the Liberation of Palestine (PFLP), a terrorist branch of the Palestinian Liberation Organization (PLO). The PFLP had formed shortly after the Six-Day War in 1967, when it became clear that the Arabs were unlikely to destroy Israel by conventional military means. This spectacular act of international sabotage, however, rebounded on the Palestinians, for it resulted in the forcible expulsion of the PLO and thousands of Palestinians from Jordan in 1970 and 1971.

The leader of the PLO was Yasser Arafat, who in the 1950s had founded Fatah (acronym for the Palestinian National Liberation Movement), the chief subgroup within the PLO. Although the PLO came to be thought of as an exclusively terrorist organization, it had its origins in a more moderate movement, and during the 1970s Arafat was struggling to reconcile the two tendencies. Moderates and extremists alike were implacably opposed to Israel, but the more moderate element was prepared to countenance a separate state for the Palestinians, alongside Israel. A younger, more militant and impatient set rejected any compromise with Israel, and joined terrorist splinter groups. Chief among these were the PFLP, a Marxist-Leninist organization founded by Georges Habash in 1967, and "Black September," which took its name from September 1970, when the Jordanian army first attempted to push the Palestinians out of Jordan during the triple plane hijack. These groups' broad agenda was to continue the struggle to destroy the Jewish state of Israel, and to replace it with a state in which Muslims, Christians and Jews would be equal.

In 1974, in Rabat, Morocco, Jordan agreed to give up its claim to the West Bank, now occupied by Israel, if it could be made into a Palestinian state. Arafat recommended the cessation of PLO terrorism outside Israel in order to garner international respectability for his organization in pursuit of this goal. But the PFLP and other radical groups rejected this compromise solution,

## TERROR AT THE MUNICH OLYMPICS

At 4:30 am on September 5, the tenth day of the 1972 Olympic Games in Munich, eight hooded figures scaled a security fence and slipped into the Olympic Village. Half an hour later they burst into the apartment of the Israeli team in a hail of machine-gun fire, killing the weightlifting team manager outright and fatally wounding a wrestling coach. A number of athletes managed to flee in the confusion, but ten remained captive. Within hours the Olympic Village had been sealed off by 12,000 German police and troops, as notes dropped from the apartment explained that the assailants belonged to Black September, the radical PLO terrorist group. They demanded the release of 200 Palestinian prisoners held in Israel, as well as a flight to an Arab capital. If their demands were not met by noon, they would kill one hostage every two hours.

The deadline was extended hour by hour, as intense negotiations proceeded through the day, led by the German chancellor, Willy Brandt. One hostage managed to jump free, dodging bullets as he dashed for cover. Finally, at 10 pm, an army bus was brought into the Olympic Village, and the terrorists and the blindfolded hostages were transported to two waiting helicopters. West German and Bavarian politicians and police chiefs mounted a third helicopter, and together they flew to the military airfield of Fürstenfeldbruck, 28 miles from Munich, where a Lufthansa Boeing 707 was waiting.

The terrorists had been assured that their demands were being met and they were about to fly to Cairo: but it was a trap. Two of them crossed the tarmac to inspect the plane, but as they returned to the helicopters the airport lights were switched off, and German marksmen opened fire. Three terrorists on the ground were quickly eliminated, but those inside the helicopters turned their guns on the hostages and threw grenades. All the hostages died, along with five terrorists and a German police officer.

The rescue attempt had gone horribly wrong. Worse still, midnight news broadcasts announced that all of the hostages were, in fact, safe, creating a great surge of joyous relief and celebration in Israel and in Germany. Three hours later, the awful truth became known.

Willy Brandt was left to explain his government's action: Cairo had refused to allow the aircraft to land, and Israel had refused to negotiate the release of prisoners. The Germans had been left with little alternative but to try using force. Furthermore, they had mistakenly believed that the terrorists would surrender when they realized that they were surrounded. The tragedy completely overshadowed the Olympic Games, and high security now became a factor for any major event.

**GUN LAW A Black September terrorist during the attack. Above: Israeli relatives mourn their dead.**

maintaining their commitment to recover the whole of Palestine by whatever means. They, and other extremist groupings, formed the "Rejection Front," and continued their terrorist activities. The PLO remained split after the leadership was forced to evacuate Beirut in 1982, but Arafat—from his new base in Tunis—gradually reasserted his authority. Israel, meanwhile, remained firm in its unwillingness to bow to terrorist violence, and retaliated with military attacks on guerrilla camps, and with its own undercover activities and assassinations directed by its intelligence service, Mossad. The raid on Entebbe in 1976 was a demonstration of this robust, uncompromising and often ruthless response.

### Separatism

The PLO was attempting to win back a homeland from which many of its people had been dispossessed. Elsewhere, terrorists were at work within their homeland attempting to achieve a separate identity or autonomy. The Basque people of northeastern Spain had been treated particularly harshly under the regime of the dictator General Franco. With their own language and cultural roots, many Basques resented being incorporated into Spain. A separatist organization called Euzkadi Ta Azkatasuna (Basque Homeland and Liberty, or ETA) had been waging a campaign of violence since the mid 1960s. Franco's government curtailed their activities through strong-arm police-state tactics of arrest, abduction and torture. Nonetheless, ETA continued to operate, killing the Spanish prime minister, Admiral Luis Carrero Blanco, in 1973 with a bomb so massive that it hurled his car over a church.

After Franco's death in 1975, Spain's new democratic governments released ETA prisoners and explored negotiated settlements, but frustration with the process simply rekindled terrorist fervor and ETA's campaign of violence escalated tenfold. Over 30 years ETA has been responsible for some 800 deaths. This also coincided with a time when northern Spain's once powerful heavy industries were gradually declining into a rust-belt. ETA's destabilizing activities frightened off new investment, fostering further malaise.

The province of Quebec in Canada shares some similarities with the Basque country. Its largely French-speaking population traces its roots to the first settlers in Canada, conquered by the British in 1779. For the most part separatism has been limited to legitimate political activities and a series of referenda, but in 1970 the Front de Libération du Québec carried out a series of kidnaps, and killed one of their hostages, the Quebec minister of labor Pierre Laporte.

Another kind of issue was raised by South Moluccan refugees in the Netherlands. The Christian Ambonese of the South Moluccas, an island group in what had been the Netherlands East Indies, had provided an important source of recruits for the Royal Netherlands-Indies army during Dutch colonial days. The Ambonese had hoped to

**DESERT HEAT** In the final hours of the PFLP hijack in Jordan in 1970, the remaining hostages were evacuated onto the airstrip (above) before the three Boeing 707s were demolished in a spectacular and expensive series of explosions.

be granted independent status when the Dutch left in 1950, but this aspiration was crushed by Indonesia. In 1975-8 South Moluccan terrorists waged a campaign of violence in the Netherlands to draw attention to their grievances. In June 1977 they hijacked a train at the town of Assen and held 55 people hostage for 20 days before Dutch marines stormed the train, killing six of the terrorists and two hostages.

These conflicts were on a minor scale compared with the problems in Northern Ireland. For decades the Roman Catholic minority had been treated as second-class citizens by the Protestant majority, who remained fiercely loyal to the United Kingdom, and held the reins of power through the Northern Ireland assembly at Stormont in Belfast. During the 1960s, inspired by the Civil Rights Movement, Catholic activists had attempted to redress the imbalance through marches, rallies and demonstrations, but were often met by violence from the Protestant-dominated police force, the Royal Ulster Constabulary (RUC).

As the confrontations between the two deeply entrenched communities escalated,

the British Government was obliged to step in, and sent troops to Northern Ireland to protect Catholics from Protestant aggression. But within months, the Catholics came to see these troops as an enemy force upholding the rule of Stormont and the British Government to their disadvantage. This played into the hands of the Republican movement, which had as its goal the complete removal of the British, and the reunification of Northern Ireland with the Republic of Ireland in the south. Two closely linked organizations fought for this goal: Sinn Fein, the political wing of the Republican movement, and the Provisional Irish Republican Army (IRA), its military wing. The IRA pursued a campaign of terrorist violence, in parallel with other extremist groups such as the Irish National Liberation Army (INLA).

The IRA campaign of bombing and assassination was met with tit-for-tat killings by Protestant loyalists, who

**BLOWN APART** The Spanish premier Admiral Luis Carrero Blanco, one of Franco's closest aides, was killed in a terrorist attack in Madrid in December 1973. The Basque separatists ETA had planted a bomb under the road.

formed their own paramilitary groups, such as the Ulster Defense Force (UDF) and the Ulster Freedom Fighters (UFF). In mid 1971 alone, there were 37 explosions in April, 47 in May, 50 in June. The Conservative government of Edward Heath was at a loss to know how to respond: it was politically difficult to reward terrorism by allowing concessions that would effectively diminish the power of the side that had remained loyal to the British.

In August 1971 the British Government used new emergency powers to introduce internment—the detention of suspects without trial. This ignited anti-British resentment even further. September marked the death of the 100th victim since "the Troubles" began—a 14-year-old

*continued on page 40*

# REBELS IN SEARCH OF A CAUSE

## THE WESTERN WORLD HAD ITS OWN HOME-BRED SCOURGE: URBAN TERRORISM FUELLED BY AN INCANDESCENT BLEND OF YOUTHFUL RAGE AND REVOLUTIONARY IDEALISM

The posters of the Marxist revolutionary Che Guevara that adorned the bedrooms of countless students around the Western world during the late 1960s and 70s signified a widely held sympathy with left-wing revolutionary activity. There was a fashionable romanticism about fighting for the world's oppressed. But some took this romanticism one step further, and put their revolutionary sympathies into practice. Their targets were not the oppressive regimes of Third World countries, but the symbols of capitalist government on their doorstep. Leading industrialists, military officers, government officials and diplomats became the victims of kidnaps and assassinations perpetrated by a new breed of ruthless revolutionary: the "urban terrorist."

One of the earliest manifestations of this trend was the German Baader-Meinhof group. In May 1970 Andreas Baader was serving a three-year sentence in Berlin for setting fire to a department store when he was dramatically sprung from prison by three machine-gun toting colleagues, Ulrike Meinhof, Horst Mahler and Astrid Proll. It was the start of life on the run for the so-called Baader-Meinhof gang, as they committed a trail of bank raids and murders. Meinhof, Baader and his girl-friend Gudrun Ensslin were captured in 1972, but the Rote Armee Fraktion (Red Army Faction) continued where they had left off, waging a campaign of violence to secure their release.

The members of the Red Army Faction were fuelled by a deep, if loosely defined, resentment toward Western civilization. They detected neo-fascism in the West German government, labeling it the "Strawberry Reich." The Vietnam War became the hated symbol of Western rapacity. They also professed solidarity with the Popular Front for the Liberation of Palestine (PFLP) and other like-minded terrorist organizations, and received arms and training from the PLO, as well as East Germany and Libya.

The trial of the imprisoned ringleaders took place in a specially constructed courthouse, built like a fortress adjacent to Stammheim prison in Stuttgart. It began in May 1975 and continued over two

years. Meinhof committed suicide in prison in 1976.

In October 1977 pro-Palestinian terrorists hijacked a Lufthansa plane with 91 passengers and crew and took them to Mogadishu, Somalia, where the pilot was shot and dumped on the runway. They demanded the release of Red Army Faction and other prisoners, but on October 18 the hostages were freed and all the hijackers were killed in a dramatic rescue carried out by a German anti-terrorist squad. The following day Baader and Ensslin were found dead in their cells in prison; they had apparently shot them-selves, though it is not clear how they had acquired guns. After this, the Red Army Faction scaled down its activities and faded from view.

At its height it had some 20 principal activists and 200 close supporters; they were responsible for more than 30 deaths.

The Red Army Faction claimed international affiliation with similar organizations elsewhere, such as the Brigate Rosse (Red Brigades) in Italy. Founded in 1970, this movement drew inspiration from disaffected left-wing intel-lectuals, notably Renato Curcio of the University of Trento, and modeled itself on Latin American liberation movements. Targeting police chiefs, judges, industrial leaders, government officials and other "enemies of the working class," it started with bomb attacks on factories and relatively short-lived kid-nappings, but its violence gradu-ally escalated into a campaign of bombings, kidnap and murder. In March 1978 they committed their most notorious act: six gunmen kidnapped Aldo Moro, president of the Christian Democratic Party and former prime minister of Italy, killing

URBAN TERROR    The Baader-Meinhof group and Red Army Faction targeted symbols of the capitalist establishment in a campaign of kidnap and murder.

five bodyguards as they did so. When the Italian government refused to accede to their demands to release 13 fellow terrorists on trial in Turin, Aldo Moro was killed. His body was found in the trunk of a car on May 9, 54 days after his abduction.

This brutal killing of a respected public figure undermined any sympathy the Red Brigades had previously enjoyed in Italy. But their activities only increased; during 1980 alone they killed 30 people. At its height, the Red Brigades probably had some 500 active members. To counteract their campaign, the Italian authorities arrested hundreds of suspects, and gradually the net closed on the ringleaders. The Red Brigades faded from view in the late 1980s, when their revolutionary posturing began to look increasingly moribund.

The Press focused on certain individuals, endowing them with cult status. Carlos "the Jackal," a Venezuelan whose real name was Ilich Ramírez Sánchez, had connections with the PLO and the Baader-Meinhof gang. Following a spate of violent attacks in France in 1974-5, in which he killed some 15 people, he evaded arrest in London where an arsenal of weapons was discovered, along with a hit-list of prominent Jewish figures in Britain. He next popped up in Vienna, where he masterminded the daring capture of 70 people at the OPEC headquarters. He and his accomplices were then flown to Algeria with 11 hostages—including Saudi Arabia's powerful oil minister, Sheik Yamani—where they were released in return for a $20 million ransom. He was eventually captured in 1994 in Sudan and brought to trial in France. When sentenced to life imprisonment, he yelled defiantly, "Long live the Revolution." France also had its own home-grown terror group, the Maoist and anarchist Action Directe, which targeted offices, factories, law courts and army barracks in more than 80 bomb attacks, and assassinated the head of Renault, George Besse, in November 1986.

Even the United States was not immune to the scourge of urban terrorism. A shadowy group called the Symbionese Liberation Army (SLA)—in fact little more than a handful of activists—kidnapped 19-year-old Patty Hearst, an heiress to the Hearst newspaper fortune, in San Francisco on February 4, 1974. They demanded a $2 million ransom to be paid in food handouts to the poor. This demand was duly met, but Patty Hearst was not released. Instead, when the SLA held up a bank in San Francisco a week later, Hearst was filmed on security cameras carrying a machine gun, apparently a willing participant in the raid. Six of the group were killed in a police stake-out in Los Angeles in May 1975, and most of the remainder, including Hearst and her captors Emily and William Harris, were arrested in September 1975. Patty Hearst claimed that she had been brainwashed, but nonetheless spent four years in jail.

The basic intention of most leftist terrorist groups was to undermine the state and create the conditions for revolution. Through their activities, they hoped to

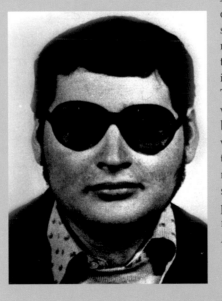

**THE JACKAL'S ARMORY** An arsenal of weapons apparently belonging to Carlos "the Jackal" (right) was found in Budapest.

bounce existing governments into an authoritarian crackdown that would show their true colors, infringe upon the liberties of all citizens and foment widespread discontent. They exploited the Achilles' heel of democracy: they abused the freedom it offered, but cried foul when their own liberties were infringed. When governments adopted strong-arm tactics to stamp out the blight of urban terrorism, the terrorists and their sympathizers enjoyed the satisfaction of having their prejudices confirmed.

Right-wing groups practiced parallel tactics. In Italy, in 1980, 85 people were killed when a huge bomb exploded in a waiting room at Bologna train station. The explosives had been planted by neo-fascists attempting to disrupt the trial of fellow terrorists who had bombed a train in Milan in 1974; they may also have intended to cause panic and a diversion for a right-wing military coup.

In 1998, when few people realized it even still existed, the Red Army Faction announced that it was winding itself down. One of their group then mused that "it was a strategic error not to build up a social-political organization in addition to the illegal, armed one." The truth is that these groups never had a fully coherent ideology capable of commanding popular support. They had dipped into the cauldron of youthful left-wing resentment and idealism; they liked the idea of being revolutionaries, but largely remained rebels without a cause. Britain experienced a short-lived terror campaign from a small group who set off a number of bombs, including two at the secretary of state for employment's house in January 1971. They perhaps had the most apt name of all the urban terrorist groups: they called themselves the Angry Brigade.

**ACCOMPLICE OR VICTIM?**
Kidnapped heiress Patty Hearst mystified police by appearing to be a willing accomplice of her SLA captors.

# WORLD TRADE CENTER BOMBING

**MASSIVE DESTRUCTION** Escalators were destroyed at One World Trade Center in New York City when a bomb exploded in the basement level of the building. Many months of building demolition and construction were required before service could be restored to the facility.

A seemingly normal day in New York City turned ominous on February 26, 1993 when a bomb planted in the World Trade Center exploded, killing six people and wounding over a thousand. The incident, caused by a group of Islamic fundamentalists, shocked and devastated New York residents as well as leaders and individuals around the world. The comforting myth that the United States was exempt from terrorism had been shattered. The two main conspirators—Ramzi Ahmed Yousef and Eyad Ismoil—had loaded three tanks of hydrogen gas, ingredients for the bomb, into a rented yellow Ryder van. The next day they drove the van into the lower-level parking garage of One World Trade Center; and at 12:17 pm, the 1,500 pound bomb exploded, which, in addition to the deaths and injuries, resulted in around $550 million of damage. Ramzi Yousef, the ringleader in the attack and a supposed trained electronics engineer and explosives expert from Pakistan, arrived in America—according to prosecutor David Kelly— with a library of terrorist manuals. At one point, Yousef allegedly said that he hoped the blast would topple one tower on top of the other, which could have killed an estimated 250,000 people. Kelly also stated that Yousef had bragged to agents about the crime he had committed, and that he had expressed regret over not killing enough people. Other conspirators in the attack included Mohammad Salameh, Nidal Ayyad, Mahmud Abouhalima, and Ahmdad Mohammad Ajaj, who were all sentenced to 240 years in prison. Both Yousef and Ismoil were found guilty of masterminding the 1993 bombing and were sentenced to life in prison. Though the attack was bungled by the bombers as well as by those who were supposed to stop them, it still led journalists to investigate whether the bombing could have been avoided. Controversy over the FBI's failure to heed their informants exists to this day.

**STRIKING AT THE HEART OF GOVERNMENT** An IRA car bomb at Westminster in March 1979 killed Airey Neave, the Conservative Party's spokesperson on Northern Ireland.

girl caught in crossfire. In December that year 15 people were killed in a Christmas bombing campaign in Ulster. Internment also led to the confrontation called "Bloody Sunday" in January 1972, when 13 Catholic demonstrators were shot dead by British troops. The IRA now openly targeted the British military establishment, wherever it operated. An IRA car bomb exploded at a parachute regiment headquarters at Aldershot, England, in February 1972; its victims

**FULL MILITARY HONORS** The highly charged funeral of hunger striker Bobby Sands in Belfast in May 1981 was attended by masked paramilitary colleagues.

were five female domestic workers, a gardener and a Roman Catholic priest.

In March 1972 the Stormont assembly—now almost exclusively Protestant—was suspended and "direct rule" imposed from Westminster, but this only encouraged the IRA to attack at the heart of the British political establishment. In June 1974, a bomb wrecked much of the 877-year-old Westminster Hall, inside the Houses of Parliament; Airey Neave, a senior aide to the leader of the Conservative Party and future prime minister, Margaret Thatcher, was killed by a bomb at the House of Commons in March 1979. In August the same year, Lord Mountbatten, the 79-year-old cousin of the Queen, was killed when a bomb exploded on his boat off the coast of County Sligo in the Republic of Ireland. The IRA, whose bomb also killed Mountbatten's 14-year-old grandson and their young Irish boatman, called this an "execution."

The pressure continued to mount in 1981 when Bobby Sands and nine other Irish Republican prisoners held in the Maze (Long Kesh) high-security prison near Belfast died when on hunger strike, becoming instant martyrs and provoking days of angry rioting. On June 20, 1982, an IRA bomb blew up a mounted detachment of the Blues and Royals regiment in Hyde Park, London, killing two guardsmen and seven horses. That same afternoon in London a military band of the Royal Green Jackets playing in Regent's Park was targeted, and six bandsmen were killed.

The people of Northern Ireland became ever more polarized in a seemingly intractable

**SONGS OF PEACE** Sickened by the seemingly endless cycle of violence, many women of Northern Ireland joined the Ulster Peace Movement led by Mairead Corrigan (center left) and Betty Williams (center right).

situation. But the majority were sickened by the violence that was touching increasing numbers of families, and claiming innocent bystanders—including children. In August 1976 two women, Betty Williams and Mairead Corrigan, the aunt of three children killed in the Troubles, founded the Community of Peace People, or Ulster Peace Movement, essentially a women's campaign that gathered a groundswell of support. Some 30,000 marched for peace in London in November that year. In October 1977 Williams and Corrigan were awarded the Nobel prize for peace (confusingly, the peace prize was also awarded that year to Amnesty International for its worldwide work on behalf of prisoners of conscience). But the forces of sectarianism proved too great, and the initial élan and optimism of the movement faded. Each new outrage produced new victims, and new recruits from among those who demanded revenge and retribution. While borders across the rest of Europe eased in the more

**URBAN CONFLICT** Armed with truncheons, tear gas, and rubber bullets, British soldiers try to control a riot in Londonderry.

relaxed regime of the European Community, those between Northern Ireland and the Republic of Ireland hardened behind military barricades, checkpoints and border patrols. A peaceful solution seemed ever more remote.

## Revolution

The Roman Catholics of Northern Ireland wanted change, but they did not want revolution. In South America a number of leftist terrorist organizations took on their governments in pursuit of revolution by waging campaigns of terror, mainly in the cities. The Tupamaros of Uruguay were founded in 1963 by a labor activist Raúl Sendic, taking their name from Tupac Amaru II, the leader of a Peruvian revolt against Spain in the eighteenth century. To begin with, they robbed banks and attacked businesses in

order to distribute the pickings to the poor, but by the 1970s they were involved in increasingly violent raids, arson attacks and kidnappings, targeting the military and foreign officials. An American adviser to the Uruguayan police was kidnapped and murdered in 1970; the British ambassador, Geoffrey Jackson, was kidnapped for eight months in 1971, but was released shortly after more than 100 Tupamaros managed to break out of jail—possibly with official connivance. In a crackdown by the military government in 1973, some 300 Tupamaros activists and sympathizers were killed and several thousand were imprisoned. Most were released when civilian democracy was restored in 1985.

In Argentina the Montoneros youth movement, founded by President Juan Perón in the early 1950s, became a militant left-wing revolutionary movement during his exile, and was disowned by Perón on his return to power in 1973. It became vehemently anti-government during the presidency of Perón's widow Isabel after 1974, but found a ruthless opponent in her commander-in-chief, General Jorge Rafael Videla, who became president after "Isabelita" was deposed in March 1976. That same month hundreds of government opponents were arrested, and later as many as 15,000 were imprisoned, tortured, assassinated by right-wing death squads, or disappeared in the government-sponsored "dirty war." This was terrorism in reverse: performed by the government to terrorize its people into conformity.

One of the most violent Marxist terrorist movements of South America was the Sendero Luminoso (Shining Path) in Peru. It was founded in 1970 by Abimael Guzmán Reynoso, a philosophy professor in the Andean city of Ayacucho. Inspired by some of the most extreme manifestations of communist revolution, such as the

**TAKING UP ARMS** Tupamaros recruits in Uruguay believed that they were joining a communist revolutionary army, as portrayed in a propaganda poster (top). In Peru, by contrast, peasants had to form their own military units to defend themselves against the Shining Path terrorist group.

# RAID ON ENTEBBE

In the terminal buildings at Entebbe Airport, near Uganda's capital, Kampala, the heat was stifling. As the night of July 4, 1976, went on, 106 Israeli and Jewish hostages sat under the nervous gaze of seven terrorists, five from the Popular Front for the Liberation of Palestine (PFLP), and two West Germans—one a woman. In the background were Ugandan troops, placed there by the country's president, Idi Amin, who visited the scene in a cowboy hat and claimed unconvincingly to be negotiating on behalf of the hostages.

The hostages' ordeal had begun on an Air France flight from Tel Aviv to Paris a week before. Four terrorists had hijacked the plane and ordered the captain to fly first to Libya, and then to Uganda. There they were joined by three more terrorists, implying Amin's complicity. During the negotiations that ensued, more than 150 passengers were released. But the situation looked grim for the remaining 106 as the deadline drew nearer. In exchange for the hostages, the terrorists demanded the release from jail of 53 fellow terrorists. If the prisoners were not released, the hostages would be killed. The Israelis, however, were not inclined to give into this kind of blackmail, and for four days during the negotiations they had been training a crack force to attempt what would be one of the most remarkable rescue operations of the terrorist era.

On Saturday, July 3, three Hercules military aircraft left Israel and flew 2,500 miles direct to Uganda. The Israelis knew Entebbe Airport well: they had built it four years previously. Under the cover of darkness, parachutists dropped to the edge of the airfield and set off a series of diversionary explosions on the far side of the runway to the terminal buildings. Then the three Hercules landed, lowering their ramps as they drew to a halt to emit a stream of jeeps carrying 150 commandos with blackened faces. They stormed the terminal, yelling instructions to the hostages in Hebrew to lie flat on the ground.

A gun battle ensued, and all seven terrorists were killed, along with 20 Ugandan soldiers and three hostages caught in the crossfire. The remaining hostages were ushered to the aircraft. Within an hour of the beginning of the raid they were on their way home, where they were greeted in jubilant triumph. The Israeli force suffered just one casualty, shot by Ugandan troops during the getaway. He was the commander, Lieutenant-Colonel Jonathan Netanyahu—the brother of Benjamin, Israel's future prime minister. Another casualty was a 75-year-old hostage, Dora Bloch. Before the raid, she had begun to choke and had been taken to a hospital. She was never seen again—apparently the victim of Ugandan revenge.

Maoist Cultural Revolution and the Khmer Rouge of Cambodia, Guzmán's followers took up arms in 1980 in a campaign that gave them control over much of central and southern Peru. While championing the rights and culture of indigenous Indians, they terrorized villagers and the poor urban underclass through a campaign of ruthless intimidation, destruction and murder. Guzmán was eventually arrested in 1992, by which time his revolutionary movement had caused the deaths of some 25,000 people.

Even this group had its supporters in the world beyond, who romanticized the role of leftist terrorists while vilifying the governments who had to contend with them. It was only at the collapse of communism at the end of the 1980s that revolutionary Marxist terrorists began to lose both practical and popular support, and the path of negotiation, persuasion and political campaigning began to look like a more promising course.

# THE NEW AGE

**T**HE RESHAPING OF ATTITUDES THAT MARKED THE 1960S ROLLED ON INTO THE 1970S, BRINGING HUGE CHANGES TO SOCIETY—IN THE POSITION OF WOMEN, IN GAY LIFE, AND THE RIGHTS OF MINORITIES. AS THE PARAMETERS CHANGED, MANY SEARCHED FOR MEANING IN ALTERNATIVE LIFESTYLES AND RELIGION. POPULAR MUSIC AND THE MEDIA EXPRESSED THESE NEW ATTITUDES, AND REFLECTED THE INCREASING GLOBALIZATION BROUGHT ABOUT BY ADVANCES IN COMMUNICATIONS.

# LIBERATION

## THE CIVIL RIGHTS ACTIVISM OF THE 1960S COMBINED WITH THE NEW FREEDOMS OF THE 1970S TO TRANSFORM SOCIAL ATTITUDES

The great era of experimental youth culture that had blossomed in the Western world during the late 1960s rolled on into the 1970s. Many young people continued to explore new patterns of social life, determined to break free from the constraints and conformity of traditional domestic life. They went to live in communes, or fled the cities to the countryside to pursue a self-sufficient life of gardening and farming, powered by alternative energy generated from the wind, the Sun and streams. They adopted vegetarian and macrobiotic diets, yoga and meditation, astrology, alternative medicines—all elements of what later came to be called the "New Age."

But lurking in the wings of these experiments was a darker side, seen in rising casualties to hard drugs, outbreaks of violence and the mind-bending aberrations of extreme religious cults. The shadow of the Manson trials in Los Angeles hung over the early 1970s: in March 1971 Charles Manson and his accomplices from his "family" of followers were convicted and sentenced for the ritualistic murder of the pregnant Hollywood actress Sharon Tate and others in Beverly Hills in 1969.

Generally, the gentle innocence and naive idealism that had marked the peace-loving era of flower power and the hippies had now been either tainted by a new vein of cynicism and commercial exploitation, or hardened by a trend toward political activism.

Broad interest in the environment, for instance, was chaneled into direct action by Greenpeace, founded in 1971, and into the political engagement of the new Green parties—such as Die Grünen in Germany, chaired in the early 1980s by the charismatic Petra Kelly, who did much to make the movement internationally respectable.

Another legacy of the 1960s was the new mood of sexual freedom, labeled "the permissive society" in the previous decade.

## STREAKING

In 1974 stripping naked and dashing through a public place became a craze, introducing a new word into the English language: streaking. The craze is said to have begun on college campuses, a vestige of the *joie de vivre* and cult of the natural of the hippie era. When police tried to stop it at the University of Delaware in March 1974, 11 students and 11 policemen were injured in the ensuing fracas.

According to British press reports, streaking crossed the Atlantic when a businessman ran naked down the aisle of a Pan-Am jumbo jet. Thereafter there were countless incidents across Europe by men and women, at university lectures, in city shopping centers, at sports events—for fun, for the challenge and for charity. "Streak for Peace" was often the accompanying slogan.

**LEGAL COVER**  Police usher a streaker off the rugby field at Twickenham in April 1974.

1970 *The Female Eunuch* is published

1971 Topless bathing comes to the French Riviera

1973 American Indian protesters occupy Wounded Knee

1974 Streaking becomes a fad

1976 *The Hite Report* is published

1977 Amnesty International wins Nobel peace prize

1981 First woman judge appointed to U.S. Supreme Court

Advertising, the media, the arts and fashion were all exploring a new interest in, and public tolerance toward, nudity and sexuality. In 1971 minuscule women's shorts called "hot pants" became the most revealing new fashion since the 1960s miniskirt, while topless sunbathing made its debut on Mediterranean public beaches. In July that year riot police were called onto the beaches of the French Riviera in a vain attempt to protect public morality from the "monokini."

Theater censorship was pushed to the limit in 1970 when the British critic and impresario Kenneth Tynan brought his highly controversial erotic revue *Oh! Calcutta* to the London stage, featuring nude dancing and sketches about orgies. Main-stream feature films also became increasingly explicit. For instance, the Italian director Bernardo Bertolucci used the established Hollywood star Marlon Brando to explore his sexuality in *Last Tango in Paris* (1972); British director Nicolas Roeg included an explicit sex scene between Donald Sutherland and Julie Christie in his thriller *Don't Look Now* (1973).

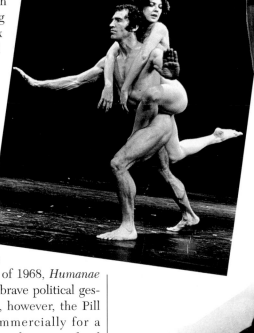

### Feminism

"I am on the Pill," declared a slogan T-shirt worn by young women in Italy in 1973. In a country that still followed the rejection of contraception enshrined in Pope Paul VI's encyclical of 1968, *Humanae Vitae,* this represented a brave political gesture. By the early 1970s, however, the Pill had been available commercially for a decade and had begun to have a radical effect on patterns of sexual behavior. More reliable than any previous form of contraception, it effectively freed women from the fear of pregnancy. This, and greater access to legal abortion, put women in control of their own fertility for the first time. It also gave them the opportunity to pursue sexuality, and demand its pleasures and rewards, in the same way that men always had. It was therefore women as much as men who were driving the new mood of sexual freedom, and female sexuality was explored with unprecedented openness in publications such as *The Hite Report on Female Sexuality* (1976) by Shere Hite. But sexual liberation was not all that women wanted: they wanted equality in all areas of their lives.

A reinvigorated current of feminism had been growing throughout the 1960s. The groundbreaking work by Betty Friedan, *The Feminine Mystique* (1963)—calling on women to define themselves outside of the terms laid down by men—had provided a major landmark and sold more than a million copies. Women no longer accepted

**ANYTHING GOES** In the early 1970s, liberation came to female fashion— women could wear almost anything, from long hippie skirts to minuscule hot pants. Clothes were abandoned in the stage revue *Oh! Calcutta* in 1970.

being restricted to, or defined by, the tasks that Western society had traditionally assigned to them: essentially the tasks of wives and mothers. They wanted to explore their own individuality and potential in a world where they had equal opportunities with men. This meant tackling the institutions that denied women equality in employment and pay, in the law, in education, in the Church, as well as challenging ingrained social attitudes. In August 1970 a demonstration of 50,000 women took place in New York; celebrating the 50th anniversary of the women's vote, they now demanded a whole raft of equal rights, such as "Equal Pay for Equal Work."

The feminist Kate Millet introduced the concept of "sexual politics" in a book of that name published in 1970: it urged women to convert their grievances into a political agenda. Another landmark book appeared that year, *The Female Eunuch*—a hard-hitting reassessment of women's position in a male-dominated world by the Australian intellectual Germaine Greer. Women, she suggested, had been effectively castrated by a male-

**VOICE OF PROTEST** Germaine Greer added a new stridency to feminist politics with her book *The Female Eunuch*, published in 1970.

dominated society. Marriage was dismissed as the legal enslavement of women. In 1972 Gloria Steinem and others founded the influential feminist magazine *Ms.*, its title broadcasting the fact that many women no longer wanted to be publicly labeled either as married (Mrs.) or unmarried (Miss).

These attitudes set the tone for the decade, in which many feminists took an aggressive stance to win greater equality. The catchphrase now was "Women's Lib," the popular abbreviation of the Women's Liberation Movement, and few women—in the Western world at least—remained untouched by its arguments.

Legislation went some way to meeting the demands of women, such as the Sex Discrimination Act passed by the British Government in 1975, which established the Equal Opportunities Commission; and the Equal Pay Act, which sought to bring women's pay into line with men's by 1976. But women's pay remained on average at 75 percent of men's for the rest of the century. In America, an Equal Rights Bill for women was passed by Congress in 1972; as it was a constitutional amendment, it then had to be ratified by the state legislatures. Many states failed to do this by the deadline of 1982, and the bill never became law. In other areas, however, tradi-

**WOMEN AGAINST THE BOMB** Thousands of women of all ages and backgrounds came to protest against the arrival of U.S. cruise missiles at the Greenham Common air base in Britain during the 1980s.

tional barriers were being broken down: women were allowed to train at the Military Academy at West Point for the first time in 1976; in 1981 Sandra Day O'Connor became the first woman to be appointed to the Supreme Court. In various countries women rose to be presidents or prime ministers, including Sirimavo Bandaranaike in Sri Lanka, Indira Gandhi in India, Golda Meir in Israel,

Margaret Thatcher in Great Britain, and Gro Harlem Bruntland in Norway. Votes for women had been the burning issue for feminist activists in the early decades of the century: latecomers to the concept included Switzerland (1971), Portugal (1976), Nigeria (1977) and Jordan (1982).

Feminism took on many causes—such as the demands for civil rights for prostitutes in France, which led to a prostitutes' strike in 1976. In 1980 a broad spectrum of feminists found common cause in Britain over the threatened arrival of American cruise missiles at an air base at Greenham Common in Berkshire. Protesters saw this as another example of male aggression, symbolized by phallic nuclear-tipped rocketry. They surrounded the base with a women's peace camp that attracted around 20,000 people.

During the 1980s, however, feminism was beginning to witness what was termed the "backlash." Men and women alike grew tired

of the stridency of militant feminism. Paradoxically, it seemed to have taken on many of the same aggressive qualities that it criticized in men; in the process, it appeared to negate or undervalue many of the distinctive values of femininity. Women still struggled to root out inequality in society, but now sought a realistic balance between the demands of a satisfying career, family life and motherhood—for those who chose it. Men, too, had become more accommodating to these demands.

By the 1990s the tone had softened further. Whereas previously feminists had argued that men and women were more or less the same and equally capable—physical differences apart—it now became permissible to

**EQUALITY AND FERTILITY** The struggle for equal pay united virtually all working women (left). The legal right of women to have an abortion, however, remained a deeply divisive and disputed issue (right).

WOMEN HAVE THE RIGHT to CHOOSE

KEEP ABORTION SAFE AND LEGAL

NERAL and MUNICIPAL WORKERS' UNION

QUALITY the struggle ALL

suggest that there were genuine and valuable differences between male and female. Indeed, in a new age of service industries and high technology, feminine skills in communication and dexterity became increasingly valued. To some degree, women now felt able to relax because many of their goals had been achieved. Not all battles had been won, and "glass ceilings" often prevented them from advancing up career hierarchies, but they now had more freedom to operate on their own terms in the world.

In many parts of the developing world, however, women remained as restricted within a patriarchal world as they ever were. In the West, too, some old feminist battles still remain unresolved. Abortion, for example, had been a key feminist issue in the early 1970s. The landmark law case

brought by "Jane Roe" and "Mary Doe"— the pseudonyms used by two women who had been refused abortion and were obliged to put their babies up for adoption—propelled the government into legalizing abortion in 1973. In Britain abortion had been legalized in 1967; France took the same measure in 1975, Italy in 1977. The emotional pain of adoption and the high casualty rate of illegal abortion fuelled the arguments of those who wanted women to have a legal choice to terminate a pregnancy—the "pro-choice" lobby. But there were many in the "pro-life" camp who were implacably opposed to abor-

**CONSENTING ADULTS** The age of consent and the legality of homosexuality varied from country to country. Gay activists fought to decriminalize homosexual activities, and to combat discrimination against gay men and women.

## EPIDEMIC OF THE AGE

**PUBLIC KNOWLEDGE** The threat of AIDS demanded a new openness about how to practice safe sex.

The late 1960s and the 1970s were the era of free love, when vastly improved methods of contraception permitted a sexual revolution, and homosexuality became more widely accepted and more openly practiced. Conservative Christian groups railed against what they perceived as the pernicious immorality of a promiscuous society, and predicted divine retribution. This seemed to have been delivered in 1981, when medical researchers in California found a new disease called Acquired Immune Deficiency Syndrome (AIDS), which attacks the human body's ability to fight off disease. The disease had undoubtedly existed prior to this, but remained unidentified and unlabeled until a cluster of victims was identified in San Francisco. All were homosexual, and the immediate conclusion was that this was a disease spread by homosexual activity. Other vulnerable groups soon emerged, such as drug addicts using intravenous injections and hemophiliacs receiving frequent blood transfusions, but the prejudice of the original conclusion proved hard to shake.

In 1985 the World Health Organization announced that AIDS had reached epidemic proportions. In America and Europe deaths occurred mainly among the gay community, but this had quickly closed ranks in the crisis, and established codes for safer conduct. All active homosexuals were advised to use condoms. Governments, meanwhile, campaigned for general public awareness, encouraging heterosexuals also to use condoms with new partners. Worldwide statistics were soon to prove conclusively that AIDS was very much a heterosexual disease: at least 70 percent of all cases resulted from heterosexual intercourse.

In 1986, 20,000 AIDS cases had been reported across the world; by 1988 there were 120,000. By 1996 there were around 23 million people infected with the Human Immunodeficiency Virus (HIV), the virus that precedes AIDS, and AIDS had been responsible for 6 million deaths. While the disease seemed to be under control in the Western world, it was rampant in developing countries. Some 20 percent of the victims lived in East and Southeast Asia, but the worst epidemic was in sub-Saharan Africa, which had 60 percent of the world's total.

**RECURRING THEME** Nine years after the Miami race riots of May 1980, police display a hardline attitude toward a black suspect. Race relations remained volatile, flaring up over real or perceived injustices.

tion, usually for religious reasons. It remains one of the most contentious issues of politics in the United States.

## Gay rights

Just as women formed their own liberation movement, so did homosexuals, who for centuries had been the victims of discrimination. The foundation of the Gay Liberation Front is usually traced back to June 28, 1969, when police raided a homosexual bar, called the Stonewall Inn, in Greenwich Village in New York City. Instead of acquiescing, the clients resisted and there were several successive nights of rioting.

The homosexual world began to organize itself into a cohesive movement that aimed to decriminalize homosexual activity, and to redress the unequal treatment of homosexuals in the law, in employment, in the armed forces and in the general prejudices of a heterosexual-oriented society. For many homosexuals, liberation also meant being able to "come out of the closet," to be able to admit freely and publicly—to family and friends—for the first time that they were "gay." Given that an estimated 4 percent of adult males are naturally inclined to be predominantly homosexual, this was welcomed by a substantial portion of the population.

Gay life—for both men and women—soon became an important subculture, with its own bars, clubs, art, magazines and even whole city quarters, such as the Castro district of San Francisco. Gay life in these self-contained environments was redefined. It was no longer subversive, timid or secretive: it often became brazen, displayed exuberantly in exotic transvestism, by wearing the macho leather outfits of bikers and cowboys, or more modestly in the short-haired look of the 1980s.

From the early 1970s on, gay life became much more generally accepted in the Western world. Governments and state legislatures responded little by little, abolishing laws against sodomy between consenting adults, lowering the age of consent, and in certain cases—as in Denmark after 1989—giving a recognized legal status in law to homosexual "marriages." Homosexual acts between consenting adults were decriminalized in Austria in 1971, in Spain in 1978, in Israel in 1988. However, homosexuality remained strictly proscribed in many other nations, notably in Muslim countries and in Africa, as well as in many areas of the United States.

The exuberance of the gay revolution in the 1970s was suddenly deflated in the 1980s by the outbreak of AIDS, which initially was perceived as a homosexual disease. The cohesive nature of the gay movement helped to bring about a rapid and disciplined response to AIDS, both in the application of preventive measures and the creation of numerous support groups to help the victims. The death toll, however, was devastating: very few people in the gay community were left untouched by the loss of friends during the early years of the AIDS epidemic.

## Ethnic rights

For many people around the world, women's rights and gay rights seemed something of a luxury: they still lived under repressive regimes or encountered widespread discrimination. International tolerance of repression was diminishing, however.

## AMNESTY INTERNATIONAL

Amnesty International was founded in 1961 by London lawyer Peter Berenson. From an initial campaign inspired by the imprisonment of Portuguese students for ill-advisedly toasting freedom in a restaurant during the dictatorship of António de Oliveira Salazar, Amnesty International grew exponentially; by the closing years of the twentieth century it had more than a million members in 160 countries and was campaigning for more than 4,000 prisoners .

Amnesty International's primary aim is to free "prisoners of conscience," men and women around the world who are imprisoned "by reason of their political, religious or other conscientiously held beliefs, or by reason of their ethnic origin, sex, color or language." It also acts on behalf of "political prisoners," those who have been arrested for political activity which has, for some reason, offended the ruling government. Here, however, Amnesty International does not necessarily campaign for release, but for a fair and prompt trial. It does not take a political view, but simply applies the tenets of the United Nations Universal Declaration of Human Rights. It also campaigns against extra-judicial killings, the death penalty and executions, and the use of torture or cruel or degrading treatment on detainees.

In recognition for its work, Amnesty International was awarded the Nobel peace prize in 1977.

**SYMBOL OF HOPE** The candle and barbed wire logo of Amnesty International.

# THE LOS ANGELES RIOTS

For all the efforts made toward multiculturalism during the 1970s and 1980s, America still retained deep undercurrents of racism. The 1992 riots in Los Angeles, a reaction to the outcome of the Rodney King trial, demonstrated the anger that had been building within the city and the nation for decades. The four cops who had brutally beaten Rodney King on March 3, 1991—their act of violence witnessed on television by millions of viewers—were acquitted on virtually all charges by an all-white jury located in Simi Valley, an area in which many cops resided. The six days of riots in South Central Los Angeles that immediately followed the verdict—one of the bloodiest American disturbances since the New York draft riots during the Civil War—essentially were a predictable reaction by an outraged minority population. At the end of the riot, 54 people were dead and around 2,000 injured; South Central Los Angeles suffered almost $1 billion in property damage, most of it to Korean groceries, liquor stores and other small businesses.

In the conventional version of the story, the brutal beating of Rodney King by a group of white Los Angeles cops, recorded on a bystander's videotape, was yet another indication of the pervasive brutality and racism of an out-of-control police department. The four cops—Sgt. Stacey Koon and officers Laurence Powell, Theodore Briseno and Timothy Wind—were charged with unlawful force, or allowing the unlawful use of force. On the basis of the videotape, they were widely expected to be convicted. However, the media's portrayal of the event was complicated and convoluted: the edited version of the videotape played on television exhibited a helpless King beaten senseless by police. It did not include King's refusal to comply with the orders of California Highway Patrol Officer Melanie Singer, nor did it include his resistance of arrest—King had violently thrown a swarm of cops off his back when they tried to handcuff him. After the jury witnessed the unedited tape and heard the story of the events that preceded the taping, they reached their verdict. The acquittal of the police officers brought mayhem to Los Angeles. The mayor of the city, Tom Bradley, inflamed the city more by issuing an angry statement denouncing the verdict; it was interpreted in some quarters as an invitation to the community to take matters into its own hands.

The four police officers were eventually dismissed. The episode changed the way Los Angeles viewed its police force, but it was a violent and destructive lesson.

**LOS ANGELES RIOTS** Two buildings on Picos Boulevard burn during riots following the acquittal of the two policemen charged with the beating of Rodney King (right). Below, a woman from Los Angeles raises her hands high, taking in the burning buildings around her during the riots.

A new emphasis on human rights was heralded by the Helsinki Accords of 1975, and nongovernmental organizations such as Amnesty International waged an ongoing battle against the abuse of human rights, torture and illegal detention.

Within the democratic countries of the West, meanwhile, minorities continued to suffer abuse, victimization and discrimination. Much had been achieved by the civil rights movement during the 1960s, but racism remained an enduring scourge. Race riots erupted periodically through the passing decades, as in Miami in May 1980, following the acquittal by an all-white jury of a white police officer accused of killing a black businessman; 18 people died in the ensuing violence.

Britain introduced its Race Relations Act in 1976, under which incitement to racial hatred became an offense. This was the start of a series of government-led strategies to improve racial tolerance and integration. Nonetheless, the country saw violent disturbances on the streets of London, Liverpool, Bristol, Birmingham and several other cities in the spring and summer of 1981. They were Britain's worst race riots of the century.

In West Germany, the racist hatred of neo-Nazi groups was directed at immigrant "guest workers" from Turkey and elsewhere, while in France the undercurrent of racism toward immigrant North Africans was exploited by the right-wing National Front led by Jean-Marie Le Pen. In South Africa racism remained official policy of the white-supremacist regime until the dismantling of apartheid began in the early 1990s.

Native or aboriginal groups in Australia, New Zealand and America also worked to redress historic grievances. American Indians in the United States had suffered under the policy known as "termination"—the ending of a special relationship with the federal government, which had progressively handed over responsibility to the state legislatures. This resulted in rising unemployment, poorer education and increased poverty, especially on the reservations. The 1980 census showed that there were 1,360,000 American Indians, 45 percent of whom lived on reservations. A quarter of the total were living beneath the poverty level.

The militant American Indian Movement (AIM), established in 1968, took it upon itself to reverse this trend, and to pursue land claims and demands for greater self-government. In a headline-hitting incident in 1973, armed members of AIM took over Wounded Knee in South Dakota, the emotionally loaded site of the massacre that had brought the Indian Wars to their dismal close in 1890. The protesters resisted the authorities for 72 days before giving up their siege, during which two of them had lost their lives.

In the closing decades of the twentieth century, native American peoples in both America and Canada won increasing support for their land claims; for instance, the Yukon Indians achieved a major land deal in 1996, and the Inuit were granted half the Northwest Territories of Canada for a new self-governing territory called Nunavut. American Indians worked hard to enhance their status in American society by developing programs to promote their arts, languages, dance, traditional religion and philosophy. A measure of their success was the change in attitude in Hollywood films, witnessed particularly in Kevin Costner's *Dances with Wolves* (1990), which portrays Indians in a respectful and sympathetic light.

Similar conflicts were being played out in New Zealand, where the Maoris represent 12 percent of the total population. One of their main contentions is land-ownership, an issue that dates back to the Treaty of Waitangi of 1840. This had been designed to protect their land rights, but the good intentions were subsequently compromised by one-sided deals, confiscations, illegal purchase, inadequate surveys and misunderstandings. Facing a growing tumult of Maori protest, in 1975 the Labor government established the Waitangi Tribunal which continues to assess Maori land claims dating back to 1840; the Office of Treaty Settlements uses the tribunal's reports as a basis for settling the claims. The Maori language was made an official language of New Zealand, alongside English, in 1987. But Maoris still suffer from disadvantage: disaffected youths form urban street gangs, fall readily into drug and alcohol abuse, and more than 50 percent of New Zealand's prison population is Maori.

The Australian Aborigines staged a major protest to coincide with bicentennial celebration ceremonies held on January 26, 1988. More than 15,000 people attended a march and rally about land rights. Unlike the Maoris, the Aborigines never had a treaty and had a different concept of land ownership from Europeans. Some progress has been made with the (limited) Land Rights Act of 1976 and the Native Title Act of

**STEPS TOWARD JUSTICE** Delegations of American Indians have brought their grievances to Washington for over a hundred years. Political activism and heightened public awareness since the 1970s have brought some redress.

1994, but the issues are far from resolved. The sacred sites of Uluru (Ayers Rock) and Kata-Tjuta (the Olgas) were returned to their traditional owners in 1985.

"Everyone is crying out for peace, none is crying out for justice," sang the Jamaican reggae star Peter Tosh in "Equal Rights" (1977). "I don't want no peace, I want equal rights and justice." It caught the combative mood of the times, and the plea for the eradication of inequality. However, many despaired of politics and sought meaning in religion.

**THE FIRST AUSTRALIANS** Aborigines on a protest march in Sydney during the bicentennial celebrations in 1988. Since the coming of Europeans they have suffered discrimination and expropriation of their land; today Aborigines are demanding equal rights and respect for their traditions.

# SEARCHING FOR MEANING

## RELIGION WITNESSED A REVIVAL, BUT THE GULLIBLE WERE EXPLOITED AND SEVERAL CULTS INVOLVED ABUSE, DEATH AND SUICIDE

At the beginning of the twentieth century, many observers predicted that religion would gradually but relentlessly be pushed into the wings by science. Discoveries in atomic physics, in astronomy, the logic of Darwinism, all appeared to be colonizing the territory that was once the exclusive domain of the godhead.

By 1970 this prediction appeared way off target: religion was still around. Leaders in the mainstream institutionalized religions worried publicly about declining participation; for many people in the Western world, in particular, attendance at weekly services was no longer the norm that it had been for their parents and grandparents. Yet it was also true that significant numbers of people, and not all of them old, continued to draw comfort and spiritual inspiration from mainstream religion.

At the same time, there had been a proliferation of sects and cults that demanded an all-consuming fervor. "Born again" was the term that Christians used to express this renewal, witnessed especially in the evangelical churches. In Islam the new vigor manifested itself in the uncompromising reappraisal that became known as fundamentalism, which had widespread political repercussions around the world.

### Looking East

At the beginning of the 1970s the "hippie trail" was still in full flourish. This overland route linked Europe to Australia, via the Middle East, Afghanistan, Thailand and Bali. But the main focus was the Indian subcontinent, where young travelers from Europe, Australia, New Zealand, America, and Canada converged in search of spiritual enlightenment from the Hindu gurus in their ashrams or Buddhist teachers in remote mountain retreats. With their ancient reverberations, philosophical wisdom, promises of personal enlightenment and whiff of exoticism, the Asian religions satisfied these Westerners' spirit of inquiry where many strands of the Christian tradition, with their insistence on the articles of faith, failed. Religious practices, such as yoga, meditation and dietary control also taught them new ways to look at both mind and body—and new perspectives were the hippie travellers' primary quest. They were searching for meaning in a world that seemed to have been derailed by rampant materialism, inequality and political strife.

Many were following the path made fashionable by The Beatles and other celebrities, who visited the ashram of the Maharishi Mahesh Yogi in the late 1960s. Since the 1940s the Maharishi had been working on a practice called "Transcendental Meditation," repackaging the ancient discipline of meditation in a form that Westerners could easily learn and adopt. Having successfully exported his

**HIPPIE TRAIL** The hippie movement spilled over into the 1970s. While most went no further than the nearest music festival, many set off on a quest for enlightenment through travel and mind-broadening experiences.

1978 Pope John Paul II elected; Mass suicide at Jonestown, Guyana

1981 Bagwan Shree Rajneesh builds Ashram in Oregon

**MANTRA TO HEAVEN** Hare Krishna devotees undertook a complete personal transformation—mental, physical and social.

During the 1970s he acquired a following of some 200,000, and in 1981 built a large center called the Rajneeshpuram in Oregon. However, this became an administrative nightmare, and collapsed in 1985 amid widespread desertions and recriminations, and charges of firearms infringements, drug dealing and fraud. His ashram back in Poona, India, continued to attract many wealthy Western devotees until his death in 1990.

## Christian revival

The old established Christian churches had difficulties squaring up to this youthful quest for renewed spirituality. The Roman Catholic Church received new impetus, however, with the appointment of Karol Wojtyla, Archbishop of Krakow, as Pope John Paul II in 1978—the first non-Italian pope since 1542 and, at 58, the youngest in the twentieth century. He soon embarked on a series of international tours, including his native Poland in 1979, attracting vast and rapturous crowds who

teachings, the Maharishi set up schools around the Western world.

Schools based on Asian religions soon became commonplace, ranging from night-school yoga classes to strictly disciplined training in Japanese Zen Buddhism. To some, however, it was not enough simply to borrow from Asian religions: they wanted total immersion. The shaven-headed and saffron-robed devotees of the Hare Krishna movement became a common sight in Western cities during the 1970s, as they went about spreading their message, begging for donations and recruiting new candidates. The movement was founded by A.C. Bhaktivedanta (Swami Prabhupada) in New York in 1965, and had spread to more than 100 centers worldwide before his death at 81 in 1977. Its appeal lay partly in its strict, uncomplicated and stringently nonmaterialistic lifestyle. Through the study and practice of ancient Vedic scriptures, and the chanting of the Hare Krishna mantra, devotees could hope to throw off the base world of the flesh and join the energy of the godhead Krishna.

Parents of Hare Krishna recruits often complained that their children were victims

of mind-control techniques or brainwashing. It was a criticism leveled, with varying degrees of justice, at a number of closed cults. Many cults also demanded large financial donations from their devotees, which led to accusations of financial impropriety. The Indian guru Bagwan Shree Rajneesh accrued vast wealth—which he openly displayed—by promoting a cult that combined ancient mysticism with sexual freedom.

**CULT LEADER** Bagwan Shree Rajneesh's following was drawn mainly from the Western nations. His cult centered upon a technique known as "loving meditation," and inspired intense devotion to Rajneesh himself.

1989 The Dalai Lama wins the Nobel peace prize

1993 Siege of Waco ranch ends in 82 deaths

1994 First manifestation of the "Toronto Blessing"

1995 Aum Shinrikyo cult releases poison gas on Tokyo underground

1997 Mass suicide of Heaven's Gate Cult

came to watch him pass in his distinctive "pope-mobile" and to hear him conduct an outdoor Mass in a park or sports arena.

In Latin America, where the gap between rich and poor, the exploiters and the exploited, was all too evident, Roman Catholic priests such as the Peruvian Gustavo Gutiérrez were looking for practical ways to alleviate the plight of the oppressed. They developed what was known as "Liberation Theology." Local self-help groups called "base communities" were set up to tackle practical problems at village level, such as water distribution, sewage, electrical supply and public health, and also to study the Bible. The movement quickly became embroiled in politics, however; it clashed with the aspirations of radical left-wing politicians and guerrilla organizations, and was considered subversive by many governments.

Liberation theology spread beyond Latin America to Africa. Initially, Pope John Paul II seemed to give encouragement to the trend, but later he showed distaste for too overt a connection between the Roman Catholic Church and politics, and the movement was outflanked by the appointment of more mainstream prelates. In theology, if not necessarily in politics, John Paul II was a conservative who reaffirmed the Church's opposition to contraception, abortion, divorce and the ordination of women priests.

Such conservative attitudes may have perplexed many Roman Catholics, but they were part of the appeal for evangelical Protestant groups that underwent massive revival throughout much of the Western world. The Southern Baptist Convention, for example, saw its membership rise from 10.8 million in 1965 to 13.6 million in 1980. This brand of Christianity appealed to many ordinary people who were dismayed by what they perceived as the moral depravity of modern liberalism. They wanted to see a reaffirmation of morality, of family values and of faith.

The evangelical movement flourished through television and radio. Strongly fundamentalist, they tended to preach moral rectitude and strict adherence to the Bible, together with a broadly right-wing, anti-liberal agenda, which includes anti-communism and support for strong military defense, and vocal opposition to feminism, abortion and gay rights. During the late 1980s, the reputation of the TV evangelists was severely compromised, however, by flagrant hypocrisy. In 1987 the Reverend Jim Bakker, head of the Christian media empire Heritage USA, confessed to having an extramarital affair

**EQUALITY OF FAITH** The Church of England accepted women as deacons from 1985 and the ordination of women as priests in 1992, but not without fierce opposition from some members.

## THE DALAI LAMA

Tenzin Gyatso was just five years old in 1940 when he was identified as the reincarnation of the bodhisattva ("buddha-to-be") Avalokiteshvara—and of the previous Dalai Lamas—before being enthroned in Tibet's capital Lhasa. He was now one of the key religious leaders in this remote land of Buddhist monks, and the head of state. In 1950, China annexed Tibet and began a long campaign of repression. The Tibetans rebelled in 1959, but when the rising failed, the Dalai Lama and 100,000 followers fled over the mountains into India, and established a government in exile in Dharmsala.

From this base, the Dalai Lama campaigned relentlessly against Chinese repression in Tibet; this became particularly severe during the Cultural Revolution, when many of the monasteries were forcibly evacuated, vandalized and destroyed. The Dalai Lama traveled the world, pleading his case, becoming ever more respected for his dignity, wisdom and lack of vindictiveness. At every turn, however, China has seen him as an enemy. When the Dalai Lama visited America in 1987, for instance, and addressed Congress, China accused the United States of meddling in its internal affairs. When he visited Taiwan in 1997, he was accused by Beijing of plotting to pull China apart. In 1987 the Dalai Lama put forward a Five-Point Plan for Tibet, in which he proposed to abandon his pursuit of Tibetan independence in return for greater autonomy, and the conversion of Tibet into "a sanctuary of peace and nonviolence where human beings and nature can live in peace and harmony." China's response has given few grounds for optimism.

In 1989 the Dalai Lama was awarded the Nobel prize for peace. The citation praised his pursuit of "peaceful solutions based upon tolerance and mutual respect in order to preserve the historical and cultural heritage of his people."

the active presence of the Holy Spirit and became known as the "Toronto Blessing." Although the meeting was originally scheduled as just one of four such gatherings, the series has continued ever since, held every night of the week except for Monday. By September 1995 the church had been visited by 220,000 people, and had to move its location to a conference center nearby that could seat congregations of 3,000.

The Toronto Blessing spread to numerous churches across the denominations and all around the world. It remains, however, deeply controversial. The Airport Vineyard Church was originally part of the Association of Vineyard Churches, a network of neo-Pentecostal

**TV EVANGELISM  The Reverend Jimmy Swaggart (left), famed for his firebrand preaching, was able to command large audiences. As he and other evangelists such as Jerry Falwell spoke on the air (above), viewers phoned in with prayer requests and donations.**

with a secretary. He was criticized by his main rival, Jimmy Swaggart, as "a cancer on the body of Christ," but just the following year Swaggart himself had to confess to consorting with a prostitute.

Nevertheless, the grass-roots revival of fervent fundamentalist and evangelical Christianity had a major impact in America. The Moral Majority, founded by the Baptist minister Jerry Falwell in 1970, formed a powerful conservative political grouping and helped to secure the election of the Republican president Ronald Reagan in 1980.

The revival of Christian fervor was witnessed particularly in the Pentecostal

churches, which first developed in Kansas at the start of the century. As in the original Pentecostal revelation to the Apostles, they seek evidence of the presence of the Holy Spirit at their gatherings, witnessed in such "charismatic" manifestations as "speaking in tongues," gifts of prophecy and miraculous healing. On January 20, 1994, a prayer meeting was held at the Airport Vineyard Church, by the runway of Toronto airport. Suddenly the whole congregation was visited by a whole range of apparently uncontrollable behavior, such as trembling, jerking, fainting, laughter, wailing and emitting animal sounds. These were interpreted as manifestations of

churches founded in Anaheim, California, by John Wimber, a former businessman and pop group manager who had experienced a dramatic conversion to fundamentalist Christianity in 1962. But even this association distanced itself from the Toronto Blessing.

## Religion on the fringe

One of the most spectacular movements of the era is the Unification Church, which blends Christian and Taoist beliefs. It was founded in 1954 by the Korean preacher and industrialist Sun Myung Moon—a name that gave rise to its members' popular label, the "Moonies." The Unification Church claims

## APOCALYPSE IN GUYANA

A bizarre and horrific story emerged from the stifling jungles of Guyana in November 1978. Scattered in family groups, bloated with the heat and decomposition, lay 913 bodies, including those of 276 children. They were the participants of the largest mass suicide in modern times.

The place was called Jonestown, a remote settlement 150 miles from the capital Georgetown, which had been established as an agricultural commune by the American preacher Jim Jones for members of his People's Temple. Jones, a former Methodist preacher, founded the People's Temple in Indiana in the 1950s before moving to California in 1965. His theology was a potent mix of fundamentalist Christianity, social welfare, racial equality and apocalyptic vision. The church grew rapidly in the 1970s, with centers in San Francisco and Los Angeles, and numerous communes and retreats all the way up the West Coast. It also ran social projects, including programs for the handicapped, drug rehabilitation schemes and soup kitchens. Jones played a significant role in public life; he was involved in the Democratic Party, and was chairman of the San Francisco Housing Authority in 1976-7.

By 1975 the People's Temple had 4,000 members, 70 percent of whom were drawn from the African-American community. Jones began to see himself as the messiah, and preached a vision of the future in which a fascist government would persecute blacks before an apocalyptic nuclear conflagration. But the press increasingly drew attention to malpractice: to financial and moral impropriety within the church, and Jones's false claims to perform miracles—such as raising people from the dead.

Feeling increasingly persecuted, in 1977 Jones moved with 1,000 Temple members to Jonestown. Here he subjected his followers to tyrannical rule, instituting a regime of mind control, surveillance, torture, public floggings and detention, enforced by guards armed with submachine guns. He also regularly rehearsed mass suicide, in preparation for the apocalypse.

Word reached America that Temple members were being held in Jonestown against their will. In November 1978 Democratic Congressman Leo Ryan went to Guyana to investigate, with four journalists and a group of relatives of Temple members. After one night at Jonestown, Ryan and his team set off for the airstrip with ten Temple defectors. Jones gave orders to his guards to annihilate the entire party. They opened fire at the airstrip, killing Ryan and three journalists and a woman defector, but the rest of the party managed to board a plane and escape. Knowing that this failed action would bring the wrath of military might on the People's Temple, Jones put his suicide plan into action. Vats of soft drink were prepared, then laced with cyanide. "The time has come to meet in another place," Jones declared, as he ordered his followers to drink the poison. This they dutifully did. Parents used syringes to squirt the liquid into their infants' mouths, while the guards shot at anyone who tried to escape. Only 34 succeeded in evading death.

out his consent. The religion developed in Jamaica, strongly influenced by the "back to Africa" philosophy of Marcus Garvey. When it became clear that Rastafarians could not practically expect to go back to Ethiopia, they turned the concept into a philosophical rather than physical journey. Their distinctive culture received worldwide exposure through the reggae music of Bob Marley and Peter Tosh.

### Armageddon

Charismatic leadership can wield unhealthy power in the enclosed world of religious cults. This has manifested itself time and again in the last three decades of the century, most notoriously when Jim Jones, leader of the People's Temple, succeeded in persuading over 900 of his followers to join him in mass suicide in 1978.

His cult was linked to an apocalyptic vision, which predicted the imminent end of the world. This was also the case at the

**AFRICAN IDENTITY** The Rastafarians in Jamaica developed a belief system that offered them independence from the corruption of the Western industrial world and a heritage linked to Ethiopia.

to further Christ's work by combating Satanism, a manifestation of which it believes to be communism. Members are required to show strict loyalty to Moon and Church, which has given rise to criticism of mind-control and indoctrination—an interpretation reinforced by the Unification Church's penchant for mass weddings.

The Unification Church claims that it is persecuted by the authorities—a claim also made by the Church of Scientology, a movement founded in the 1950s by the science-fiction author L. Ron Hubbard. The central concept of the Church of Scientology is that we suffer the residual legacy of bad experiences when young. These "engrams" have to be removed by a form of psychotherapy called dianetics in order to lead more balanced, healthy and self-determined lives, and to tap into the life energy of the universe. Scientology came under scrutiny for financial mismanagement in the 1980s, but claims 8 million members worldwide,

including the Hollywood film stars Tom Cruise and Nicole Kidman.

Rastafarians have consciously put themselves on the other side of the law by insisting on smoking marijuana or "ganja." To them, however, the law is just another pernicious factor of Babylon, the corrupted world and living hell that exists outside the sacred land of Ethiopia. Rastafarians believe that the blacks are a superior race, the disinherited descendants of Israelites, who have temporarily been dominated by the inferior whites. But their day will come, led by their god-like figurehead, Emperor Haile Selassie of Ethiopia, the "Lion of Judah," who claimed to be descended from King Solomon. Haile Selassie's pre-coronation title was Ras (Prince) Tafari, giving rise to the name of the religion that deified him as the messiah of black people, but with-

**LIVING NIGHTMARE** The Aum sect released sarin nerve gas on the Tokyo underground on March 3, 1995, killing 12 people and harming thousands.

ranch at Waco, Texas, which served as the headquarters of the Branch Davidians. The cult had been founded in 1935 and was directed by a series of leaders who identified themselves with the Biblical King David and the Messiah. The last of these was Vernon Howell, a one-time rock guitarist and former Seventh Day Adventist with a lust for power, who changed his name in 1990 to David Koresh (after the ancient Persian King Cyrus). Koresh created his own highly authoritarian regime, ruling and abusing his band of 130 or so submissive followers. He taught that the world would be taken over in an apocalyptic battle with nonbelievers, and only the chosen ones would survive. Over a year or so in 1992-3, the ranch became heavily armed with $200,000 worth of guns, grenades and ammunition, and the members, including children, underwent military training.

It was to search for illegally held arms that the federal Bureau of Alcohol, Tobacco and Firearms (ATF) sent a 200-strong team of agents to the ranch on February 28, 1993. The result was an armed confrontation in which four government officers and six cult members were killed. The federal agents were forced to retreat to the perimeter of the Waco ranch, and a 51 day siege began. During this time 37 cult members were released, but 91 remained inside when the authorities decided to act. Thinking that the cult members would surrender, on April 19, 1993, the federal forces sent armored vehicles in to puncture the ranch walls, then fired tear gas. The ranch went up in flames, perhaps deliberately torched by cult members, and Koresh along with 81 others—including 25 children—died in the conflagration.

The Branch Davidians were just one of several cults whose apocalyptic teachings lead to multiple deaths. In 1994, 53 robed members of the Swiss-based Order of the Solar Temple, led by Luc Jouret, were found dead from gunshot wounds and suffocation in their

**COMMUNAL DEATH** The Heaven's Gate cult lived in San Diego, communicating with the outside world through the Internet. Their belief in an extraterrestrial destiny was apparently so absolute that all the members volunteered to commit suicide in unison.

lodges in Switzerland and Canada.

In March 1995, 12 people were killed and 5,500 were injured by the release of the deadly nerve gas sarin on the Tokyo underground. The Japanese police traced it back to a cult called Aum Shinrikyo (meaning Church of the Supreme Truth), led by Shoko Asahara, who styled himself as the Messiah. He claimed to have 30,000 followers in Japan, America, Germany and Russia. In Japan he built up an armory that included military aircraft and the chemical ingredients to manufacture sarin. Even before the underground attack, Aum was implicated in a number of murders, including those of several lawyers investigating the cult. The net closed in on Aum, and Shoko Asahara was arrested in May 1995.

In March 1997 all 39 members of the Heaven's Gate cult were found dead in a suburban villa in San Diego, California. The celibate group made a living by designing web-pages, while pursuing their belief in extraterrestrial powers. When the Hale-Bopp comet appeared in the night skies, they believed that it was a cover for an alien spaceship—this being their opportunity to join it. Dressed in uniforms, they drank a cocktail of sedatives and vodka, then lay on their bunk beds with their heads covered in plastic bags. It was a cult suicide for the modern age.

# THE MUSIC INDUSTRY

## THE MUSIC INDUSTRY BURGEONED INTO A MULTIMILLION DOLLAR BUSINESS, WITH A MAJOR IMPACT ON LIFESTYLES AND FASHION

**JOHN AND YOKO** Former Beatle John Lennon with his second wife, the Japanese-born artist Yoko Ono, in 1971.

The last few years of the 1960s had seen an extraordinary flourishing of musical innovation, transforming the music world into an industry catering for a rainbow spectrum of tastes. A sharp distinction was drawn between "pop" on the one hand, which focused on chart hits, and "rock" on the other, which centered on vinyl albums and live performances, and attracted the earnest and loyal devotion of its fans. Many of the leading rock performers in 1970 had cut their musical teeth in the late 1960s, and were now enjoying the benefits of an increasingly wealthy and sophisticated industry.

But the atmosphere had subtly changed, corrupted by money, by the uncritical adulation of fans, and the pressures of a business that was now judging success less by talent and innovation and more by the size of the venues and the number of tickets sold. The Beatles split up in April 1970, the result of business pressure and artistic differences.

Hard drugs and alcohol also took their toll. In September 1970 the brilliantly innovative guitarist Jimi Hendrix died in his sleep due to an excess of alcohol and barbiturates.

**ROCK CASUALTIES** The careers of Jimi Hendrix (left), Janis Joplin (center) and Jim Morrison (right) were all cut short at the age of 27. Although the role of drugs in these deaths remains disputed, they were certainly victims of pressure, and of the excesses now expected of rock stars.

He was 27. Then in October the raucous white blues singer Janis Joplin, also 27, died of a drug overdose. Jim Morrison, singer and leading light of the ground-breaking band *The Doors,* became another casualty of drugs and fast living in June 1971, also at 27.

### Serious music

Rock became a victim of its own vanity. A number of "supergroups" formed in the early 1970s, drawing together proven stars who were expected to achieve new heights of innovation. Emerson, Lake and Palmer (ELP) tried to elevate rock by fusing it with the classical music of composers including Bartók and Janácek. They had considerable success with their *Pictures at an Exhibition* album based on Mussorgsky (1971), but the enterprise lacked musical conviction and proved something of a cul-de-sac. This trend in "soft rock" also explored the possibilities of jazz fusion and electronic music, seen for instance in the Moog synthesizer work of the German group Tangerine Dream, one of the few bands from continental Europe to break through to an international audience. Pink Floyd found a more successful formula: their *Dark Side of the Moon* album (1973) sold over 25 million copies.

Other groups took their cue from Jimi Hendrix to produce ear-splitting loud guitar-based rock that soon acquired the label "heavy metal." Led

1970

| 1970 The Beatles split up | 1971 First stage production of *Jesus Christ Superstar* | 1972 David Bowie produces *Ziggy Stardust* | 1974 Abba wins the Eurovision Song Contest | 1975 Punk rock is born | 1977 John Travolta stars in *Saturday Night Fever* | 1979 Rap is launched | 1982 Michael Jackson promotes *Thriller* with a feature-film-style video |

Zeppelin was at the more gifted end of the spectrum: their ballad "Stairway to Heaven" became one of the classic tracks of all time.

In contrast, the mood of the gentle 1960s was maintained by "folk rock"; Fairport Convention, Steeleye Span, and the Incredible String Band looked for inspiration in traditional folk songs, but applied the new twist of jazz, rock and electrification. The French harpist Alan Stivell also had considerable success with his *Renaissance of the Celtic Harp* (1971). The exceptional songwriting skills of francophone performers such as Jacques Brel and Georges Brassens were rarely matched in English, with the major exception of Bob Dylan, who produced a string of albums containing some of his best work in *Planet Waves* (1974), *Blood on the Tracks* (1974) and *Desire* (1975).

Just as the tail-end of the hippie era was descending into a gloomy, introspective drabness, a new generation of musicians

**SOUND AND LIGHT** The British band Pink Floyd, playing to mass audiences in sports stadiums, mounted ever more elaborate stage shows.

bounced onto the music scene in a splash of glitter, sequins, outrageous bell-bottoms and towering platform heels. The Sweet, Marc Bolan and Queen all formed part of what became called "glam rock." At the more serious end of the spectrum was David Bowie, whose *The Rise and Fall of Ziggy Stardust and the Spiders from Mars* (1972) intro-

**STARMAN** Both innovative showmen, David Bowie and Elton John (inset) provided a welcome antidote when rock music began taking itself too seriously in the early 1970s.

## POP VIDEOS

It was television that first began to explore the visual possibilities of pop and rock music. Filmmakers used inventive camera techniques and adventurous cutting, synchronized to the music, to portray performers in an upbeat, novel way. Then in 1971 the video recorder was launched. Here was a format that could be readily packaged and sold to the public. One of the earliest true pop videos was Queen's *Bohemian Rhapsody* (1975), which used multifaceted lenses and other camera techniques to enhance the visual impact of the song.

It soon became clear that the pop video could be seen as an art form in its own right, and interaction between visual imagery and soundtrack could range from a straightforward recording of a performance to a highly personalized imaginative flight of fancy. Pop videos represented a blank canvas, and directors ransacked the archives and toolboxes of film to find novel and exciting ways to fill it. The montage techniques evolved in the 1920s by Sergei

**COSTLY THRILLS** Michael Jackson's high-budget video *Thriller* was a landmark production.

Eisenstein proved a particularly rich vein—inspiring a rapid-fire series of disparate images to create a kaleidoscopic effect. Other filmmakers turned to animation, others still to Hollywood to create the grand spectacle. Pop songs became the basis of 4-minute feature films, with budgets to match. As a measure of how much the visual aspect of the music business had moved on, for his famous *Thriller* video (1982) Michael Jackson created a 10-minute mini-horror movie, complete with state of the art special effects, directed by John Landis.

By the 1990s, the pop video had become an essential part of the business: indeed, it became hard to promote a chart-topping song without one.

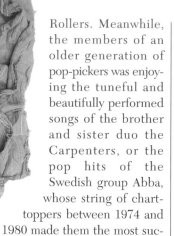

duced wacky, futuristic imagery in songs of startling inventiveness. Another outrageous dresser was Elton John, who produced his first album in 1970 and the psychedelic *Captain Fantastic and the Brown Dirt Cowboy* in 1975; he remained a leading figure of the pop world for the rest of the century.

Around 1972, the music industry had identified a new teenage market—the teenyboppers—and proceeded to feed it with a series of young stars, such as David Cassidy, the Osmonds, the Jackson Five and the Bay City Rollers. Meanwhile, the members of an older generation of pop-pickers was enjoying the tuneful and beautifully performed songs of the brother and sister duo the Carpenters, or the pop hits of the Swedish group Abba, whose string of chart-toppers between 1974 and 1980 made them the most successful group since The Beatles.

## The arrival of punk

By 1975 a younger generation had become disenchanted with the gentle legacy of the hippie era, and the blatant commercialism of the rock and pop world. A subculture of alienated British youth erupted in an explosive reaction called "punk rock." The British group, the Sex Pistols, led the way. Foul-mouthed and provocative in interviews, raucous and uncouth and unmusical on stage, they presented a deliberately challenging and unsettling image, which had as its main merit a raw and angry energy. Other groups such as the Clash, the Damned and the Jam echoed this trend, playing to audiences who banged their heads and spat and drank to a mindless oblivion. Their clothing was appropriately provocative: torn jeans, T-shirts with abusive slogans, hair dyed vivid red, blue and green set in spikes or with a Mohican mane, and adorned with chains and body piercings, most famously the safety pin through the nose.

Punk rock had a limited shelf life, and soured when Sid Vicious of the Sex Pistols took his anti-social agenda to its logical conclusion by killing his girlfriend in New York; he then died of a drug overdose. But punk's new energy had a collateral effect, and galvanized a new set of songwriters and performers such as U2, the Boomtown Rats and Adam and the Ants. This coincided with a separate trend in clubbing and disco dancing, which took its lead from New York, where the

ultra-fashionable Studio 54 attracted the rich and famous. The hugely successful film *Saturday Night Fever* (1977), starring the newcomer John Travolta, charts the transfiguration of a shop clerk through his startling ability on the dance floor in New York. It also marked a new lease of life in disco music for the Bee Gees, whose 60s hits had come mainly from tuneful ballads.

Just as the blues and jazz had been a decisive influence on the

development of pop music earlier in the century, black music continued to have a major impact. During the late 1960s and early 70s a new kind of Caribbean music was being forged in Jamaica. It had a sedate, lilting rhythm, with a strong base line, and a four-beat bar with heavily accented upbeat. Called reggae, it came to prominence through the soundtrack of the Jamaican film *The Harder They Come* (1972) starring Jimmy Cliff, but really took off with the sudden rise to fame of Bob Marley.

By the early 1980s music-lovers could listen on their new Sony Walkmans to a range of softer, more song-based groups such as Culture Club and Depeche Mode, who became known collectively as the New Romantics. At the same time a novel kind of black music called "rap" was taking America by storm. A product of the disco world, where DJs used rhythmic improvised poetry to talk over edited excerpts from recorded music, it was heralded in 1979 when American music critics voted "The Message" by Grandmaster Flash and the Furious Five as the single of the year. Rap was soon associated with distinctive dance trends, such as hip-hop, body-popping and breakdancing.

Highly inventive, if more mainstream, black artists included Michael Jackson, formerly the child star of the Jackson Five. His album *Thriller* (1982) became one of the best-selling ever. He was one of many artists to see the potential of the pop video as a powerful tool to manipulate public image. Increasing budgets were spent on pop videos by stars such as Michael Jackson, Prince, Elton John and Madonna.

**RASTA MAN** Bob Marley's trance-like performances behind the microphone suggested that his musical confidence was purely instinctive.

In contrast, a new set of post-punk bands from Seattle appealed to disillusioned youth by their harsh, grinding, angered sound and downbeat dressing, labeled "grunge." The leading band was Nirvana, led by the angst-ridden Kurt Cobain, who killed himself in 1994. Around the same time, a distinctive, hypnotic dance music called "acid house" was keeping pace with the thousands of young people who, fuelled with the drug Ecstasy, turned up for impromptu "raves" in old warehouses and aircraft hangars.

By the 1990s popular music tastes embraced a broad spectrum—jazz, soul, blues, rock, folk, country and western. A trend in "world music" opened the field yet further. Pioneers such as Peter Gabriel, formerly of Genesis, David Byrne of Talking Heads, and Ry Cooder went out in search of musical integrity wherever it

## BOB MARLEY

By far the greatest star of reggae was Bob Marley, who almost single-handedly raised reggae music from a distinctive local sound to the world stage. Marley formed his first group in 1964 in Kingston, Jamaica, with two school friends, Bunny Wailer and Peter Tosh. Calling themselves the Wailers, they remained a minority interest until 1972, when they caught the attention of promoter Chris Blackwell, who signed them up to his Island Records label. Their first album with that label, *Catch a Fire* (1972), was an international success, and songs such as "I Shot the Sheriff" and "No Woman No Cry" became hit singles.

One aspect of Bob Marley's appeal was the strong sense of integrity that permeates his music. He sang with a committed intensity, often through a cloud of ganja (marijuana) smoke—songs about the poor and oppressed, and about his native Jamaica, seen from the perspective of a committed Rastafarian. His words echoed the toughness and violence of Third World urban life, and contained a burning sense of justice, while also touching on the universal qualities of tenderness and love.

When cancer cut his life short at the age of 36 in May 1981, he was given a state funeral in Jamaica.

## ANDREW LLOYD WEBBER

From an early age Andrew Lloyd Webber was driven by a vision—to revive the theatrical magic of musicals of the classic era of Rodgers and Hammerstein. In 1965 he met the lyricist Tim Rice, and together they wrote a number of pop songs before launching their *Joseph and the Amazing Technicolor Dreamcoat,* a reworking of the Biblical story of Joseph. Their next venture put them in the big league: *Jesus Christ Superstar* was a huge popular success. Never shy of exploring new subject matter for musicals, in 1978 Lloyd Webber and Rice produced *Evita,* the story of the wife of Juan Perón, President of Argentina during the late 1940s and early 1950s.

Lloyd Webber worked without Rice from then on. *Cats* (1982), a song and dance version of T.S. Eliot's *Old Possum's Book of Practical Cats,* was a huge success in the West End of London, on Broadway in New York City, and around the world. This was followed by *Starlight Express* in 1984, *The Phantom of the Opera* (1986), *Aspects of Love* (1989), *Sunset Boulevard* (1993) and *Whistle Down the Wind* (1998).

Lloyd Webber had struck a rich vein: his tunes were often called bland and unoriginal, but each show had its fair share of hummable hits. The formula worked: in 1983 Lloyd Webber had three shows running simultaneously on both sides of the Atlantic. In 1991 six of his musicals were being performed in London, a theatrical record.

**GILDED YOUTH** Andrew Lloyd Webber (right) and his lyricist Tim Rice were in their early twenties when they struck success.

could be found. As a result, Western music received new impetus from South American folk music, African praise singing and guitar rhythms, Indian bhangra dance music, choral music from Eastern Europe, rai club music from Algeria, from artists such as Youssou N'Dour and Cheikh Lô of Senegal, Nusrat Fateh Ali Khan of Pakistan, and the Lady-smith Black Mambazo of South Africa. The last was introduced to a world stage by Paul Simon on his *Graceland* album (1986).

Although constantly refreshed with new talent, rock produced some long-lasting stars. The Rolling Stones, in particular, showed how resilient a band could be: in 1999 they completed a mammoth two-year world tour during which they played to packed stadiums, 35 years after scoring their first hits.

### A musical revival

The theaters of many large cities have been increasingly taken over by musicals—notably those of Andrew Lloyd Webber and Tim Rice. The French composer Claude-Michel Schönberg and the librettist Alain Boublil formed another successful partnership: their musical *Les Misérables,* based on a novel about revolutionary France by Victor Hugo, was first produced in Paris in 1980, and became a runaway success in both New York and London.

Modern classical music could not hope to match the popularity and financial muscle of rock and pop music. Leading contemporary composers such as the German Karlheinz Stockhausen, a pioneer of electronic music, captured comparatively small if dedicated audiences. The major exceptions to this trend were the Americans Steve Reich and Philip Glass. They started as minimalists after the fashion of composer John Cage, and worked together for a while in the 1960s before pursuing separate paths. Both use repetitive phrasing, intoned like mantras or like Balinese gamelan music, but insert small shifts to produce a sense of progression. Using classical orchestral instruments and

**REVOLUTIONARY MUSICAL**
The dramatic intensity of *Les Misérables* cast the concept of the stage musical in a new light.

**THE THREE TENORS** Through their acclaimed performances of popular arias, Placido Domingo, José Carreras and Luciano Pavarotti helped to awaken public interest in opera, and in classical music.

choral singers, as well as exotic and electronic instruments, talking and clapping, their music has a unique and meditative poise that has won it wide appeal.

Just as the obituary of opera was about to be written, it underwent a massive revival. This was largely thanks to television and soccer: Puccini's aria "Nessun Dorma" from *Turandot* was used as the theme song for the soccer World Cup in Rome in 1990. Three of the world's leading opera singers, the Italian Luciano Pavarotti and the Spaniards Placido Domingo and José Carreras, sang it at the closing festival, and the "Three Tenors" became a worldwide success. Opera—at least, its most popular elements—has since generated a hugely enlarged following. A popular interest in classical music was fueled by dedicated radio stations. One product of this was the rise to prominence of the exquisitely melancholic Third Symphony: Symphony of Sorrowful Songs by the Pole Henryk Górecki. First produced in 1976, it was recorded in 1992 by the soprano Dawn Upshaw and the London Sinfonietta and became a runaway success—evidence of the world's increasingly eclectic musical tastes at the close of the twentieth century.

# A WORLD OF IMAGES

**TELEVISION, MAGAZINES, BOOKS, FILMS AND FASHION BECAME INCREASINGLY INTERNATIONAL AS MEDIA EMPIRES WENT GLOBAL**

When the Ramayana series was broadcast across India by a state-run television channel in 1987, it was followed avidly by an estimated 70 million viewers. This lavishly produced retelling of a classic of ancient Hindu mythology generated a significant revival in Hinduism across

**SWEET TASTE OF SUCCESS** The cast of *Dallas* celebrates the 250th episode. A glossy saga of wealth and marital misdemeanor, *Dallas* demonstrated the international money-spinning potential of the soap opera.

India; it also contributed to the rise of the militant Hindu political party, the Bharatiya Janata Party (BJP), and inspired a number of intercommunal riots.

The power of the media to reach people and influence them has become ever more global since 1970. As the century closes there are some 855 million homes with televisions across the world, over a quarter of them in China. The global media world is expanding at a colossal rate, and for successful communications companies the pickings —in sales and advertising revenue—can be vast. Audience ratings for the most popular

broadcasts are counted in tens of millions. The American soap opera *Dallas* was translated into 90 languages and seen in 137 countries. The episode in which it was disclosed who shot the lead character JR, first broadcast in November 1980, was watched by 41 million viewers in the United States, 27 million in the United Kingdom, and an estimated 125 million worldwide.

## Media empires

The rapid expansion of the global media market was foreseen back in the 1960s by leading figures in the field, such as Rupert Murdoch. The son of a celebrated war correspondent and newspaper owner, he was brought up in his native Australia, then went to Oxford University before taking his first

job on the *Daily Express* in London in the early 1950s. Here he developed his theories about what makes a successful newspaper, ideas he was able to put into practice when he returned to Australia to run his late father's Adelaide-based business.

He revitalized the fortunes of these papers by injecting more sex, crime, scandal, gossip and sports, but always overlaid with a conservative editorial viewpoint. By driving them downmarket, he increased sales, and was able to use the profits to buy up a handful of other Australian newspapers. In 1969 he acquired the downmarket British Sunday paper the *News of the World*, and in the following year he bought the *Sun*, Britain's biggest selling daily. He promptly applied the same formula: the first of the Sun's "Page Three Girls"—a naked or semi-naked girl facing the first inside page—was introduced that same year.

In 1981 Murdoch raised his sights and bought *The Times* and *The Sunday Times*. These famous institutions of the British

**AIR POWER** Rupert Murdoch launched Sky Television in 1989, offering a four-channel service received through a satellite dish.

**MAVERICK DUO** Ted Turner's unconventional approach to life and business earned him the nickname "Captain Outrageous." In 1991 he married the film actress Jane Fonda, who had achieved notoriety in the 1970s for her anti-establishment sympathies.

press had been ailing from protracted industrial action, victims of the stranglehold of restrictive practices and high labor costs exerted by the print unions. Murdoch applied the kind of ruthless action that is his hallmark: he built modern premises in Wapping, east London, and in 1986 moved the papers out of Fleet Street, shedding 5,500 jobs. This resulted in a violent industrial dispute, but Murdoch emerged victorious, and with a modernized, computer-based industry. After that, the British press was transformed as other papers and their proprietors followed his example.

Murdoch had bought a handful of American papers in the 1970s, starting with the *San Antonio News* in Texas, and later the *New York Post*. He subsequently concentrated on his American interests, and took American citizenship in 1985, the same year that he acquired the Twentieth Century Fox Film Corporation, and founded Fox Television. In 1987 he bought the publishing company Harper & Row, and subsequently Collins in the United Kingdom, merging them as a transatlantic giant HarperCollins. He also set up Sky Television for the expanding satellite and cable television business in the United Kingdom. He developed his Asian interests by acquiring Star TV, based in Hong Kong, as the first stage in reaching the massive and underdeveloped Chinese television market.

There were other major players in this lucrative field, such as the American Ted Turner. He started out with ownership of a small TV station in Atlanta, but recognized the value of syndicating sports transmissions to cable operators via satellite, in this way building a powerful base. Against all market advice, he established the Cable News Network (CNN) in 1980, which broadcast a 24 hour news service using satellite communications. This came into its own in major crises, when CNN was able to transmit constant updates from the scene of action. CNN rapidly established itself as the network that anyone with an interest in up-to-the-minute news had to have. In the late 1980s he created the cable channel Turner Network Television (TNT), and acquired a library of 4,000 classic films from the old MGM studios; he also founded the Cartoon Network. In 1996, the media giant Time Warner acquired Turner's holding company, Turner Broadcasting System (TBS), for $7.5 billion. In January 2000, Time Warner was acquired by the Internet company American Online, the first media/online merger of its kind.

Meanwhile, the lower profile German publishing giant Bertelsmann—owners of the book publishers Random House, Bantam Doubleday Dell and Transworld, and a number of lead-ing book clubs and various printing and multimedia interests—had built up annual profits of $960 million on sales of $12 billion.

A number of concerns were raised about the growth of these media empires, which threatened to monopolize the distribution of information, to drown smaller independent rivals, to drive down standards in the effort to reach a broader mass market and to crush local enterprise with blander, American-oriented content. Press intrusion became an issue, as journalists and photographers pressed ever harder to grab the scoop that could drive up sales and earn fortunes through international syndication. The British royal family was among the victims, especially as the marriages of the younger generation collapsed. Prince Charles and Lady Diana Spencer were married in 1981 in a fairy-tale wedding, but as their marriage ran into difficulties, exacerbated by media intrusion, and ended in separation in 1992, the Press picked over the pieces.

The balance between public information and intrusion remained a delicate issue. One of the most celebrated trials of the era was filmed for television and broadcast live around the world. It involved the popular football star, actor, TV personality and broadcaster O.J. Simpson. On June 12, 1994, his wife Nicole was found stabbed to death in her home in Los Angeles, along with Ronald Goldman, a waiter and acquaintance

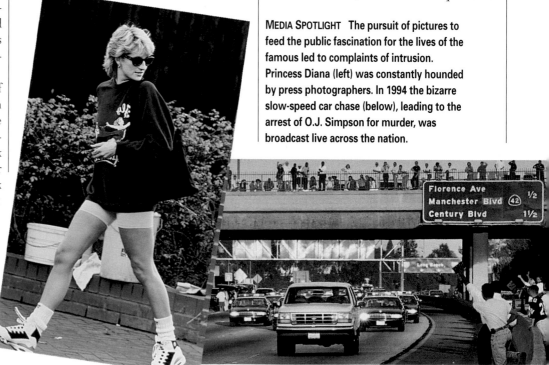

**MEDIA SPOTLIGHT** The pursuit of pictures to feed the public fascination for the lives of the famous led to complaints of intrusion. Princess Diana (left) was constantly hounded by press photographers. In 1994 the bizarre slow-speed car chase (below), leading to the arrest of O.J. Simpson for murder, was broadcast live across the nation.

1970

1974 Last episode of *Monty Python's Flying Circus*

1975 Steven Spielberg has first major hit with *Jaws*

1976 *The Muppet Show* begins

1980 Ted Turner launches CNN

1981 Rupert Murdoch buys *The Times*

**MASTER PUPPETEER  Jim Henson was the creative genius behind _Sesame Street_ and _The Muppet Show_.**

aspects of the global media market, other elements drew almost universal praise. In children's television, the work of the inventive American puppeteer Jim Henson was particularly well received. Henson had created his star character Kermit the Frog in 1955, but it was not until 1969 that he was invited by the Children's Television Workshop to work on the ground-breaking _Sesame Street_, in which Kermit was joined by Bert and Ernie, Grover, Big Bird and Cookie Monster. _Sesame Street_ has appeared on television for more than 30 years and has been translated into dozens of languages. The first show that was truly Henson's own, however, was _The Muppet Show_, which ran from 1976 to 1981, and was seen by an estimated 235 million people worldwide at its peak. Henson died suddenly in 1990, at 53, but his legacy has lived on.

### World literature, world film

The effect of global television and communications is to make the world seem ever smaller. Satellite communications mean that film and radio reports can be broadcast around the world from just about anywhere within hours of a story breaking. Nature and travel programs enable viewers to build up a detailed view of the rest of the world that was inconceivable in previous decades.

In the face of this kind of competition, the death of the book has long been predicted. In fact, more new books are published every year, but often in smaller quantities, a factor made economically viable by improved techniques of printing and distribution.

As the media has become more global, so too has literature. One aspect of this is the emergence of writers who have come to the broader world market through

translation, especially writers with a proven track record such as the Italian Primo Levi, whose work _The Periodic Table_ appeared in 1975; the Czech Milan Kundera, whose _The Unbearable Lightness of Being_ was published in translation in 1984; and the Colombian writer Gabriel Garcia Márquez, whose _One Hundred Years of Solitude_ was published in 1967. Asian writers, in particular, have shone: Salman Rushdie's _Midnight's Children_ was published to great acclaim in 1981, and won the coveted Booker Prize in England. Vikram Seth's epic _A Suitable Boy_ (1993) achieved international success, despite its great length. Arundhati Roy won the 1997 Booker Prize with _The God of Small Things_, set in southern India.

The world of fiction was still dominated, however, by the blockbuster, and authors such as John Grisham, Michael Crichton, Jeffrey Archer, and Danielle Steel. The same applied to the movies, which increasingly looked to authors like these to supply ideas. One of the key figures of the era was the Hollywood director Steven Spielberg, who

**ONE-OFF  After publishing her award-winning novel _The God of Small Things_, Arundhati Roy announced that she had no intention of writing another.**

who had come to deliver a pair of glasses left in the restaurant where he worked. A trail of blood led to a glove found on the property nearby where Simpson lived alone since separation from his wife. The evidence seemed to suggest that Simpson killed his wife in one of the fits of jealous rage to which he was prone, but when the police attempted to arrest him five days after the murders, Simpson had left. He was found on the freeway driving in a Ford Bronco with a friend, and was escorted by scores of police cars back to his home—a remarkable scene caught and broadcast by television cameras. At the trial, which lasted nine months, Simpson's "dream team" of lawyers argued that the forensic evidence was flawed, that the Los Angeles Police Department contained white racists who may well have wanted to frame Simpson—and so successfully undermined the prosecution's case that the jury was given little choice but to acquit Simpson. It was a case that fascinated the world—but was treated more like entertainment than a story about real people in crisis.

But while many felt queasy about some

## AND NOW FOR SOMETHING COMPLETELY DIFFERENT . . .

All across the English-speaking world in the early 1970s, students could spend many a night recalling and re-enacting their favorite Monty Python sketches. First produced in 1969, *Monty Python's Flying Circus* rapidly acquired a cult following. It was a breath of fresh air in television comedy—anarchic, absurd, original and often just plain silly. It poked fun at British attitudes, at the Establishment, and particularly at the traditions of television such as news broadcasting and talk shows. A newsreader behind a desk in an incongruous location introduced sketches with the famous words "And now for something completely different . . ."

**POLITICAL PUPPETS** *Spitting Image* was unsparing in their caricatures of public figures, such as Margaret Thatcher.

The main actors and writers emerged from university cabaret, notably the Cambridge Footlights: John Cleese, Graham Chapman, Eric Idle, Michael Palin and Terry Jones. Idiosyncratic cartoon-like graphics were supplied by American Terry Gilliam, who often amalgamated cut-out Victorian prints to create short and absurd narratives. The series ran until 1974. Thereafter the team came together for various shows, and made two successful feature films: *Monty Python and the Holy Grail* (1974), which poked fun at films on the Arthurian legend; and *Monty Python's Life of Brian* (1979), a spoof Bible epic. John Cleese, with his wife Connie Booth, went on to write the highly successful series *Fawlty Towers* (1975-9), in which he played the sometimes rude, sometimes obsequious, always eccentric owner of a small private hotel.

**MINE HOST** John Cleese in his role as Basil Fawlty, the infuriating but hilarious owner of *Fawlty Towers*. The name became a synonym for any eccentrically run hotel.

A new generation of British comedians emerged in the early 1980s with *Not the Nine O'Clock News*. They included Mel Smith, Gryff Rhys Jones, Rowan Atkinson and Pamela Stevenson, who performed a program of witty, often profane sketches that poked fun at contemporary life. But new levels of topical, satirical humor were reached by *Spitting Image*, launched in 1984, which used rubbery puppets designed by Roger Law and Peter Fluck to mimic and mercilessly mock the famous.

In 1983 the newly launched Channel 4 sponsored the first of a series of short television films made by a group of "alternative comedians" called *The Comic Strip*, who had cut their teeth in the London Comedy Store, a popular venue for stand-up comedians. They included Rik Mayall, Adrian Edmondson, Nigel Planer, Peter Richardson, Dawn French and Jennifer Saunders, who later achieved international success with *Absolutely Fabulous*, launched in 1993, which mocked the contemporary fashion and PR worlds.

Perhaps the greatest international star to emerge from this era was Rowan Atkinson, who starred in *Blackadder* and *Mr. Bean*. Because the humor of *Mr. Bean* is virtually all visual, it was readily appreciated around the world.

**SILENT STAR** The comic capers of the disaster-prone Mr. Bean, played by Rowan Atkinson, have the same universal appeal as the comedy classics of the silent movie era.

shot to fame with the killer-shark story *Jaws* (1975). He had struck a kind of magic formula, which was essentially to use B-movie style stories, but to enrich them with state of the art special effects and production techniques. He went from strength to strength, with a chain of box-office successes including *Close Encounters of the Third Kind* (1977), the *Indiana Jones* series (1981-89) and *ET: The Extraterrestrial* (1982). His *Jurassic Park* (1993), which used computer-generated imagery to create credible dinosaurs, is estimated to have grossed $912 million worldwide. Another highly successful director was George Lucas, whose *Star Wars Trilogy* (1977-83), and its prequel *Star Wars: The Phantom Menace* (1999), were an international success. The James Bond series continued through the decades, as Sean Connery was replaced by Roger Moore (1973), who was succeeded in turn by Timothy Dalton (1987) and Pierce Brosnan (1995). The 19th Bond movie—*The World Is Not Enough*—was released in 1999.

The film world was dominated by the immense power of Hollywood, but there were plenty of excellent filmmakers elsewhere. Australian directors such as Peter Weir and Phillip Noyce had a run of success in the 1970s with films such as *Picnic at Hanging Rock* (1975) and *Newsfront* (1978). French filmmaking remained strong, with work such as *Day for Night* (1973) by François Truffaut reaching an international audience. Italy had Frederico Fellini (*Roma*, 1972; *Amarcord*, 1973) and Bernardo Bertolucci, who made multi-language films using an international cast, as in his epic *1900* (1976). The Cannes Film Festival awarded its Palme d'Or to some surprise successes, such as the Chinese film *Farewell my Concubine* (1993). There were some low-budget successes from Britain: *Four Weddings and a Funeral* (1994) and *The Full Monty* (1997) were hits on both sides of the Atlantic. India, meanwhile, feeding a huge public appetite for films, remained the country with the world's

cloths and minimizing the lining. Japanese designers, such as Issey Miyake and Yohji Yamamoto, brought a fresh oriental eye to body shape. The catwalk shows became increasingly theatrical and dramatic, notably when the august Paris houses of Dior and Givenchy decided to revitalize their images in 1996-7 by bringing in two *enfants terribles* of British design, John Galliano and Alexander McQueen respectively.

The challenging and controversial designs of the catwalks may seem far

**HOLLYWOOD HITS** Bond films such as *The Spy Who Loved Me* (left) maintained their popularity. Steven Spielberg directs one of the stars of *Jurassic Park* (above); Bernardo Bertolucci (right) directs Keanu Reeves in *Little Buddha*.

highest output—averaging over 750 films per year in contrast to America's 680.

The merits of European-style director-led films were recognized in Hollywood, in films such as *Blue Velvet* (1986) by David Lynch, and *Pulp Fiction* (1995) by Quentin Tarantino, which won the Palme d'Or in Cannes in 1994. But *Pulp Fiction* also displayed another evolving feature of films, the increasing use of graphic violence, and the influence of film violence remained a subject of controversy.

The world of film, and indeed television, was greatly influenced by the introduction of the video recorder. First produced in 1971, it became widely used during the 1980s. Film-makers could now expect to make a substantial part of their income through the sale of videocassettes. Meanwhile the arrival of lightweight and accessibly priced video cameras helped to democratize filmmaking: now almost anyone could make a film.

## Changing styles

The wealth and glamour of the film and media worlds exerted a worldwide fascination, seen in the success of magazines such as *People*, and the development of new journals focusing on style—in clothing, interior design, gardens or lifestyles in general. This was the age of the supermodels, celebrity beauties who travelled the world, earning colossal sums to act as mannequins for the top couturiers.

The world of fashion went through a number of significant transformations. Punk was launched as an anti-fashion statement in the mid 1970s by Vivienne Westwood and Malcolm McClaren from their King's Road boutiques in London. Its iconoclastic and subversive approach had a lasting effect on high fashion, an approach Westwood took to Paris in the 1980s. The Italian designer Gianni Versace applied a new panache to color and fabric, while Giorgio Armani reworked the classic men's suit into something more relaxed and casual by using softer

removed from fashion on the street, but style filters down from them. And there were other influences afoot, such as the use of sportswear as daily clothing. Track suits and "shell suits" reflected a more casual approach to dressing, while the cross-trainer became the ubiquitous form of footwear for the young, and even the not so young.

Image also became an increasingly important element of commercial products, projected through television, magazine and poster advertising. Denim jeans, for instance, were once working clothes, and old jeans became part and parcel of the hippie era. In 1985 the original manufacturer, Levi Strauss, decided to revitalize its image, and used an advertising campaign that showed the muscular young model Nick Kamen stripping in a launderette. Jeans were reborn as an upmarket fashion item. The use of sex in advertising became increasingly blatant, notably when it was used to promote luxury ice cream—a product not previously associated with sex—in a Häagen-Dazs campaign launched in 1991.

## GIANNI VERSACE

On July 15, 1997 Gianni Versace was gunned down by a serial killer outside his palatial home in Miami Beach, Florida. He was 50 years old.

He had risen from a humble beginning in southern Italy, where he helped his mother in her dressmaking business from the age of nine. It was here that he learned his supreme skills in cutting cloth so that it responds to the body of the wearer. In 1972 he went to Milan and worked for a number of big labels, before launching his own business in 1978. From the start his clothes were showy and opulent: he used richly printed silks and other luxury cloths. He combined classical shapes with the ostentatious theatricality of Hollywood, tinged with sensuous vulgarity—a flamboyant mixture of high and low culture that mirrored the taste of his younger sister Donatella, who became a partner in the business.

Versace courted the rich and famous. He was friends with Diana, Princess of Wales, Madonna and Elton John. At his villas and houses in Milan, on Lake Como, in Miami Beach and New York, he played the generous host, but he was also relentlessly hardworking. By the early 1990s his business included fragrances, accessories and home furnishings—at the time of his death, it was estimated to be worth $1 billion.

**KING OF THE CATWALK** Gianni Versace brought a new pizzazz to fashion—glittering, exciting, luxurious, with a faint hint of vulgarity.

Repackaging became a familiar ploy to add value, even to basic products. The McDonald's fast food chain sells burgers and french fries, but their branding and promotion made their chain instantly recognizable, and their emphasis on standardization of product meant that customers could rely on comparable quality wherever they were in the world.

The formula proved hugely successful, and McDonald's gradually spread around the world to serve 26 million customers every day.

### The art scene

During the 1960s Andy Warhol and Pop Art had cheekily explored the proximity of commercial art to high art. It may have seemed that the art world was becoming ever more commercially oriented, especially when auction prices for the Old Masters began to break all records dramatically. The Japanese proved avid buyers: in 1990 Ryoei Saito of Daishowa Paper Manufacturing bought *Portrait of Dr. Gachet* by Van Gogh for a record-breaking $75 million, and *At the Moulin de la Galette* by Renoir for $71 million.

But contemporary artists were in fact moving away from commercially oriented product toward art that could not readily be bought, or could not fit into galleries or homes. At the most extreme end of this trend, Christo was wrapping up pieces of landscape, and "Land artists" such as Robert Smithson and the Briton Richard Long were making marks in the countryside as an artistic statement. Art was being redefined: it was no longer about pictures on a wall or even a product, but as Duchamp had suggested as early as 1913, about selection and concept.

Two contrasting movements were in evidence in the 1970s. The Minimalists, notably the American sculptors Donald Judd, Richard Serra and Carl Andre, created works out of industrial materials such as rusted steel and firebricks. Expression, decoration and even

**PUBLIC IMAGE** Increased exposure through television and magazines brought celebrity status to models such as Naomi Campbell, here wearing an outfit by Alexander McQueen, part of his first collection for Givenchy.

the creative input of the artist was minimized, and the setting around the work became almost as important as the work itself. Such minimalist pieces were nonetheless considered art objects to be looked at.

Conceptual art took this idea one stage further, proclaiming that art was not so much about the object as the idea: "Actual works of art are little more than historical curiosities," said Joseph Kosuth, whose conceptual art manifestoes had much influence in the 1970s. This was a liberating moment for modern art: it was about to shift into an era of dramatic revision—of "anything goes."

First, however, came a counterattack mounted by a number of artists who still believed in paint. While David Hockney, one of the leading British figurative painters, began experimenting with photocollage and photocopies, the "neo-Expressionists"—such as the Germans Anselm Keifer and Georg Baselitz, and Julian Schnabel—took painting into a new, reinvigorated dimension, fusing abstraction with figurative imagery, sometimes on a monumental scale.

But painting was rapidly becoming just one form of expression in the diverse set of trends that came under the broad label of "Post-Modernism." Photography, video film, found objects, temporary installations, performances by the artists—all could be harnessed for the purpose of artistic expression. One of the leading figures of this trend was the veteran German artist Joseph Beuys, who made decomposing sculptures out of animal fat. His installation *Plight* (1985) consisted of a grand piano in rooms lined with thick rolls of felt.

The new generation of artists reveled in their liberty, freed from the shackles of traditional art concepts: they could use any medium, technique or format to make a statement. Whether it was good art remained the burning question—but this controversy was central to its appeal. The British artist

## WRAPPING THE WORLD

Christo is one of the world's best-known artists, if only for the daring of his work. He started wrapping small objects when an art student in Paris. The habit just grew and grew, to trees, cars, buildings and whole swathes of landscape. In 1969 he wrapped 1½ miles of the Australian coastline in plastic sheeting, a work entitled "Wrapped Coast." His next major project was "Running Fence" (1976), a flimsy wall of white plastic, 18 feet high, stretching across 24 miles of Sonoma and Marin Counties in California. It took months of planning, teams of workers to construct it, and it lasted just two weeks—but won critical acclaim for its transient beauty. Perhaps his most visually appealing work was "Surrounded Islands" (1980-3), a vast tribute to Monet's water lily paintings that involved encircling 11 islands off Florida in 670,000 square yards of pink fabric. Since then Christo has wrapped the Pont Neuf in Paris (1985) and the Reichstag (parliament) building in Berlin (1995). The cost of the projects is funded by collectible spin-offs such as sketches, photographs and prints.

**IT'S A WRAP** Christo wrapped the Pont Neuf bridge over the Seine in Paris in 1985. His wrapping creates vast, temporary, semi-abstract forms.

Damien Hirst, for example, made large glass boxes, called vitrines, in which he exhibited dead animals preserved in formaldehyde. In an early vitrine called *A Thousand Years* (1990), flies buzzed around a severed cow's head and an electric insect killer, posing questions about life, reproduction and death, beauty and revulsion, and art itself. Fellow Briton Rachel Whiteread made concrete and plaster casts of real rooms; in the case of *House* (1993-4), she cast a complete house in situ in east London. Artist Jeff Koons questioned the idea of taste in playful works that are banal to the point of absurdity. His *Puppy* was put on display outside the new Guggenheim Museum at Bilbao in northern Spain: it is a giant Yorkshire terrier planted with 60,000 living pansies.

The ephemeral nature of art was a recurring theme, although the work of British sculptors Antony Gormley and Anish Kapoor expressed profound ideas in glass fiber, concrete, clay, stone and metal, and may have a greater chance of standing the test of time.

By the late 1990s, much of modern art was baffling and inscrutable, and often deliberately obscene and shocking. It was nonetheless forged in a dynamic atmosphere of radical rethinking and questioning, and the best works carried that electric charge delivered when artistic insight is perfectly and inseparably matched by the chosen medium.

**IS IT ART?** In *Away from the Flock* (1994) Damien Hirst presents a real lamb preserved in formaldehyde. The use of real components had a shock value that caught the public's attention.

# THE GLOBAL VILLAGE

## THE RAPID DEVELOPMENT OF INFORMATION AND COMMUNICATION TECHNOLOGY MADE THE WORLD SEEM EVEN SMALLER

Looking into the crystal ball in 1949, the magazine *Popular Mechanics* predicted that "computers in the future may weigh no more than 1.5 tons." Even in the 1970s few people thought that computers would become so compact and affordable as to find a place in homes as well as in virtually every office. Besides, there seemed little point. Computers were big machines, occupying large areas of floor space, if not whole rooms, in multinational companies, where they crunched vast numbers and recorded the results on whirring magnetic tapes. Smaller offices got by perfectly well with adding machines, typewriters, carbon paper, Xerox machines and ledgers.

But radical change was on the horizon — change that has been labeled a "revolution" without excessive exaggeration. In 1971 the California company Intel produced the first microprocessor or "silicon chip." Capable of processing data much faster than its predecessor, the transistor, it was also more economic, both in terms of space and mass-production costs. Miniaturization and the mass market beckoned.

The silicon chip was designed initially for use in calculators: Texas Instruments produced the first pocket calculator in 1972. Combined with a liquid-crystal display (LCD), invented in 1970, calculators not only became genuinely pocket-sized, they also dropped radically in price. The pioneering Sinclair Executive cost $150 in 1972; by 1982 significantly more powerful calculators were available for just $10.50. While teachers and commentators in the media predicted that the human brain would atrophy as a result of such technology, ordinary people were happy to abandon their slide rules and logarithm tables and let their new calculators take the strain.

### The PC

The true revolution came with the advent of the personal computer (PC). Although the logical outcome of miniaturization, made possible by increasingly powerful silicon chips, the concept initially proved hard to sell. Steven Jobs and Stephen Wozniak were turned down by both Atari and Hewlett-Packard before they set up their own company, Apple, in California in 1976, and produced the ground-breaking Apple II in 1977. They deliberately chose an approachable, organic name for their company to set it apart from the more steely, business-suited world of the multinational corporations, such as IBM. Apple's team looked relaxed, they wore jeans, and had a counter-culture air reminiscent of the 1960s youth movement. Essentially they promoted the concept that computer technology was not an alienating force, but rather something that could be harnessed for the benefit and amusement of ordinary people. They were appealing to the individual.

Their concept quickly caught on. Before long all the major players—including IBM—were producing compact personal computers, while small workshops around the world were mercilessly pirating their ideas with identical "clones" which, without the

**APPLE OF HIS EYE   When the California-based company Apple Computer, co-founded by Steve Jobs (below), produced the Apple II in 1977, it brought computers within the reach of small businesses and individuals for the first time.**

1970

1970 First jumbo jet crosses Atlantic

1971 First viable "silicon chip" produced

1972 First pocket calculator goes on the market

1973 Bar codes patented

1976 Concorde begins passenger service

1977 Apple launches first PC

1978 Space Invaders launched

1979 First successful word-processing program introduced

1983 French launch first TGV train services

1984 Term "cyberspace" is coined

research and development costs, they could sell at much lower prices.

The public came to see that the personal computer held distinct advantages, and word processing was the most persuasive factor in this. Computers allowed anyone who could type the possibility of drafting, altering and rearranging text before committing it to paper —a massive advantage over the traditional typewriter. There were intermediate developments: advanced or "intelligent" typewriters were produced after 1978, incorporating some computer technology, small amounts of memory and narrow LCD screens showing text. But PCs had not only a much larger capacity for processing information, they also had television-sized Visual Display Units (VDUs). These advantages were exploited in the launch in 1979 of WordStar, the first successful word-processing program for PCs that remained the market leader until the mid 1980s.

Many people bought PCs only for their word-processing facilities, although well aware that they were using just a tiny percentage of their machine's capabilities. However, other programs—notably the hugely successful Lotus 1-2-3, launched in 1983—showed how other office functions such as accounting could be performed on the same machine. These programs had the huge built-in advantage that spreadsheets (a

**DOWNSIZING** The 1976 Portable from IBM reflected the trend toward making computers smaller, but the company did not engage fully in the PC market until 1981.

term coined in the 1980s) could be produced instantaneously by the computer's powerful calculating facilities.

## PONG AND PAC-MAN

The first modern video game was a kind of table tennis called Pong. Created in California in 1972, it consisted of a black-and-white screen with two stick-like bats that were used by players to knock a square dot back and forth. Simple it may have been, but it caused a sensation. Its inventor, Nolan Bushnell, founded Atari to market the idea, creating a business that made him $15 million when he sold it to Warner Brothers a decade later.

Video games were, nonetheless, slow to develop, while the main outlet remained largely the coin-operated machines in amusement arcades and bars. Space Invaders was launched in 1978 and rapidly became a craze: the task was to shoot down invading alien spaceships. In 1980 the Japanese company Namco produced Pac-Man, in which a gobbling head had to navigate a maze to munch dots and avoid dangerous ghosts. It was another instant success.

Building on the experiences of Atari and other video-games producers, Hiroshi Yamauchi—the dynamic head of the 90-year-old Nintendo playing card manufacturers—developed his own arcade game called Donkey Kong in the late 1970s, and then the Super Mario Brothers in the early 1980s. They soon won an enthusiastic audience not only in Japan, but also in America. Meanwhile, handheld battery-powered games using liquid-crystal displays had begun to emerge. Nintendo pushed this trend to new limits with its GameBoy in 1990; it offered the possibility of using interchangeable games cartridges on the same handheld console, like miniature versions of the games consoles linked to TVs.

Nintendo's dominant position in the market was challenged by Sega in the 1990s, and later by Sony. By the mid 1990s they were vying for a share in a business estimated to be worth $10 billion a year.

**INTERACTIVE OBSESSION** Video games ousted "one-armed bandits" from amusement arcades (right), took over the TV set in the home (above) and created a market for dedicated games machines such as the pocket-sized GameBoy (left).

1989 Term "information superhighway" becomes current

1994 Channel Tunnel opened

1995 Microsoft launches Windows 95

**COMPUTER LITERATE** Bar codes were first devised in 1973. Optical scanning equipment can "read" the bar code to identify both price and product.

Computers, however, presented a daunting learning curve to all new users. Purchasers taking their machines out of their boxes were faced with an array of wires and plugs, thick manuals and a whole new vocabulary that included words such as compatibility, megabytes, boot, DOS and crash. But the market was expanding exponentially, and with it came rapidly advancing and more user-friendly technology at decreasing prices. Manufacturers knew that the public had little ambition to be computer experts: they simply wanted machines and programs that did the work they promised with the minimum of fuss. This was delivered by software such as Windows, developed by Microsoft in the 1990s, which, following in the footsteps of Apple, made a virtue of the screen-navigation potential of the mouse. The keyboard remained one of the few unchanging features of the system, with the letters of the alphabet still presented in the old QWERTY format developed in the 1920s to prevent mechanical typewriter keys from jamming.

Meanwhile, the process of miniaturization continued: portable battery-powered "laptop" computers emerged in the early 1980s, shortly followed by "palmtop" mini-comput-

**CREDIT ON LINE** The use of credit cards has grown in tandem with the development of computers from the 1950s up to the present.

ers combining a calendar, address book and calculator with word-processing facilities.

Printers, too, became ever more sophisticated as the laser printer replaced the noisy and more limited daisy-wheel and dot-matrix printers. In 1977 Xerox launched a laser printer costing $350,000. When Hewlett-Packard produced its first desktop laser printer, the HP Laserjet, in 1984, it sold for $7,000. Ten years later laser printers were selling for one-tenth of this price. The improvement in print quality allowed businesses and individuals to produce professional-looking documents, without recourse to an outside printing business, and the term "desktop publishing" became current in the late 1980s. Authors were now able to deliver manuscripts on disk, which saved the publisher from having to retype it. These innovations transformed the printing industry, and pushed the old profession of typesetting to the edge of extinction—just one of many areas of business deeply affected by the rising tide of computer technology.

Meanwhile, the applications of personal computers widened, from the work-oriented word-processing and accounting programs to education and entertainment. At the same time, portable for-

mats for storing information moved progressively from the fragile 5½ inch "floppy" disk to the 3½ inch disks and formats with increased capacity such as the CD-ROM, Jaz and Zip disks. However, the exchange of data on disks also carried a new anxiety: the

### CYBERSPACE

William Gibson used the word "cyberspace" in his novel *Neuromancer* (1984) to describe the virtual reality experienced by people whose brains are linked to networked computers. Cyberspace evolved out of the word cybernetics, coined in the 1940s— from the Greek for a steersman—to denote the science of communications and automatic control. As Gibson put it, people using computer-based machines "develop a belief that there's some kind of actual space behind the screen . . . some place that you can't see but you know is there."

transmission of computer viruses, a concept that became widespread in the late 1980s as destructive programs, created largely by malicious pranksters, were surreptitiously passed from computer to computer through corrupted disks.

Slowly but surely computers were entering all areas of public life, in offices, hospitals, airlines, the military. In factories the drudgery and physical labor of some assembly-line tasks were taken over by robots, dispensing with human intervention altogether:

during the 1980s major car manufacturers modernized by introducing computer-linked robotic machinery capable of pressing steel, welding, paint-spraying and polishing. Computers were also increasingly used in design. Bar codes (or the "Universal Product Code"), first patented in the United States in 1973, began to be used in supermarkets around the world for pricing and stock control. Banking and commerce made increasing use of communication systems connected to data bases, such as Electronic Funds Transfer at Points of Sale (EFTPOS), to spread the culture of ATM cards and credit cards. During the 1980s both the "paperless office" and the "cashless society" seemed just around the corner, although traditional patterns of behavior remained resistant and, at the end of the century, neither had arrived quite as thoroughly as had been predicted.

## World Wide Web

All the while, communications across the globe had become more efficient and cost-effective. In 1970 it became possible, for the first time, to telephone directly—without the mediation of an operator—between New York and London by International Direct Dialling (IDD). Gradually IDD reached most countries around the world. Mobile or cellular phones evolved in the late 1970s. But as the web of telephones and telephone links continued to spread, there remained great disparity between the developed and the less developed countries. In the early 1990s there were 380 telephones per 1,000 people in developed countries, but in sub-Saharan Africa there were just 10 per 1,000.

Satellites played an increasingly significant role in communications, as telephone systems and television used geo-stationary satellites (orbiting at such a speed that they remain above fixed points on Earth) to bounce information around the globe. These were originally all launched by rocket, but the advent of the Space Shuttle in the 1980s provided a more secure means of delivering these delicate craft to their orbital positions some 22,300 miles above the Earth's surface.

Meanwhile, on the ground the arrival of fiber-optic cables—first developed in the 1970s—permitted the delivery of faster, clearer telephone, television and computer signals, and in significantly greater volume. The fax machine, although invented at the
*continued on page 76*

## BILL GATES: SOFTWARE SUCCESS

A little over 20 years after 19-year-old Bill Gates founded his Seattle-based software company Microsoft, the media was struggling to find ways to communicate the magnitude of his vast personal fortune. By 1998 he was clearly the richest man in the world, and his fortune was stated as $47 billion one day, $51 billion the next. It was estimated that he was nearly twice as rich as the Sultan of Brunei, previous holder of the title; and that his fortune in dollar bills would require 304 jumbo jets to transport it.

Bill Gates has become the single greatest beneficiary of the computer revolution—and his colleague and co-founder of Microsoft, Paul Allen, is estimated to be the third richest man in the world with a fortune of some $7.5 billion. Back in 1975 Allen saw an advertisement for the Altair self-assembly computer, and persuaded Gates—then a Harvard undergraduate—to help him to write an operating program for it. They created GW-Basic (GW for Gee Whizz) and licensed it successfully to Altair's manufacturer. They founded Microsoft that same year, but their real break came in 1981, when they persuaded IBM—the market-leaders of the 1980s—to buy their MS-DOS (Microsoft Disk Operating System), which Gates had in turn bought outright for $50,000 from another Seattle company the year before.

Gates' genius lay not so much in technical innovation—comparable ideas were being evolved by others—but in his business acumen. He did not sell exclusive rights in MS-DOS to IBM, thereby leaving open the possibility of licensing the system to other software and hardware manufacturers who wanted to feed into IBM's structure. By the mid 1990s, 80 percent of PCs operated on Microsoft software, and with each sale came a royalty. Then, in 1995, Microsoft launched Windows 95, a user-friendly program for organizing and navigating around programs and files. Its operating concepts of icons, drop-down menus and on-screen presentation through "wysiwyg" ("what you see is what you get") were not original; Apple had developed similar systems for their Macintosh as early as 1984. But crucially Microsoft now had a dominant slice of the market into which to launch this product.

Gates is an enigmatic figure. On the one hand, he represents the immense power and ingenuity of the software business; on the other hand he has the classic persona of the "computer geek," with an awkward and temperamental public image. He also incites jealousy and resentment among his rivals, and accusations that he uses Microsoft's dominance of the software market to stifle rivals and innovation. Thus in 1998 his company came under scrutiny from the government applying anti-trust legislation, mainly because Microsoft insisted on giving away its Internet Explorer program with Windows. This piece of unsubtle marketing ensured that Microsoft controlled users' access to the Internet to the detriment of the producers of other Internet browsers, notably Netscape.

**SOFTWARE BARON** By June 1998 when Microsoft launched Windows 98, Bill Gates had become the richest man in the world.

# SPEED AND GRIDLOCK

### TRAVEL BY PLANE AND TRAIN BECAME FASTER AND MORE EFFICIENT, BUT AS MORE AND MORE PEOPLE BEGAN DRIVING CARS, THE ROADS JAMMED UP

Just as the world appeared to shrink with the mounting speed and efficiency of faxes, the Internet and satellite communications, physical distances also evaporated with the relentless improvement of transportation. In 1970, the first Boeing 747 jumbo jet crossed the Atlantic to land at Heathrow Airport, London, with 362 passengers on board—nearly double the carrying capacity of other planes. Airlines were catering to hugely increased demands in mass travel—for business and for vacations—by opening up new destinations, and reducing flight times and costs.

The jumbo jet represented one side of an argument about air travel: about whether the future lay in speed or in volume. Back in the 1960s, speed had beckoned, and in 1962 the British and French had entered into an uneasy joint-venture project to produce a super-sonic airliner, Concorde, ahead of the Americans and the Soviets. In 1969 this slimline delta-winged, droop-nosed wonder of engineering began its test flights, and made its first Heathrow landing in 1970. It swiftly received criticism over noise levels. Then the 1973 oil crisis hit, and gradually all the 74 provisional orders placed by international airlines were withdrawn. Concorde eventually began passenger flights in 1976. Meanwhile its rivals had faded away: the United States' project was abandoned in 1971, and a prototype of the Soviet TU-144 (nick-named "Konkordski") crashed spectacularly and fatally at the Paris airshow in 1973. Konkordski was withdrawn by the Soviets in 1978 after just 102 passenger flights.

So Concorde stood unrivaled, but the British and French governments had to foist it onto their national airlines, and foot the immense bill. Only 16 Concordes were built—not the 1,370 once envisioned by the planners—and in the end, only the transatlantic route proved commercially viable. It was an engineering triumph that still won admiring gazes 25 years later; but it was a finan-cial disaster. The public was simply unwilling to pay a heavy premium for the privilege of chopping off a few hours of flying time, espe-cially when the rest of air travel was so

**FLYING HIGH** The Boeing 747 jumbo jet (below) and Concorde (right) were the talk of the aviation industry in the early 1970s, representing respectively the quest for high-volume passenger transport and time-saving speed. The growth of mass air travel and the economies of scale favored bulk over speed, but both remained at the forefront of air travel until the end of the century.

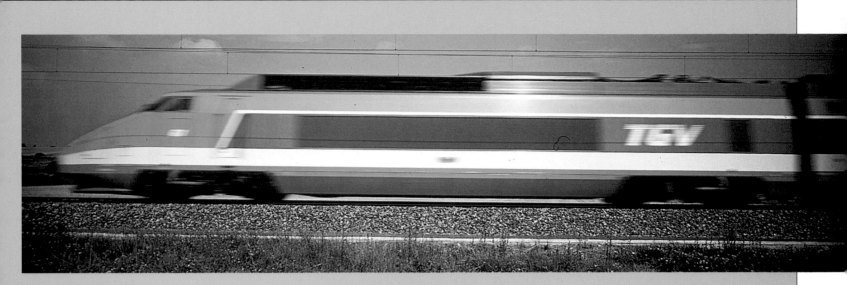

cumbersome. The comedian Bob Hope quipped: "Concorde is great. It gives you three extra hours to find your luggage."

Speed, however, did prove attractive on the railways. In 1983 the French launched the first high-speed *Train à Grande Vitesse* (TGV) on the Paris-Lyon route. Traveling at up to 170mph, the TGV rivaled flight times over short distances. Meanwhile, the Japanese continued to expand the Shinkansen (bullet train) routes, first developed in the 1960s, throughout the main islands, linked by a variety of increasingly ambitious tunnel and bridge projects.

One of the greatest engineering feats of the period was the construction of the Channel Tunnel between Britain and France. Another Anglo-French joint venture, work began in 1986 and was completed in 1994. The expense of the project, however, made Concorde's balance sheet look rather favorable: the Channel Tunnel's costs rose inexorably, piling up debts of $12.6 billion, which its operators cannot reasonably hope to recover.

The Channel Tunnel was built for rail transport, but over the last three decades of the century the automobile was in the ascendant. Its only setback was the 1970s oil crisis. In response to the massive hike in fuel costs, manufacturers produced smaller, more efficient cars. The large "gas guzzlers" were replaced by trimmer vehicles of more modest scale, many made by Japanese manufacturers. The "hatchback" was introduced in 1974 with the Volkswagen Golf, one of the most successful models of the era. By the early 1990s there were estimated to be nearly 600 million cars in the world. But the inexorable rise of the car led to another new term, coined during

**FAST TRACK** The French *Train à Grande Vitesse* (TGV) combined new engine technology with specially built high-speed lines.

the 1970s: "gridlock." While Concorde could whisk passengers from London to New York in well under 4 hours, the jaunts from the airports to the city centers could take almost as long.

Another downside of the growth in mass transport was the increasing scale of disasters. In 1977 two jumbo jets collided on the ground at Tenerife in the Canary Islands, and 583 passengers died. In 1987 the British roll-on roll-off car ferry, the *Herald of Free Enterprise,* keeled over in the sea off Zeebrugge, Belgium, and 193 people drowned. But it was not always the numbers that captured attention in transport disasters. In an incident in 1972 the 16 survivors of an air crash in the Andes found that they could survive only by eating the remains of their dead fellow passengers—a story that graphically reminded the world that, behind all the benefits that technology brings lie the eternal harsh realities of human existence.

**POWER BOAT** In 1990 the multihulled SeaCat *Great Britain* won the trans-Atlantic Blue Riband trophy by crossing in 3 days and 7 hours.

**BUMPER TO BUMPER**
Rush hour, Vauxhall Bridge, London: traffic congestion became an increasingly familiar feature of urban life across the world, fuelled by growing consumer wealth and car dependency.

beginning of the century, became ubiquitous in the 1980s, when it began to take over from the more cumbersome and less adaptable telex. But already a system of linking computers directly to the telephone network had been developed. One initial concern that this raised was the security of information, and another new word entered the vocabulary: hacking—gaining unauthorized access to a computer database through telephone links. In 1983 hackers succeeded in breaking into the American main defense computer, presenting a new nightmare scenario in a world already coming to terms with a downturn in Cold War relations.

Nonetheless, the telephone linkage of computers was to provide one of the most significant developments in communications of the century: the Internet. It was the rapid growth of the market in personal computers in the 1980s and 1990s that facilitated this development, and thrust the Internet out of the cocoon of university research and into

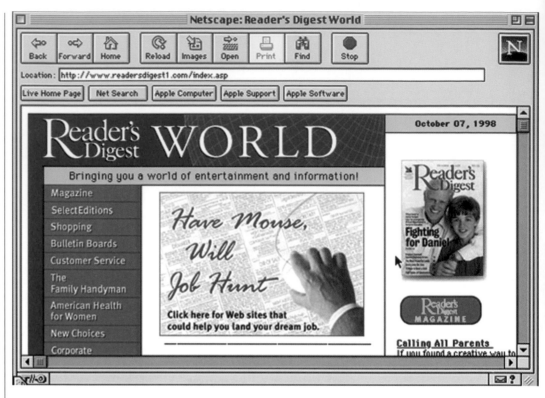

### ANY TIME, ANY PLACE, ANYWHERE
A Shanghai businessman keeps in touch. "Mobile" phones were introduced in the 1940s, but the development of cellular phones in the late 1970s gave them a new lease of life and by the end of the century they were ubiquitous.

the public domain. With millions of computers linked through the telephone system, suddenly an unprecedented volume of information became available to subscribers, assisted by the user-friendly presentation of the World Wide Web and rapidly accessed through search engines. Electronic mail (email), forums and discussion groups put people in touch across the world.

More sinisterly, it could also be used to access unregulated information on anything from child pornography to instructions on how to make bombs. The issue of censorship remained unresolved at the end of the twentieth century, but the Internet made real and tangible the concept of the electronic "superhighway" that had been envisaged in the late 1980s—a comprehensive system of interlinked communications capable of delivering a

**WEB OF INFORMATION** The Internet provides access to a vast—and continually growing—amount of information. Some is supplied by experts in communication, such as Reader's Digest, but much is posted by individuals.

### THE SPREAD OF THE NET
The Internet had unlikely origins in ARPANET, a linked computer system developed in 1969 for the Department of Defense to improve communications, share research and survive nuclear attack. It was broadened to other research bodies and universities, and took off with the rapid use of personal computers in the 1980s and 1990s. By 1995 the Internet was linked to 7 million computers worldwide; by 1997 some 11 million businesses and 60 million private users had hooked up to it. Presently, over 240 million individuals are connected to the Internet.

wide range of multimedia services on-line, including the telephone, television, video links, research databases, games, movies, and shopping resources. The Internet may prove to have as great an impact on the twenty-first century as the development of the automobile, powered flight and radio had on the twentieth century.

# THE WORLD OF SPORT

## UNDER THE EYE OF TELEVISION, SPORTS WERE FACED WITH GROWING PRESSURES, LEADING TO ABUSES AS WELL AS MOMENTS OF MAGIC

**GOLD STAR** The 22-year-old American swimmer Mark Spitz was the hero of the 1972 Munich Olympics, winning seven gold medals and breaking four world records.

The year 1992 was considered a vintage one for the Olympic Games. They took place in Barcelona, and—unlike previous years—there were no outstanding, dominant stars. That was part of their success and charm. But more important, these were the first Olympics for over two decades not to be clouded by politics.

Back in 1972 at Munich, the swimmer Mark Spitz had been the outstanding performer of the Olympics, winning a record seven gold medals. The story was less rosy, however, for American athletes as a whole, who lost ten of the titles their team had won at the previous Olympic Games in Mexico City. Dominating the medals table at the Munich Olympics were the contenders from the Soviet bloc, and the Russian sprinter Valery Borzov, in particular, while the young Soviet gymnast Olga Korbut captured the world's heart on her way to winning three gold medals. On a bleaker note, these were

also the Games that saw a PLO terrorist attack on the Israeli team in the Olympic village that left 11 Israeli athletes dead. None of the prowess of the competitors could restore the shine that was so brutally erased by this tragedy.

In 1976 in Montreal, the prestige and spirit of the Games was dented by a boycott by 22 African nations objecting to the presence of New Zealand, whose rugby team had flouted the sports boycott of South Africa. The outstanding personality that year was the diminutive Romanian gymnast Nadia Comaneci, age

**BREATHTAKING BALANCE** The Soviet bloc excelled in women's gymnastics. The Soviet gymnast Olga Korbut (inset), age 16, stole the show at the 1972 Olympics; but in 1976 she was eclipsed by the 14-year-old Romanian Nadia Comaneci (below).

**JUMP FOR JOY** At the Los Angeles Olympics in 1984 Carl Lewis showed his all-round talent by adding the long-jump gold to his three golds for sprinting.

14, the first competitor in Olympic history to achieve a perfect score—the maximum ten—and also win three gold medals.

The United States led a boycott of the 1980 Moscow Olympics in protest against the Soviet invasion of Afghanistan—a boycott supported by all West European nations bar Great Britain. As a result, the U.S.S.R. overwhelmed the medals table with 80 golds, and East Germany took second place with 47. But one of the highlights was the contest between rival British athletes Steve Ovett and Sebastian Coe in the middle distance track events. It ended with a draw, Ovett taking the 800 m and Coe the 1,500 m.

The Soviet Union took its revenge on the

### BORN TO RUN

African nations produced a string of world class middle and long-distance runners. At the 1968 Olympics Kenya's Kip Keino and Naftali Temu won the 1,500 m and 10,000 m respectively. In 1980 Ethiopian Miruts Yifter won the 5,000 m and 10,000 m, earning him the nickname Yifter the Shifter.

United States by boycotting the Los Angeles Olympics of 1984. The hero of this Games was the sprinter and long-jumper Carl Lewis, who won the 100 m, 200 m and long jump, and was a member of the winning team in the 4 × 100 m relay—an achievement matched only by Jesse Owens in the 1936 Olympics. It was the

beginning of Lewis's phenomenal Olympic record in which he won nine gold medals over the next 12 years, including an unprecedented four consecutive gold medals for the long jump. The 1984 Games will also be remembered for an incident in the women's 3,000 m, when the barefooted South African runner Zola Budd, controversially representing Great Britain, accidentally tripped and eliminated America's darling, Mary Decker.

Cold War rivalry returned in the 1988 Seoul Olympics, where the Soviet Union dominated the medal table and drug-taking became an increasingly urgent issue. Accusations were leveled in particular at East German athletes. But it was the Canadian Ben Johnson, winner of the 100 m, who hit the headlines when he was found to have taken anabolic steroids and was stripped of his medal. The diver Greg Louganis won acclaim when he hit his head on the diving board during the competition but, after receiving stitches, went on to retain the gold medal that he had won in Los Angeles.

A radical shift in world politics brought a fresh breeze to the Barcelona Olympics in 1992. Following the collapse of communism, countries such as Latvia, Lithuania and Estonia could compete under their own name. North Korea had stayed away from the 1988 Seoul games, backed by two communist allies, Cuba and Ethiopia. All three countries now abandoned their boycott. South Africa, in the process of dismantling apartheid, was allowed to compete for the first time since 1960.

A star emerged at the 1996 Olympics in Atlanta: the sprinter Michael Johnson won gold in the 400 m, and broke the world record in the 200 m. Perhaps one of the most poignant memories of those Games was the lighting of the

Olympic flame by the veteran boxer Muhammad Ali, himself a gold medal winner in the 1960 games, now debilitated by Parkinson's disease.

### Big prizes

With huge revenues from television, and ever-increasing financial rewards for top professional players, it indeed

**FALLEN HERO** Diego Maradona led Argentina to victory in the 1986 World Cup. At his peak he was rated the best and most valuable player in the world, but his record was marred by his temperamental nature.

1972 PLO raid sours Munich Olympics

1974 Muhammad Ali regains heavyweight boxing championship in Zaire

1976 Nadia Comaneci is the darling of the Montreal Olympics

1980 Moscow Olympics boycotted by many Western countries

1981 John McEnroe takes Wimbledon title from Björn Borg

1984 Torvill and Dean win gold at the Winter Olympics with *Bolero*

**TOWER OF STRENGTH   At 6 feet 9 inches tall, Earvin "Magic" Johnson was a real giant of basketball. He led the Los Angeles Lakers to five championships.**

was inevitable that sports appeared to be corrupted by commercialization, money and performance-enhancing drugs. Transfer fees in soccer give a measure of the rise in the sums exchanged: in 1982 the Argentine star striker Diego Maradona moved to Barcelona for a record $7.5 million; by 1995 the record had trebled to $22.5 million when British player Alan Shearer moved from Blackburn Rovers to Newcastle United. At the same time the rewards rocketed for top players in sports that had become the passion of millions, largely fuelled by television presentation. During the 1980s, the Super Bowl could command television audiences of more than 40 million, nearly half of all households. Basketball, the world's most popular indoor sport, made stars out of players such as Kareem Addul-Jabbar (Milwaukee Bucks and Los Angeles Lakers) in the 1970s and 1980s, and Magic Johnson (Lakers) in the 1980s and 1990s. By the late 1990s sportsmen in the United States numbered among its richest citizens. In 1996 the basketball player Shaquille O'Neal (Orlando Magic) was estimated to be worth over $24 million, and fellow basketball player Michael Jordan (Chicago Bulls) $52 million. The top earner was the boxer Mike Tyson with $75 million.

Boxing remained a key television sport, and high-profile, gladatorial combats continued to be waged even after the championship became diluted by the splits between the World Boxing Association (WBA), World Boxing Council (WBC) and International Boxing Federation (IBF) during the 1980s. Muhammad Ali dominated the 1970s, but the new focus of attention in the 1980s was the tough young New Yorker Mike Tyson. He became the youngest world champion ever in 1986 when, at the age of 20, he took the WBC heavyweight title by beating Trevor Berbick. Tyson was considered insuperable until he was knocked out by James "Buster" Douglas in 1990. Then his career went into a tailspin as he was first convicted to six years' imprisonment in 1992 for raping a beauty queen, and then in 1997 banned from boxing after biting the ear of Evander Holyfield in a comeback fight.

The media revels in the bad boys of sport. Tennis in the 1970s had its temperamental

## "RUMBLE IN THE JUNGLE"

Muhammad Ali had declared himself "The Greatest" when he reigned supreme as world heavyweight boxing champion in the 1960s, and in 1970 he was still indisputably the world's most famous sports personality. He had, however, spent three years in the wilderness, victim of a court ruling in 1967 that banned him from boxing because of his refusal, on Muslim religious grounds, to be drafted into the army at a time when the Vietnam War was raging. In 1971 the Supreme Court lifted the ban and, in what was billed as the "Fight of the Century" against the current champion, Joe Frazier, Ali was defeated for the first time in his career.

By 1974 the new champion was 25-year-old George Foreman. Ali now had a new manager, the dynamic Don King, who proposed another "Fight of the Century." Furthermore King managed to sell the idea of a championship fight to President Mobutu of Zaire and raised a purse of $5 million for both boxers. Mobutu saw this as a political opportunity to enhance the status of his nation, across Africa and the world, by bringing the eyes of a vast international TV audience to Kinshasa. For Ali the fight was a daunting prospect. At 32 he was past his prime. Foreman had defeated his previous 35 opponents and many thought that he was invincible. But Ali was always a gifted strategist and he had a plan, which he called—with characteristically mocking disdain for his opponent—"rope-the-dope."

The fight was staged at 2 am to fit prime-time television. Beneath the stars on a sweltering October night, the ring was surrounded by an excitable audience of 62,000, while beyond the stadium the capital buzzed to the ripple of Zairean electric guitars and the throb of imported American soul music. There was a mood of rebellion and anarchy in the air, and Mobutu chose to stay away and watch the match on close-circuit TV in the safety of his palace.

In the ring Ali forced Foreman to come at him for the first four rounds, absorbing punches and gradually sapping his opponent's energies. Then in the eighth round he struck. After a series of right-hand punches Foreman was floored and counted out. In what the Press crudely dubbed the "Rumble in the Jungle," Ali had regained the world championship a decade after his original stunning victory over Sonny Liston. Commenting on this surprise result, Ali announced: "The bull is stronger, but the matador is smarter."

**THE GREATEST ONCE MORE   In the sweltering heat of Kinshasa, Ali took Foreman to the eighth round before launching the attack that would regain the world title.**

1986 Mike Tyson becomes world heavyweight boxing champion

1994 Ayrton Senna is killed at Imola

1995 South Africa wins rugby World Cup

1998 Tour de France clouded by charges of drug use

## THE BATTLE OF THE SEXES

No one has ever won more Wimbledon titles than Billie Jean King, the tennis star who not only dominated women's tennis in the 1970s, but also helped to propel the women's game forward and place it on a par with the men's. She won 20 Wimbledon titles in all, and was singles champion in 1966-8, 1972, 1973 and 1975.

Small in stature, shortsighted and prone to breathing difficulties, she overcame a number of

**SOMETHING TO PROVE** Billie Jean King and Bobby Riggs indulge in some playful arm-wrestling at the press conference to announce their challenge match.

personal hurdles to reach the top. This may in part account for her feisty attitude, which often had her dubbed by the media as the feminist voice of tennis. She was angered by the patronizing approach of the tennis authorities toward the women's game—a stance that led to a famous tennis event in 1973.

Her great predecessor in women's tennis was the Australian Margaret Court, who had dominated the game in the 1960s and made a famous comeback in 1973, after the birth of her first child. That year the veteran champion Bobby Riggs, age 55 and a self-proclaimed "male chauvinist pig," declared that men would always be superior to women in tennis and challenged Court to a match, which he won.

Billie Jean King would have none of it. She in turn took up Riggs' challenge, and a match was scheduled for September 20 that same year, to be held at the Astrodome in Houston, Texas. This "Battle of the Sexes" became a cause célèbre, watched by an audience of 30,472 in the stadium, still a record for tennis, and 50 million on television. After formalities in which Riggs gave King a giant lollipop as a "sucker," and King gave Riggs a live pig, the match began. Billie Jean King emerged triumphant, winning in three straight sets, and taking home a prize of $100,000.

players, such as Jimmy Connors and the Romanian Ilie Nastase, but the real champion of that decade was the contrasting Swede Björn Borg, who was so cool that he was nicknamed "Iceborg." In 1981 the game's true *enfant terrible*, John McEnroe, put an end to Borg's run of five Wimbledon victories in succession, incurring as he did so a $7,500 fine for misconduct. McEnroe went on to dominate men's tennis in the 1980s. Meanwhile, Martina Navratilova was building up her unprecedented record of nine Wimbledon singles victories, only to be succeeded in turn in the late 1980s by the German Steffi Graf.

The late 1970s and 1980s was a classic period for cricket, with countless records achieved by such prominent stars as the Australian Allan Border (11,174 runs in 156 Tests), the Indian Kapil Dev (434 wickets in 131 Tests), the New Zealander Richard Hadlee (431 wickets in 86 Tests), and other leading players such as Ian Botham (England), Viv Richards (West Indies), Imran Khan (Pakistan), Dennis Lillee (Australia) and Sunil Gaviskar (India). In a controversial effort to exploit the commercial potential of cricket, in 1977-9 the Australian TV tycoon Kerry Packer invited a selection of top international players to break rank and partake in a tournament, dubbed a "circus," in Australia. Money also lured English cricketers to South Africa in 1982, breaking the international sporting boycott raised in protest against South Africa's apartheid policies. The players earned $75,000 each, but back home they were banned from Test cricket for three years.

**SUPER-SERIOUS CONTENDER**
John McEnroe won his first major title, the U.S. Open, in 1979, age 20. His stormy behavior brought a drama and tough competitive edge to the game, which fascinated the public.

In continental Europe the greatest passion was reserved for cycling. The outstanding hero of the early 1970s was the Belgian Eddy Merckx, winner of the Tour de France five times (1969-72 and 1974), and of a record 38 classics overall. He was nicknamed "the Cannibal" for his propensity to devour all other riders

**CYCLING SUPREMO** The overall record of Belgian cyclist Eddy Merckx remains unmatched. Five times winner of the Tour de France, he dominated the sport in the early 1970s. His modesty about his achievements remains part of his mystique.

in his path. Other great cyclists of the era included Miguel Indurain of Spain, Bernard Hinault of France and Greg LeMond of the United States. Drug-taking, however, came to haunt this, one of the most gruelling of sports, turning the 1998 Tour de France into a fiasco. Cycling, meanwhile, gained a new dimension after the off-road mountain bike was developed in California in 1973.

## Sports go global

Several sports took on an increasingly international flavor as the professional circuit traveled around the world pursued by television cameras. Heroes of the international golfing tour included Jack Nicklaus and Tom Watson, Severiano Ballesteros of Spain, Bernhard Langer of Germany and the British player Nick Faldo, who won the Masters two years in a row in 1989 and 1990. By 1997, when Eldrick "Tiger" Woods became the youngest player ever to win the Masters at the age of 21, no fewer than ten

**DRIVING TO WIN** The German Michael Schumacher won the Formula One world championship in 1994 and 1995. In 1996 he joined the Ferrari team, but has yet to win the championship for them.

American players were able to command earnings of more than $1 million a year.

In Formula One motor racing the opening years of the 1970s were dominated by the British driver Jackie Stewart, who was then succeeded by the Brazilian Emerson Fittipaldi. The Austrian Nikki Lauda came back from a near fatal accident at the Nurburgring in West Germany in 1975 to retake the world championship title in 1977. He remained a leading driver until the mid 1980s, when his place was taken by Alain Prost of France, Ayrton Senna of Brazil, and Nigel Mansell of Britain, before the German Michael Schumacher began to stake his claim as the leading driver after 1994. Although motor racing had become safer through technical improvements and regulations, that same year saw the tragic death of the great Brazilian hero, Ayrton Senna, at Imola in Italy.

Accidents must be accepted as part of a dangerous sport like motor racing. They are less expected in soccer. A series of stadium disasters cast a pall over the game in the 1980s. In 1982, 340 fans were crushed to death in the Lenin Stadium in Moscow. At the final of the European Champions' Cup in 1985, held at the Heysel Stadium in Brussels, Liverpool played the Italian team Juventus; rioting Liverpool fans caused a wall to collapse killing 41 Italian and Belgian supporters. Some 80 died in a stampede in a stadium in Kathmandu, Nepal, in 1988. And in 1989, 96 Liverpool supporters died at Hillsborough in Sheffield, England, through

overcrowding in one part of the ground at the start of an FA Cup semifinal match between Liverpool and Nottingham Forest.

Soccer hooliganism, particularly associated with English fans, blighted many European matches, but the World Cup in general was conducted in a spirit of joyous festivity. The 1970 World Cup final between Brazil and Italy, held in Mexico, is rated by many to be the best ever, not least because it starred the great Brazilian Pele, playing in his fourth consecutive World Cup, and bringing home the trophy for a record third time. Argentina, West Germany and Italy subsequently became leading contenders. Argentina won the Cup for a second time in Mexico in 1986, the year that saw the arrival of the "Mexican Wave"—a ripple around the stadium created by bands of spectators standing in succession and waving their hands.

That same year Diego Maradona famously scored a goal against England in the quarter final by illegally using his hand—he later said that the goal had been scored by the "hand of God." Maradona, acknowledged as one of the most gifted soccer players of all time, proved to be the victim of his own success, and his career nose-dived after traces of cocaine were found in his urine in 1991. This stunned the city of Naples, whose team he was playing for: the Neapolitans had taken him into their hearts, even renaming the number 11 in their centuries-old bingo game after Maradona's shirt number.

Rugby celebrated its first World Cup in 1987, by which time the game was becoming

increasingly dominated by Australia and New Zealand. Perhaps the most memorable of the series was the World Cup played in 1995 in South Africa, a nation newly emerged from the trauma of apartheid. When the South African Springboks triumphed against their old rivals New Zealand in the final, Nelson Mandela celebrated by wearing a Springboks' shirt—a symbolic gesture of national joy and reconciliation.

Among the aggression of high-pressured sports there were moments of pure aesthetic beauty. The British ice dancers Jayne Torvill and Christopher Dean won a perfect score and international acclaim when they gave

a mesmeric performance to the music of Ravel's *Bolero* at the 1984 Winter Olympics in Sarajevo in Yugoslavia. This memory proved all the more poignant when the host city became the focus of a region collapsing into civil war in the following decade.

## Keeping fit

Among ordinary people, leading increasingly sedentary, office-oriented lives, the need to keep fit and healthy was made repeatedly clear through government campaigns, magazine articles and leisure programs on television. Scores of people joined aerobics or keep-fit classes, or went to the gym to "work out" on the growing array of fitness machines. Jogging—a supposedly gentle

FUN RUN **The first New York Marathon began in 1970, as a race around Central Park for 27 runners. By the late 1990s, there were over 25,000 runners. Some competed to win and break records, like this determined racer in the wheelchair marathon (left). Below, the throng on the Verranzano Narrows Bridge at the start of the 1985 New York Marathon.**

form of exercise—became a common sight in city parks and streets after the late 1970s.

But perhaps the most remarkable innovation was the development of city marathons. The idea began in New York City, where in 1970 Fred Lebow, an immigrant from Czechoslovakia, organized a race for 27 runners around Central Park. Within five years 2,000 runners were taking part, and the route passed through all of New York's boroughs. Each year it became bigger, joined by top professional runners as well as amateurs. Meanwhile, the idea had spread to other cities. More than 7,000 runners took part in the first London Marathon in 1981. By 1996 there were major city marathons across the world, notably in Osaka, Tokyo, Boston and Rotterdam. This phenomenon preserved the virtues of the old adage: "It's not winning that counts, so much as taking part."

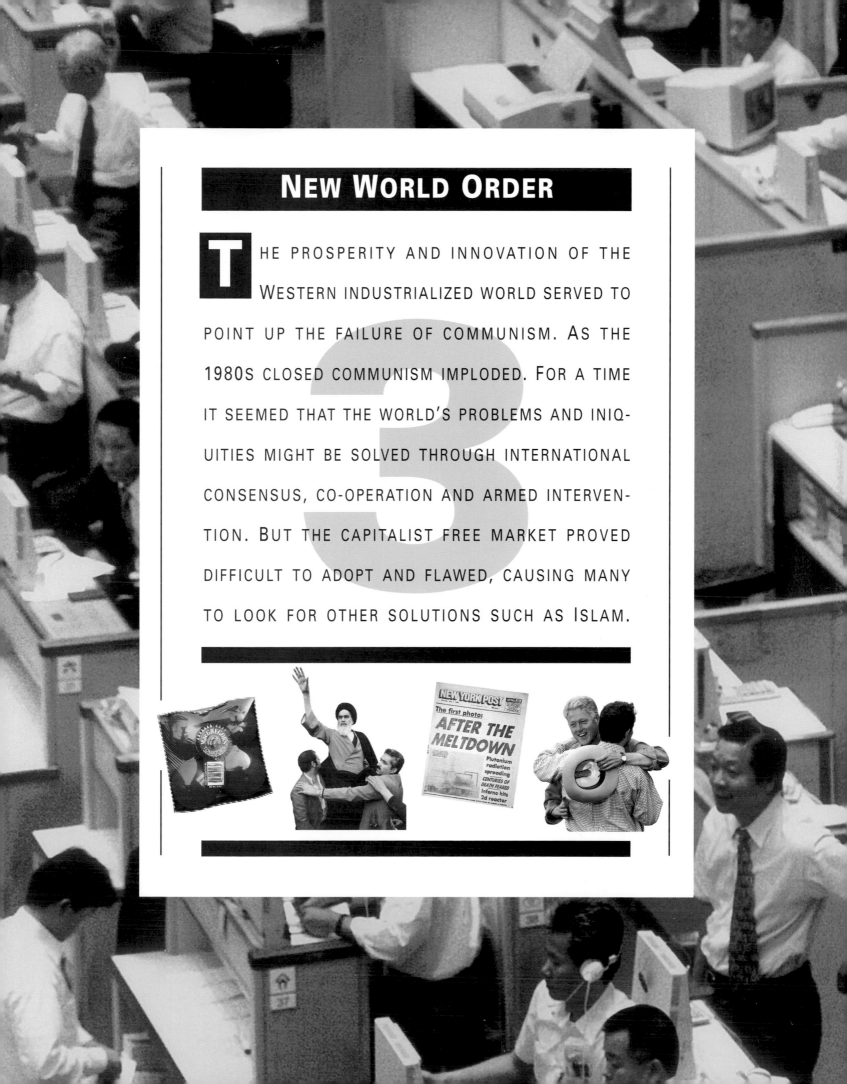

# New World Order

**T**HE PROSPERITY AND INNOVATION OF THE WESTERN INDUSTRIALIZED WORLD SERVED TO POINT UP THE FAILURE OF COMMUNISM. AS THE 1980S CLOSED COMMUNISM IMPLODED. FOR A TIME IT SEEMED THAT THE WORLD'S PROBLEMS AND INIQUITIES MIGHT BE SOLVED THROUGH INTERNATIONAL CONSENSUS, CO-OPERATION AND ARMED INTERVENTION. BUT THE CAPITALIST FREE MARKET PROVED DIFFICULT TO ADOPT AND FLAWED, CAUSING MANY TO LOOK FOR OTHER SOLUTIONS SUCH AS ISLAM.

# THE MARKET ECONOMY

## WESTERN INDUSTRIALIZED NATIONS HAD TO ADAPT TO AN INCREASINGLY GLOBAL ECONOMY TO BE SURE OF RETAINING A STAKE IN IT

THE INTERNATIONAL CAR  The Ford Fiesta, first produced in 1976. It was designed as an economic family car for a European market still struggling to come to terms with vastly increased oil prices.

In 1973 the American sociologist Daniel Bell suggested that the Western industrialized nations were at the threshold of a new era: the postindustrial society. First there had been agriculture, then trade and industry leading to the factory production of the industrial revolution. Now the Western world had exported the factory to the developing world, and could not compete with the developing world's low labor costs. To maintain the wealth they had once earned from industry, the older industrial nations had to look for new sources of income. The answer lay in services, such as banking, insurance, accounting and education, and in technological know-how—all of which can be priced and sold just like manufactured goods. The postindustrial society did not dispense with industry: goods still had to be produced. But this would happen in low-cost factories abroad or in high-tech computer and robot-assisted ones at home.

The concept of the postindustrial society is directly linked to the revolution in information and communications technology, and to the increasing globalization of trade and industry. Since the 1970s the meaning of the term "multinational" has grown. It refers to companies that not only manufacture and trade in more than one country, but also source their materials from around the world. In 1976, for example, the car manufacturer Ford launched a new car for the European market: the Fiesta. It was assembled in Ford plants in West Germany, Spain and Great Britain—but parts came also from France, Northern Ireland and ten other locations. By the early 1990s the Ford Escort contained parts from 15 different countries.

This same approach was taken by many household names, such as Siemens, Philips, Mitsubishi, Glaxo, Nike. Multinationals have a reputation for being ruthless: they take their business wherever its makes economic sense, and remove it from wherever it does not. A dispassionate, objective global strategy is essential to their survival.

The multinational perspective was a burning issue for the older industrial nations in the 1970s. Their heavy industries were in decline; their modern industries could not compete with Japan and the burgeoning industrial economies of South Korea and Taiwan. There were two lines of thought. One was that the Western industrial economies should protect their home industries with tariffs or import duties. But many also argued that tariffs simply isolated the symptoms; they did not provide the cure. The alternative, by contrast, was free trade. Starting in 1947, when the world was still recovering from the effects of the Second World War, the United Nations had sponsored seven rounds of talks on the General Agreements on Tariffs and Trade (GATT). These aimed to win a consensus among participant nations for the reduction of trading barriers. In 1995 GATT was officially superseded by the World Trade Organization, with headquarters in Geneva. By this time it had 125 nation signatories covering 90 percent of world trade and had managed to reduce tariffs to about 5 percent of market value: they had stood at 40 percent in 1947.

Free trade, however, seems like a threat to countries in recession or those unable to produce enough exports to balance the

RUST BELTS  Industry ground to a halt in many parts of Europe in the mid 1970s, as emphasis shifted from labor-intensive manufacturing. This affected factories up and down the supply chain, such as this oil refinery and chemical plant in Mestre, near Venice in Italy.

1973 Oil crisis begins, bringing about world recession

1979 Margaret Thatcher becomes British prime minister

1980 Ronald Reagan becomes U.S. president

1981 President François Mitterrand attempts sweeping socialist reforms in France

**THE WINTER OF DISCONTENT**
Uncollected garbage piled up in London's streets in February 1979, during a strike by public sector workers. For many, it was all too symbolic of the crisis gripping Britain.

influx of imports. This was the situation in Britain in the 1970s. In 1976 Britain, once the world's leading industrial nation, had to apply to the International Monetary Fund (IMF) for a loan of $4.5 billion to cover its balance of payments deficit.

### Anatomy of decline

A handful of explanations was adduced. The 1973 oil crisis had struck deep, affecting the whole of the Western industrialized world. The British Government was saddled with high public spending and loss-making nationalized industries. It was also racked by industrial disputes. In 1970, 8.8 million days of work were lost to strikes—the highest since the General Strike of 1926. In 1972 and 1973, the Conservative prime minister, Edward Heath, was forced to put the country on a three-day working week because striking miners effectively blockaded the power stations and prevented coal from reaching them. When further industrial unrest threatened in 1974, he called an election and lost. The succeeding Labor government—under Harold Wilson until 1976, then James

**GAS CRISIS** Tempers flare due to the gas shortage of 1974, as demonstrated by this man who waves his fist at another motorist blocking his way as he tries to drive into a service station in Chicago.

Callaghan—fared no better. Industrial unrest culminated in wide-ranging strikes among the public services in early 1979, which left garbage piled high in city streets during what was known as the "Winter of Discontent."

Heath's successor as Conservative leader, Margaret Thatcher, capitalized on Labor's troubles to win the 1979 election. She identified several causes of the malaise, proposed solutions for each, and convinced the strike-weary electorate to give her ideas a chance. Her overriding conviction was that only a free market could restore Britain's fortunes. In this, she was influenced by the theory of monetarism, proposed notably by the economist Milton Friedman. Essentially this held that money supply management, regulated by inflation, is the key to output, prices and employment, which tend naturally toward equilibrium. By contrast fiscal policy—government attempts to steer the economy by taxation and price-and-incomes policy—is a far less reliable tool. Margaret Thatcher intended to liberalize the economy and let market forces do their work.

One of her first moves was to reduce income tax. Then she began a long and bruising battle with the trade unions. Through their wage demands and strikes they had effectively held the country hostage, and caused the downfall of three successive governments. Their restrictive practices and strict job demarcation made employment cumbersome and expensive: in the British shipyards men from five separate unions

were needed to fit a porthole. Not surprisingly, South Korea and Taiwan were making deep inroads into the shipbuilding industry.

### Taking on the unions

With her rallying call "Who governs Britain?" (the government or the unions?), Margaret Thatcher initiated a series of legislative reforms to curtail the power of the unions, such as secret strike ballots, compulsory cooling-off periods, the outlawing of secondary picketing, and punishments for contravention which included fines or the sequestration of union funds.

The Thatcher government also began a campaign to reduce government spending across the board. This meant cutting back on welfare spending, reducing subsidies to "lame-duck" industries and beginning the process of "privatizing" nationalized industries. It was a bitter process, during which factories all over Britain closed as financial support dried up. Unemployment rose to 3 million; inflation rose to 21 percent, at a time when inflation in France and Germany stood at 4 percent. During Margaret Thatcher's first administration, her promise of an upturn seemed to be receding. Britain remained the "sick man of Europe." But the hardships were, she implied, the bitter pill that Britain had to swallow for recovery.

Her policies toward nationalized industry and the unions came to a head in the miners' strike, which began in March 1984. When it was revealed that the government intended to close a large number of unprofitable pits, the National Union of Mineworkers, under their left-wing leader Arthur Scargill, called for a strike. The union hoped either to win a reprieve or bring the country to its knees, as it had done in the 1970s; for Arthur Scargill this was a political battle, a kind of class war against capitalism. However, when the strike began there was a long summer ahead, when the demand for coal falls, and the power stations had huge stockpiles. Furthermore, not all miners agreed that confrontation would bring the desired results, and a breakaway Democratic Union of Mineworkers was formed, whose members ignored the strike call. The strike divided communities, even families. After months of violent confrontation, in which thousands of police faced picket lines of strikers, the miners started to drift back to work. In March 1985 the strike was called off. The leaders told their loyal men that they could go back to work "with

**COAL NOT DOLE**
Arthur Scargill, president of the National Union of Mineworkers. Below: Pitched battles between pickets and police were a disturbing feature of the 1984 miners' strike.

## THE INTERNATIONAL CROSS-TRAINER

Back in the early 1960s American business-school graduate Phil Knight began selling sports shoes out of the back of a van at athletics events. Soon he started manufacturing his own shoes: in 1964 he founded Nike in Oregon. By the 1990s his company was selling goods worth more than $4.7 billion a year.

This extraordinary success story can be attributed to a combination of three factors: innovation, promotion and foreign manufacture. In the 1960s Knight had asked his old college coach Bill Bowerman to come up with some new ideas for sports shoes. Bowerman is said to have used his wife's waffle iron to develop the idea of a novel kind of cellular sole that was lighter, bouncier and had better traction than the traditional sports shoe. The modern cross-trainer was born. Nike kept up the flow of innovation, producing for instance the "air-conditioned" Nike "Tailwind" in 1979, designed by an engineer.

Knight also had a keen eye for publicity, recruiting top stars—including John McEnroe and Michael Jordan—to promote his footwear and sports clothes in poster campaigns, in fashion magazines, and in forceful television advertisements akin to pop videos. Nike positively courted controversy as it sought to outplay its rivals, such as Reebok and Adidas, in this lucrative market. By the late 1990s, Nike was spending nearly a $1 billion a year on promotion. Its "swoosh" logo, designed in 1971, is now instantly recognized the world over.

Nike can afford to spend so much on promotion because its profit margins are so high. From the start Knight contracted out the manufacture of his sports shoes, to Japan in the 1960s, then to South Korea and Taiwan in the 1970s. By the late 1990s Nike products were being made by 450,000 people in 33 countries, benefiting from low labor costs. By this time, Nike's suppliers in South Korea and Taiwan had themselves subcontracted work to companies in China, Vietnam and Indonesia. In 1998 it was revealed that conditions in some of these factories were dangerous and unsanitary. Workers were being subjected to humiliating and authoritarian regimes, and earning as little as $45 a month—less than the price of one pair of Nike shoes. It was the classic dilemma of foreign investment in the Third World, where low costs attract inward investment. As its international reputation came into question, Nike claimed that it was being unfairly singled out by allegations of exploitation.

Before Nike, people walked.

**REINVENTING THE SHOE** Nike's ingenious and aggressive advertising helped to forge a broader market for running shoes.

their heads held high." In fact, they faced utter defeat. Mines were closed, and old mining communities withered and died a slow death, tragic testimony to the harsh lesson about "who governs Britain."

The Conservatives, meanwhile, pushed on with their policy of privatization. State-owned low-rent houses and apartments were put on the market, so their occupiers could buy them cheaply and put a foot in the door of property ownership. They could also buy shares in the newly privatized industries, which were opened to all comers in a bid to democratize the stock market. British Airways was put up for sale in November 1980, and was turned from an ailing recipient of government subsidies to one of the world's most successful and profitable airlines. The privatization of British Telecom in 1984 involved the largest share issue in the world, bringing $6 billion to the government's coffers.

### Investing in Britain

Britain seemed leaner and fitter. It was attracting inward investment, notably from Japan. Companies such as Nissan and Sony not only liked the inducements offered by Britain, and the potential of a toehold in Europe: they also liked the new and constructive labor relations. By the 1990s there were 275 Japanese manufacturing companies operating in Britain, responsible for creating 650,000 jobs. The global economy had come to Britain.

They were boom times for many property-owners, who made colossal profits on house-price increases, while a new breed of young City men and women were leading a life of champagne and fast cars. It was the age of the Yuppie (Young Upwardly Mobile Professional)—rich, carefree and uncaring.

The downside of this trend was that employees became simply part of the market-economy equation, to be hired in good times and fired when commercial pressures demanded. The old idea of a safe "job for life" in a secure, established company or institution withered away, as all jobs fell under the mercy of the vicissitudes of the global economy. In this more hard-hearted world many of the most vulnerable citizens were cast out of mainstream society. The extreme consequences of this trend were witnessed in the sharp rise in homelessness. Welfare cuts, unemployment, the closure of

mental hospitals—in a move toward "care in the community"—all contributed to a growing band of the dispossessed who felt that they had little stake in Thatcher's Britain.

### The spreading of "Thatcherism"

The logic of Thatcher's approach nonetheless remained persuasive, even with its unpalatable social consequences. The prevailing wisdom was that high government spending hurts the economy and hence the people's well-being. By the end of the 1980s, some 50 countries around the world had launched policies to reduce state expenditure, privatize state assets and promote a market economy. Brazil provided a good example. Emerging from military rule into economic foment in the late 1980s, it

embarked on radical economic reforms after 1990, when the new president, Fernando Collor de Mello, began privatizing state companies and opening up the heavily protected domestic economy to foreign competition. Collor was forced to make an undignified exit over a corruption scandal in 1992, but after 1994 the economic reforms continued under President Fernando Cardoso.

Back in Europe, countries with generous welfare programs—such

as the Netherlands and Sweden—found their economies under intense strain with every economic downturn. Any shortfall had to be made up by increasing the tax burden— which penalized the income earners, reduced their spending power and depressed the economy yet further. It was a question of balance: governments had to choose between rolling back the state to allow the market to thrive unfettered, and carrying out their duties in protecting the most vulnerable. As the 1980s progressed most countries in the

**HAVES, HAVE NOTS** The realities of the market economy in the 1980s led to escalating numbers living in "cardboard cities" (below). At the same time yuppies (right) in the financial world celebrated huge salaries and perks.

European Community gradually adopted "Thatcherite'" policies—although they may not have liked to see it in those terms: Margaret Thatcher's outspoken opposition to many of the EC's policies made her a controversial figure in Europe.

France for a short while bucked this trend by introducing radical socialist policies after François Mitterrand was elected president in 1981. His government embarked on a left-wing agenda, nationalizing banking groups and various key industries. But the growing trade deficit, rising inflation and tax burden were reflected in the vote of the electorate, which swung to the right in 1986. Mitterrand was forced to accept more market-oriented policies; in the late 1980s, under the socialist prime minister Michel Rocard, the state-owned banking giant Crédit Agricole and the defense and electronics firm Matra were sold off in a program of cautious privatiza-

tion. Even so, one in four workers in France was still employed by the state, 50 percent more than in Britain. Meanwhile, moderate socialist and social democratic governments in Portugal, Spain, Italy, Austria, Greece and Sweden were all juggling with similar issues.

## Reaganomics

A similar pattern was evolving in America. The Republican Ronald Reagan had come to power in 1980, following the irresolute presidency of Jimmy Carter. A former Hollywood actor, Reagan had been governor of California from 1967 to 1974, and presided over a remarkable transition in that state's economy. He too was an admirer of Milton Friedman's monetarism, and of Margaret Thatcher. He pushed tax cuts through Congress in August 1981, with the support of the Democrats, then set about liberalizing the economy by reducing government intervention in business, and cutting government expenditure on welfare, while increasing defense spending. "Not since the first six months of Franklin Roosevelt's Administration has a new President done so much of such magnitude so quickly to change the economic direction of the nation," enthused *Time* magazine. These policies, however, caused deep resentment among those at the lower end of the economic scale as the gap between

rich and poor widened.

Nonetheless, Reagan remained a popular president, especially after a failed assassination attempt on March 30, 1981, when he was shot by John Hinckley in Washington. Reagan showed calm heroics in the John Wayne mold, joking with surgeons before an operation: "I hope you guys are Republicans." He made light of the incident to his wife, Nancy, saying: "Honey, I forgot to duck."

But his popularity was not tied to the performance of the economy. The budget deficit widened, and then everything came to a grinding halt on Monday, October 19, 1987, "Black Monday," when stockmarket prices went spiralling downward. On one day during the Great Crash of October 1929, the Dow Jones Industrial Index dropped by 12.8 percent; on Black Monday 1987 it fell by 22.6 percent. Stock markets around the world followed suit, fueled by computerized systems geared to sell automatically when a market fell below certain preset values. Some $500 billion in stock values vanished.

## The gap between rich and poor

For America and Europe, the good times of the 1980s seemed to be over. In fact, the better management of international finances meant that a deep recession, like the Great Depression of the 1930s, was avoided. Western nations continued to prosper, though in a newly chastened climate.

Meanwhile, as the gap between the rich and poor within these nations continued to grow, so did a similar gap on the global scale: the poorer nations of the Third World suffered from increased impoverishment, rising populations, growing foreign debt, and concomitant corruption and political turmoil. Geared to hard-hearted market economics, the wealthy nations were not inclined to bail out foreign countries that did not contribute to the market. Foreign aid from the world's principal donors—America, Japan, France, West Germany, Britain and Italy— fell as a percentage of gross national product, from 0.99 percent in 1982 to 0.83 percent in 1994. By 1992 the average income across the Western industrialized world was $15,000, whereas in much of the Third World, including Africa, China and India, it remained below $500.

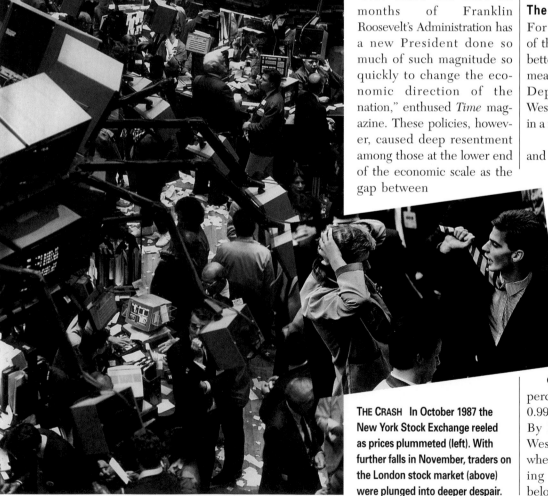

THE CRASH  In October 1987 the New York Stock Exchange reeled as prices plummeted (left). With further falls in November, traders on the London stock market (above) were plunged into deeper despair.

## ASSASSINATION ATTEMPTS: MARGARET THATCHER AND RONALD REAGAN

Margaret Thatcher became the Conservative leader of Britain in 1975, when Edward Heath was ousted. Republican Ronald Reagan was elected president of the United States in 1980, after the faltering presidency of Jimmy Carter in the 1970s. Both figures saw economic booms during their leadership, as well as economic disasters. Both had platforms that brought forth a widening gap between the rich and poor. And both conservative leaders almost had their lives taken from them by assassins.

Nicknamed the "Iron Lady" by the Soviets, or a more cozy "Mrs. T." by the British, Margaret Thatcher rose to become Britain's longest-serving prime minister this century. She established a worldwide vogue for the market economy and became a leader of international standing. Her reformist zeal attempted to put Britain back on the path to prosperity, as she targeted the trade unions, government spending and the inefficient nationalized industries, and promoted self-help and ambition. Ms. Thatcher showed her fortitude in October, 1984, when the IRA blew up the Grant Hotel in Brighton, where leading conservatives were staying for the annual party conference. Her bathroom was destroyed only moments after she had left it. Four people died in the explosion.

On March 30, 1981, just over two months after being sworn in as president, Reagan was shot in the chest by 25 year-old John Hinckley, Jr., as he left a Washington hotel. Also wounded in the attempt were press secretary James Brady (who suffered permanent brain damage and became, along with his wife, a vocal advocate for handgun control), a Secret Service agent, and a police officer. Reagan, who made a quick recovery, won massive support for the way he handled the ordeal: with quips and winks. ("Honey, I forgot to duck!" he joked to his wife Nancy.) Hinckley, who offered the shooting as a twisted tribute to actress Jodie Foster, was acquitted by reason of insanity.

**REAGAN IS SHOT**
**Police and Secret Service agents wrestle with an assailant after president Reagan is wounded in an assassination attempt.**

**AFTERMATH  Brighton's Grand Hotel after the bombing in 1984. Right: Thatcher with Ronald Reagan.**

There were, however, a handful of "emergent nations" in the Far East that fit well into the global economy, through an abundance of raw materials, cheap and willing labor and well-focused ambitions. They also practiced policies of low government expenditure, spending around 20 percent of GDP compared with an average of 50 percent among Western European nations. At the time, they inspired admiration from the industrialized nations, which dubbed them "the Tiger economies."

# DRAGONS AND TIGERS

## FOLLOWING THE LEAD OF JAPAN, THE EAST ASIAN NATIONS DEVELOPED ONE OF THE WORLD'S FASTEST GROWING ECONOMIC ZONES

Japan had led the way and provided the model. In the 1950s it had launched a vigorous campaign of industrialization and modernization, attracting foreign investment and focusing on light industrial exports, such as textiles, before establishing heavy industries such as steel, as the foundation of a broad industrial base that soon included shipbuilding and cars. By the 1960s other Pacific nations were eager to follow suit: South Korea, Taiwan, Hong Kong and Singapore. Their story really took off in the 1970s, and together they became known as the "Four Dragons."

Initially, the key to their success was a cheap and diligent workforce. Manually dextrous, eager to work and to learn and with high literacy rates, their workers provided a reliable and low-cost source of products for the multinationals, whose presence and investment were actively courted. Gifted students were sent to America to train, and brought back with them an understanding of Western industrial techniques, economic strategy and marketing. In South Korea, it was the authoritarian government of Park Chung Hee that initiated the modernization, and native conglomerates such as Daewoo, Samsung and Hyundai took up the challenge. The government invested in a massive steel works at Pohang, completed in 1973, the same year that Hyundai produced its first ship, a supertanker. Ten years later, Hyundai had become the largest shipbuilder in the world.

What the Four Dragons did not have was raw materials in any great quantity; unlike countries such as Australia, they could not rely on the export of these to ensure reasonable prosperity. Their goal, therefore, was to create sophisticated industrial bases, and to do this they concentrated on improved education and training, and negotiated deals by which foreign investors would also bring technological transfer.

By 1976 Japan and the Four Dragons were producing 60 percent of the world's manufactured exports. Throughout the 1970s and 80s, the productivity growth in these countries was at least twice, and in some cases six times, that of the United States. Japan had become a leading industrial nation, able now to make inward investments in Europe and America—a remarkable turnaround since the 1950s when the flow of capital was entirely in the opposite direction.

Japan and the Four Dragons found most of their raw materials in the countries around them, notably Thailand, Indonesia, Malaysia and the Philippines—all belonging to the Association of South East Asian Nations (ASEAN) and soon dubbed the Four Tigers. The tide of prosperity soon reached their shores, too. Not only did they provide raw materials, but they also had resources of low-cost labor: they, in their turn, began manufacturing, and benefited from technological transfer. Japan and the

WORK ETHIC By the 1980s, the Japanese had placed much of their basic manufacturing in neighboring countries where labor costs were lower. At home, the workforce concentrated on high-tech manufacture, and research and development, as in this prototype of a marine observation satellite (left). Employees, including factory workers (above), enjoyed good conditions and job security. In return companies expected a high degree of commitment and loyalty.

1976 Japan and the Four Dragons produce 60 percent of the world's manufactured exports

1981 Mahathir becomes prime minister of Malaysia

1983 Hyundai of South Korea becomes the world's biggest shipbuilder

## DENG XIAO-PING

An old Sichuan proverb goes: "It doesn't matter if the cat is black or white. If it catches the mouse it is a good cat." Deng Xiao-ping was fond of saying it, and it suited him well. He was above all a pragmatist, and in search of a system that would give his country economic stability. By choosing a delicate path somewhere between communism and capitalism, in the closing years of his life he saw China reach the threshold of prosperity.

Deng was one of the old guard of the Chinese Communist Party (CCP). He joined the party in 1925, and took part in the Long March, the anti-Japanese war and the civil war. He rose to power in the 1950s, but during the 1960s chose to side with fellow pragmatist Liu Shaoqui. Mao Zedong, however, was too much of the romantic revolutionary to countenance such compromise. Shortly after Mao launched his Cultural Revolution in 1966, Deng was sidelined and disappeared from view in 1969. He was recalled by Zhou Enlai in 1973, purged again by the "Gang of Four" in 1976, then brought back to center stage in 1978 by Hua Guo-feng. After 1980 Deng operated from powerful positions as Chairman of the CCP's Central Military Commission and a member of the Standing Committee of the Political Bureau. By the early 1980s his protégés were in power, and Deng had become the de facto ruler of China.

Through Deng's policy of economic liberalization, China began rapidly to transform. There was pressure also for concurrent democratic liberalization, but Deng—ever the pragmatist—recognized that this was unpalatable to the conservative wing of the CCP. He was obliged therefore to stamp hard on the movement that came to a head in the massacre at Tiananmen Square in 1989. By this time he was 84 years old, and in the years that followed he became increasingly frail. He eventually died in 1997, at the age of 92. To many he is the architect of the modern Chinese economy, but others cannot forgive him for the path of repression that he took in 1989 and the years that followed.

**POLITICAL SURVIVOR** Deng grew up in troubled times, as China lurched from imperial rule to republic and civil war. Part of his revered status derived from the fact that he had taken part in every phase of communist rule since its inception.

Four Dragons now concentrated on high-tech, high-cost goods, while the Four Tigers took on the low-cost manufacturing. In the 1980s, Vietnam began slowly to emerge from years of war and communism, and it, too, started to attract inward investment for low-cost manufacturing in the pattern set by its neighbors.

### Pacific Rim

The prosperity of the western Pacific soon pulled in the whole of the region known as the "Pacific Rim," which included Australia and New Zealand, and the western coasts of Canada and America. These places not only offered eager markets for Asian goods, they also had valuable resources of raw materials. In addition, the western United States was a

world center for computer and communications technology. Previously the world's economy had centered on the Atlantic, spanning Europe and the eastern seaboard of America. The emergence of the Pacific Rim, centering on Japan, represented a major role reversal.

During the 1980s China also added its considerable weight to regional prosperity.

With its massive population of over a billion (a fifth of the world's entire population), it represented a huge source of low-cost labor, as well as a vast potential market should its economy ever become prosperous enough to absorb imports.

This process was put in motion by the veteran politician Deng Xiao-ping, notably after

**OLD WAYS** More than 60 percent of China's workers in the 1980s were engaged in agriculture, feeding a population of more than a billion. Yet many of the farming methods were antiquated and labor intensive.

1986 President Marcos ousted in the Philippines

1989 China crushes democracy movement in Tiananmen Square

1996 Singapore ranks as the seventh wealthiest nation in the world

1997 Britain hands Hong Kong back to China

1998 Economic collapse engulfs the Far East; Suharto steps down

2000

risen by an annual average of 10 percent over ten years. The city of Shanghai underwent massive redevelopment in the 1980s, and trebled its industrial output. The economy, meanwhile, was generally liberalized: in agriculture, for instance, farmers could become tenants once again and take responsibility for their own land with the incentive of keeping any surplus. By 1985 China had increased agricultural production by almost 50 percent and had begun to export food. It was also now possible to own private businesses, and similar incentives were offered. In 1978 there were 100,000 private businesses; by 1985 there were 17 million. The government, however, still retained complete or partial control over 80 percent of the economy.

With this growing prosperity, China became more self-confident and adroit in its foreign relations. In 1984 Deng negotiated a deal with Britain by which Hong Kong would be handed back to China in 1997, against guarantees that for 50 years the basis of Hong Kong's distinctive economic and social framework would be respected. Britain was forced to relinquish the colony because its lease on the New Territories in mainland China—essential to the survival of Hong Kong Island—was due to end. As a result of its pragmatic approach to negotia-

**END OF EMPIRE**   As the last British governor of Hong Kong, Chris Patten oversaw the process of giving the colony back to China. Below: On June 30, 1997, Patten receives the Union Jack, which had just been lowered for the last time at the Governor's official residence. Above: Workers in a toy factory in the Guangdong Enterprise Zone.

he began to take over the reins of power during the 1980s. A series of Special Economic Zones (SEZ) were set up around the foreign ports of Hong Kong and Macao, along the eastern coast and up the Yangtze valley. Here foreign investors were given financial inducements to establish manufacturing bases, while the Chinese gained technical knowledge from the experience. By 1992 this investment amounted to more than $36 billion, and China's Gross National Product had

tions, China won itself the prize of one of the region's most prosperous enclaves, and the British bowed out in a final grand gesture of imperial pomp.

## Tiananmen Square

By this time, however, China had given cause for concern that, while its economy was becoming more liberal, its political system was not. Pressure for democratic reform rose under the more relaxed rule of Hu Yaobang, General Secretary of the Communist Party, and his successor Zhao Ziyang. Hu Yaobang was dismissed by Deng in 1987, but when he died in 1989 students and workers used his funeral as an opportunity to demonstrate their support for his liberal tendencies, and to make evident their dissatisfaction with the current regime. There were several bones of contention, including rising unemployment, the detrimental effects of rural migration into the cities, and the growth of corruption. The groundswell of opinion placed the solution for these ills in greater democracy. From April, demonstrators gathered in huge numbers in Tiananmen Square, close to the Forbidden City in the center of Beijing. This was a site of great symbolic significance in Chinese history: it was where students had rebelled in 1919, and where Mao had declared his victory in 1949. To one side was the Great Hall of the People, and on another was Mao's Mausoleum.

The demonstrators—mainly students, but supported by teachers and workers—set up tents, podiums, broadcasting units and even erected a 30 foot plaster statue of the "Goddess of Democracy." Change seemed to be in the air, and the government prevaricated, unwilling to use force to disperse this essentially nonviolent protest. Government ministers argued that China was not ready for full democracy: they sensed they were looking down the barrel of anarchy, but did not know how to resolve the matter without incurring the wrath of their own people, and the censure of Hong Kong, Britain, America and other investor nations.

To the discomfort of the Chinese authorities, the Soviet leader Mikhail Gorbachev was scheduled to come to Beijing in May, the first official visit by a Soviet leader since 1959. On May 14, the day that he was due to attend ceremonies at the Great Hall of the People, Tiananmen Square filled with students and workers buzzing with expectation. In the event he was ushered in through a side door. To mark his visit, 300,000 people marched through the streets of Beijing on May 16, a million on May 17 and 18. It was the sort of humiliation the Chinese leadership does not take lying down.

So in early June it reinforced the People's Army encamped around central Beijing, and

**WELCOMING THE FUTURE**
Many in Hong Kong greeted the hand-over with optimism. China promised to preserve Hong Kong's status under the "one country, two systems" slogan.

## TIANANMEN SQUARE

A documentary film entitled *The Gate of Heavenly Peace* (1995) told the story of the Chinese anti-government protests of 1989 using interviews with those who took part. Here they recount their experiences on the night of June 3-4:

Zhao Hongliang (a worker): "Workers and Beijing residents stopped it [the personnel carrier]. Someone hit it with a Molotov cocktail and it caught fire. The fire hardly slowed it down. Frankly, I was scared and got out of its way. Everyone got out of its way . . . We wanted to see what was happening, so we headed south and ran smack into some soldiers. They weren't shooting into the sky or at the ground. They were shooting straight at us.

"Five workers beside me fell. At first, we said, 'Come on, guys, stop fooling around and get up!' But then we saw the blood. Some had been shot in the chest, some in the head . . ."

Feng Congde (a student): "At around 3:00 in the morning, several thousand students sat down at the Monument. They wanted to stay to the very end. A lot of blood had already been shed that night, but most of the students in the Square hadn't seen anything, so they didn't know what to believe . . .

"At around 3:30 the four people on hunger strike came to talk to the students. They said, 'Blood is being spilled all over the city. More than enough blood has already been shed to awaken the people. We know you're not afraid of dying, but leaving now doesn't mean that you're cowards.'

"I was in charge of the vote to determine whether we should leave. I said, 'On the count of three, those who want to go, shout "Go!"; those who vote to stay, shout "Stay!"' I couldn't tell which side was louder . . . Because of this situation, I felt that when the two sides sounded about the same, most likely more people voted to leave. So I announced the decision to leave."

Liang Xiaoyan (a teacher): "We filed out of the Square from the southeast corner. I was near the end of the line. When we turned the corner at the Concert Hall, several tanks came up from behind. Suddenly we heard shouts of panic. We looked back and saw people scrambling to get away, as a tank turned around right in the middle of the crowd. Then we heard screaming and crying. We ran as fast as we could, afraid that the tank was going to run over us. A student I knew . . . practically crawled out from under the tank. Two of his classmates were crushed."

**UNEQUAL FORCE**  In an act of desperate defiance, a lone figure armed only with a shopping bag tried to halt the march of tanks along Beijing's Avenue of Eternal Peace, 1989.

on June 3 troops made a concerted effort to break into Tiananmen Square. That night the shooting began, and the demonstration was crushed. Estimates vary as to the number of deaths: some put it at 3,000, others at 400-800. The Chinese authorities proposed the figure at 23, but they had lost all credibility. On June 5, as a line of 18 tanks drove down the Avenue of Eternal Peace, one lone student stood in their way, trying in vain to block their advance—a gesture of despair and defiance witnessed on film around the world. He jumped on to the tank, exchanged brief words with the driver, then was pulled away by the crowd and to an unknown fate.

A long period of political repression and retrenchment followed, which lifted only in the mid 1990s with reforms under President Jiang Zemin, whose "socialist market econo-

my" produced a sustained period of econom-ic stability and growth. The shadow of Tiananmen Square hung over all questions of political reform in China until the end of the century.

### 2020 vision

To some degree, obedience to authority is part and parcel of the Confucian work ethic that has made the Chinese prosper else-where. In the late 1990s the World Bank was predicting that by the year 2002 the "Chinese Economic Area" (China, Hong Kong, Taiwan and Singapore) would have a greater Gross National Product than the United States.

Singapore, under the premiership of Lee Kuan Yew from 1959 to 1993, rose from lit-tle more than a trading port to one of the world's most prosperous countries. Lee Kuan Yew ran a tightly controlled, central-

**WARNING CLOUDS  In late 1997, fires from uncontrolled forest clearance in Indonesia, coupled with unusual weather conditions, spread a pall of acrid smoke across the entire region. Children in Sumatra had to attend school wearing face masks.**

## THE FALL OF PRESIDENT MARCOS

**SYMBOLS OF RAPACITY  After Marcos had been overthrown, rebels discovered his wife's vast collection of fashion shoes. Press photos of these spoke eloquently of the couple's greed and excesses.**

Strangely, it was perhaps his wife Imelda's collection of thousands of pairs of shoes that most shocked the world about the Marcos regime. While the urban poor of the Philippines raked over the rubbish heaps for scraps, President Marcos and his coterie of family and cronies were looting the nation's wealth to live a jet-setting high life.

When Ferdinand Marcos came to power in 1965, he initially brought about successful reforms to agri-culture, industry and education. But these were undermined by mounting student revolt and con-tinued guerrilla campaigns by communist insurgents and Muslim separatists in the southern islands. In 1972 Marcos used these activities as a pretext to impose martial law, giving himself supreme power. He also attempted to nurture a cult of personality by creating a fantasy past for himself as a resistance fighter during the 1942-5 anti-Japanese war. Martial law was lifted in January 1981, but his government still bore the stamp of authoritarianism, and became flagrantly corrupt.

Along with many others, the popular opposition spokesman Begnino Aquino was arrested in 1972 and imprisoned for seven years before being permitted to travel to America for an operation. He eventually returned to the Philippines to head the opposition in August 1983 but was shot dead as he stepped from his plane. A com-mission of inquiry set up by Marcos blamed an assassination plot by an army chief and 25 other officers; then a court, also appointed by Marcos, acquitted them.

Aquino's crude assassination and casual cover-up turned the tide against Marcos, and crucially the army split between his loyal supporters and those who backed the opposition, now led by Aquino's widow, Corazon. Marcos held an election in 1986, of which he was declared the winner— but only as the result of massive election fraud. America withdrew its support for Marcos. As pro-Aquino sup-porters and troops stormed the Malacanang Palace in Manila on February 25, 1986, U.S. helicopters whisked the president and his wife, Imelda, to safety. Marcos was already a sick man and had to be carried away on a stretcher. He died in 1990 after four years in exile on Hawaii. Imelda Marcos was acquit-ted in a U.S. fraud trial and returned to the Philippines to try to revive the Marcos cult. She met with only partial success, despite the failure of Corazon Aquino's government, and she was indicted on further corruption charges. Few could ever divorce her from the memory of those shoes.

**NEW DAWN  For many, the collapse of the Marcos regime signified the end of more than two decades of struggle.**

## THE AUSTRALIAN BICENTENNIAL

In 1988, 200 years after the men of the First Fleet raised the British flag on the shores of Port Jackson, Sydney, Australia was ready to celebrate its remarkable history. The Australian Bicentennial was a year-long festival, a hectic round of concerts, dance festivals, sporting events, exhibitions, and historical re-enactments.

Among the most memorable events was the Tall Ships Race from Hobart to Sydney in January, and the Parade of Sail in Sydney Harbor on Australia Day, January 26. A Travelling Australia Exhibition toured the nation, carrying screens and displays in a caravan of 60 trucks. Numerous building and landscape projects carried memories of the bicentennial into the future, such as the Chinese Garden at Darling Harbor, Sydney, and the Gladstone Tondoon Botanic Gardens in Queensland. The new Parliament House was inaugurated by the Queen and Duke of Edinburgh in Canberra. The government also completed a huge network of highways to link all the mainland state capitals.

Not everyone joined in the fun unequivocally. The Aborigines used the celebrations to express their very different perspective of European settlement, and to voice grievances over their treatment historically and in current land settlements. They, after all, had been in Australia not 200 years but 50,000.

SAILING BY   The Tall Ships Parade in Sydney harbor on January 26, 1988, recalled the arrival of the first European settlers 200 years before.

HIGH RISE   Singapore's thrusting modern architecture reflects its economy. During the 1980s it emerged as one of the world's most dynamic financial centers.

ized regime, but he kept taxation and public spending to a minimum. Instead of state welfare, individuals were obliged to put aside a substantial percentage of their income to create their own personal welfare and pension funds. The result was a high degree of public saving, and high net wealth. By 1996 Singapore ranked as the seventh wealthiest nation in the world, with a per capita income higher than in France and Britain.

The Four Tigers, meanwhile, were built on weaker foundations than Singapore, starting with greater poverty, poor infrastructure and political systems prone to corruption. The economic potential of the Philippines was squandered during the rule of President Marcos, which ended in 1986. Since then no government has been able to create the stability needed for full economic development. Indonesia was ruled by Thojib Suharto for more than 30 years, from 1967 to 1998. Over that period his family controlled increasing slices of the nation's wealth—in industry, mining, banking and services. This was acceptable while the economy grew and everyone seemed to receive the benefits, but it became unsustainable when the boom faltered.

Malaysia witnessed an unprecedented rise to prosperity under the leadership of Prime Minister Mahathir bin Muhammad, who came to power in 1981. Reducing trade tariffs and welcoming foreign investment, he announced what he called his 2020 vision: a transformation of the Malaysian economy that would place the nation on a par with the Western industrialized countries by the year 2020. He was on track until the unexpected downturn of East Asian economies after 1997. A host of structural and economic reasons were given for this damaging slump, which saw massive unemployment, the collapse of businesses, banks and whole currencies, and the kind of civil unrest that ousted Suharto after 22 years of rule. The Chinese, however, always tend to take a long-term view of these cycles, and what others see as a blip or slump, they see as an opportunity.

# ISLAM TAKES POWER

## WHEN AYATOLLAH KHOMEINI TOOK POWER IN IRAN, HE GAVE HOPE TO MUSLIMS AROUND THE WORLD, AND PUT FEAR INTO WESTERN NATIONS

The ink was barely dry on the Camp David peace agreement, signed by Egypt and Israel in Washington in September 1978, when another storm blew up in the Middle East—one that was to confirm American prejudices that this region was forever destined to be the nadir of their foreign policy. The new location of anguish was not Palestine, nor Israel, nor Lebanon, nor Libya, but Iran, homeland of the Americans' loyal ally, the Shah of Iran.

Since taking power in 1941, Muhammad Reza Shah Pahlavi had set about modernizing his nation with an élan only possible through the benefit of vast oil wealth. Into a once backward country came industry and investment, and with them luxury cars, Coca-Cola, whisky, television, Hollywood films and Paris fashions. The major city centers, and Tehran in particular, were rapidly transformed. But in the poorer towns and villages, in the souks and mosques, there was a festering resentment among all those who did not share in this bonanza—a resentment that was relentlessly kept

in check by the shah's ruthless and ubiquitous secret police given the name of SAVAK.

The shah ruled imperiously from his "Peacock Throne." His crown jewels could be seen in a heavily fortified museum in Tehran, with piles of spare gems waiting to be set into more crowns and tiaras. In 1971 he organized a party to celebrate 2,500 years of Persian monarchy at the ruined city of Persepolis, the ancient ceremonial capital built by Darius I in the 6th century BC. Dignitaries and royalty were flown in from all around the world, lodged in luxury tents, refreshed with champagne. The event cost $20 million. Meanwhile, rural Iran and its industrial backwaters remained in dreadful poverty.

The one area that SAVAK could not or would not penetrate was the mosques, and these became hotbeds of dissent. It was from this background that the shah's nemesis arose, a great holy man or Ayatollah, and a leader of the Shiite Muslims—who make up a minority group in Islam overall, but the vast majority of the Iranian population. Ayatollah Khomeini inspired revolution from exile, first from Iraq and then from Paris. He had a very real presence in Iran: his speeches, views and edicts circulated in leaflets and cassette tape recordings. He called for the shah's downfall to make way for an Islamic state, free of corrupting Western influences and ruled by Islamic sharia law. He also developed a deep loathing of the United States, the shah's ally and sponsor, and the source of so many of the corrupting Western influences. He called

**REGAL SPLENDOR** The shah in bejewelled pomp officiating at a state occasion (left). He did much to modernize Iran, but his regime was both autocratic and tainted by corruption.

## AYATOLLAH KHOMEINI

For millions in Iran Ayatollah Khomeini was a beloved hero, a man who gave Islam the dignity of political power. To the West he was an enigma.

Ruhollah ("Inspired by God") Khomeini was 75 years old when he achieved power in 1979, but he had been active in religious politics since the 1960s. He was a vocal critic of the shah's regime, opposing the secularization of Iran that came with industrial modernization, while developing a vision of an Islamic nation, free of the corrupting influences of the West, and closer to God. In 1963 the shah had Khomeini expelled. Khomeini settled in Iraq and became the focus of opposition to the shah. In 1978, the shah leaned upon the Iraqis to expel Khomeini, and he moved to Paris. Shortly after the shah fled his throne in January 1979, Khomeini returned to Iran as the appointed figurehead of the new Islamic regime. He set about ridding the country of vestiges of the shah's regime, and purging it of opponents. He also pursued a policy of exporting the Islamic revolution, nurturing fanatical opposition groups and terrorist organizations.

When Khomeini died in 1989, he was still the object of fanatical devotion in Iran. He was little mourned in the West.

**THE HERO'S RETURN** Ayatollah Khomeini received a tumultuous welcome when he returned to Iran in February 1979 after 15 years of exile.

was forced to impose martial law, and he put pressure on Iraq to expel Khomeini, which was when the Ayatollah moved his headquarters to Paris. Further demonstrations and strikes in Iran led to more bloodshed. Islamic vigilantes began attacking non-Islamic targets such as bars, or women not wearing the veil. The situation was spiralling out of control. The army was beginning to waver. Soldiers were not facing ordinary political dissenters and agitators: they were facing a movement inspired by a vision of Islam. To oppose it, argued the mullahs, would be tantamount to blasphemy.

In December, during the Shiite festival of Muharran, crowds of 5 million gathered around the grandiose Shayyad Monument erected by the shah in Tehran. The swell and force of public opinion was incontestable. On January 16, 1979, the shah and his family

## DEBACLE IN THE DESERT

Ten months into Khomeini's Islamic revolution, the atmosphere in Iran remained highly charged and vengeful. On November 4, 1979, a crowd of Revolutionary Guards and students stormed into the U.S. embassy and took over the building. They demanded that the shah—then in the U.S.—should be returned to Iran to stand trial, and announced that the 100 embassy staff would be held hostage until that event.

President Jimmy Carter might have expected to receive assistance from the Iranian government, but instead it seemed that the student kidnappers had Khomeini's approval. He intervened only to gain the release of all women and black hostages on November 17, leaving 53 imprisoned.

President Carter decided to authorize a rescue. The elite Delta Force was dispatched to snatch the hostages with helicopters. On April 25, 1980, they landed in the Dasht-e-Kavir salt flats 200 miles to the south of Tehran. The helicopter force immediately encountered mechanical problems, and the mission had to be aborted: there were not enough operational helicopters to bring out all the hostages. As the planes refueled on the ground a helicopter crashed into a fuel tanker causing a massive explosion and killing eight Americans. The remainder fled the scene and headed for home.

Operation Eagle Claw had been a fiasco, and President Carter took the blame personally. His handling of the hostage crisis contributed to his subsequent election defeat. The hostages were released on January 21, 1981, after 444 days of captivity. The shah had died in Cairo in July the previous year.

**ANTI-AMERICANISM** A young girl joins in protests against Americans besieged in the U.S. embassy in Tehran in December 1979.

the United States "the Great Satan."

It was a tempting vision. For long, Muslims in the Middle East and elsewhere had felt wounded by the indignity of adopting a way of life borrowed from the West, and of being treated disdainfully by the West to boot. Now was an opportunity to show the world the dignity, spirituality, intellectual purity and originality of Islam by rooting out not only the shah, but all Western influences in Iran.

Riots broke out in 1977 and 1978. Despite savage repression, the nation was racked by demonstrations and strikes. Women took an active part in the revolt, showing their loyalties by wearing the veil (or headscarf). At the end of Ramadan in September 1978 a crowd of 750,000 assembled in central Tehran. They were confronted by troops who fired on them, killing more than 100. After this "Black Friday" the shah

**HOPES DASHED** Photos of blindfolded U.S. embassy hostages contributed to the sense of humiliation that drove the U.S. to make its rescue bid. But it ended in abject failure in the desert (below).

1971 Shah of Iran celebrates the monarchy at Persepolis

1978 "Black Friday" demonstrations in Tehran

1979 The shah flees and Ayatollah Khomeini assumes power in Iran; Siege of U.S. embassy in Tehran

1980 The Iran-Iraq War begins

**INFLAMED PASSIONS** Anti-American feeling in Iran was exacerbated by the U.S.'s tacit support for Iraq during the Iran-Iraq war. But it emerged later, during the Iran-Contra scandal, that the U.S. had made covert arrangements to supply Iran with arms.

left Iran on the pretext of taking a vacation. He never returned.

Ayatollah Khomeini was ushered in from Paris to an ecstatic reception on February 1, 1979: 3 million gathered to greet him with the clamorous chant "Allah ho Akbar!" (God is Great!). He immediately began reforming the nation. He was assisted by zealous mullahs and Revolutionary Guards who arrested former supporters of the shah, punished women not wearing a veil, destroyed theaters, banned alcohol. Estimates suggest that 10,000 opponents were executed, and 40,000 imprisoned. In November 1979 a mob invaded the United States embassy and held 53 members of its staff hostage for 444 days.

The tumult and fervor in Iran worried the president of neighboring Iraq, where 60 per-

cent of the population was Shiite, though most of this 60 percent was excluded from political power. The president was Saddam Hussein, a member of the Arab nationalist Ba'ath Party, running a secular state. From his point of view, however, the revolution in Iran was not simply a threat to his internal security, it was also an opportunity—the opportunity to snatch the Shatt al'Arab Waterway (the mouth of the Tigris and Euphrates rivers) to give Iraq complete control over a vital strategic link to the Gulf. On September 23, 1980, the Iraqis invaded southern Iran and torched the oil refinery at Abadan, the largest in the world. But after initial gains they became bogged down in

**MOMENT OF TRIUMPH** Iranian soldiers celebrate the capture of the strategically important Iraqi port-city of Al-Faw.

murderous trench warfare, faced by a determined opposition inspired by the revolution and fighting a jihad (holy war) with the promise of martyrdom. What followed was the longest war in the twentieth century between two sovereign nations. It ended in

**WHO DARES WINS** On May 5, 1980, the SAS dramatically ended a terrorist siege at the Iranian embassy in London. Their initial bomb set fire to the first floor; 11 minutes later, four of the five terrorists were dead.

1988, with no victor, and cost the lives of 370,000 people.

### Spreading the word

Saddam Hussein received arms and financial support from the United States, Great Britain, France and the U.S.S.R., and he saw himself as the defender of Arab interests against the tide of Islamic extremism. Certainly, there was strong evidence of Khomeini's desire to spread the revolution beyond the borders of Iran. In Lebanon the Iranian-funded Hezbollah terrorist group was founded in 1983; this and other shadowy terrorist groups, such as Islamic Jihad, were responsible for a wave of kidnappings of Westerners, bringing a new and ugly twist to the civil war that had wracked the country since 1975. By the end of 1987, there were 17 Western

**BOOK BURNING** Even before Ayatollah Khomeini imposed a *fatwa* on Salman Rushdie, his novel *The Satanic Verses* had caused outrage across the Islamic world. In January 1989 British Muslims publicly burned copies of the book in Bradford.

hostages in Lebanon. Among the kidnap victims was the Archbishop of Canterbury's special envoy Terry Waite, who was himself trying to negotiate the release of Western hostages when he was taken prisoner on January 20, 1987. He had to endure four years of captivity in virtual isolation. Some hostages were executed, but all the surviving ones were eventually released by December 1991, the last in response to Israel's release of prisoners—the principal purpose of the hostage-taking.

There were Shiite terrorist outrages in Bahrain and Kuwait. In Syria Shiite revolutionaries attempted an insurrection against the regime of President Hafez al-Assad in the city of Hama in 1982, only to be quashed in a massacre that claimed over 15,000 lives. In 1987, 150,000 Iranian Shiite pilgrims to Mecca rioted, probably incited by Khomeini's condemnation of the Saudi royal family as heretics. Some 275 Iranians were killed in the bloody clashes between the rioters and Saudi police and security forces. The disruption of the annual pilgrimage or haj, one of the most sacred duties of all Muslims, was greeted by outrage across most of the Islamic world.

The reverberations of the Iranian revolution were mystifying and complex. In London on April 30, 1980, counter-revolutionary gunmen took over the Iranian embassy and held 21 staff and visitors hostage. They demanded the release of 91 Arab prisoners in Iran. When, after six days, they killed a hostage and showed every intention of killing more, a British SAS anti-terrorist squad was sent in. They blasted their way

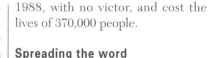

## HOSTAGE IN BEIRUT

Both Terry Anderson and Terry Waite faced conflict in the 1980s in the Middle East. The Iranian-funded terrorist group Hezbollah was founded in Lebanon in 1983 and was responsible for the surge of abductions of Westerners, causing a horrible distortion to the civil war that had pervaded the country since 1975. By the end of 1987, 17 Western diplomats and newspeople were being held captive in Lebanon. Terry Waite—the Archbishop of Canterbury's special envoy and a tenacious humanitarian known for his negotiations in Africa and the Middle East—was taken captive on January 20, 1987, while trying to negotiate the release of Western hostages. Upon Waite's imprisonment, he endured four long years of confinement while in complete isolation. A few hostages during this time were executed and others became gravely ill during the

tense negotiations with Israel for the release of prisoners convicted of terrorism. By December 1991, after Israel released many prisoners, the surviving hostages were released.

Terry Anderson was abducted by pro-Iranian Shiite Muslim extremists in Lebanon and was held hostage for over seven years. Anderson, a Middle East Correspondent for the AP, was captured in Beirut on March 16, 1985, and was held hostage in Lebanon until December 1991—the last hostage to be released.

Upon his release, Anderson remarked that he and his fellow hostages were heroes through adversity: "We were a random assortment of men—a priest, a diplomat, a minister, some educators. It is this randomness, this ordinariness, if you will, that proves the toughness of the spirit of all of us."

**FREE AT LAST** Terry Waite, above, helped negotiate the release of several hostages in the 1980s after his own release. Terry Anderson, left, speaks at a press conference after his release by his Lebanese captors in 1991.

into the embassy and then killed four out of the five terrorists to release the hostages.

In July 1988, the American naval ship *Vincennes* stationed in the Gulf thought it was under attack from the air, and shot down an Iranian Airbus carrying 290 passengers. The United States claimed it was a regrettable error; Iran raged at their deceit. "We will resist the plot of the Great Satan," declared Tehran radio, "and avenge the blood of our martyrs."

Six months later, in December 1988, a Pan Am jumbo jet flying from Heathrow to New York just before the Christmas holidays was destroyed by a bomb, and fell on the Scottish village of Lockerbie. All 259 passengers and crew were killed, as well as 11 residents of Lockerbie. Initially, this was thought to be a revenge attack by Iran. Later, however, fingers were pointed at Libya, which had been accused of state-sponsored terrorism and been the victim of a punitive bombing raid by the United States in April 1986.

In 1989, shortly before his death, Ayatollah Khomeini pronounced blasphemous a novel

called *The Satanic Verses* by Salman Rushdie, a British author of Indian origins. Rushdie was declared the subject of a *fatwa*, an edict of proscription; whoever killed him would be blessed. A price of $1 million was put on Rushdie's head, and he had to remain under police protection for the rest of the century. Passionate anti-Rushdie demonstrations took place across the Islamic world, from India and Pakistan to Bradford in England. Arguments raged about whether the book was indeed blasphemous, but it was a brilliant political coup: thereafter the West remained aware that Islamic militancy could reach to the heart of its institutions, and that none of its sacred liberties, such as freedom of the press, should be considered sacrosanct.

Fundamentalism became an issue across the entire Islamic world, and was hotly debated by the Islamic Conference Organization, set up in 1971 to promote unity and solidarity among its 49 member states. It was often hard to distinguish between the genuine and the opportunistic. Critics of existing regimes could easily rally around the banner of Islam to

foment opposition: it appealed to the masses because of its cultural roots, and played on their resentment about social conditions. Islam represented an attractive blend of pride, humility, dignity and purity. Furthermore, any opponents could easily be dismissed as unbelievers. On a government level, the response to this groundswell of religious fervor varied. In Pakistan, the military regime of President Zia al-Huq introduced Islamic law after 1979, and Sudan's government followed suit in 1983.

Indonesia, the world's most populous Islamic nation, trod warily, allowing certain developments such as the wearing of veils, but curtailing the political power of the mosques on constitutional grounds. In

### SENSE AND SENSIBILITIES

In December 1998, U.S. and British forces halted a bombing campaign on Iraq before the start of Ramadan. This effort to appear respectful was greeted with scorn in the Islamic world, because Ramadan is not primarily a time of peace. The Yom Kippur War, for example, was fought in Ramadan.

Turkey, which was founded as a secular state, the government found itself increasingly under pressure from Islamic political parties, notably Refah (Welfare). Having been successful in local elections in 1994, Refah won the largest number of votes of any party in the 1995 election—nearly 25 percent. Other parties, however, were able to combine to keep Refah out of power until 1997, when

Refah formed an alliance with Tansu Ciller's right-of-center True Path Party, and Refah's leader Necmettan Erbakan became prime minister for 11 months. The Turkish military, however, with a record of one coup a decade, holds the ultimate balance of power and does not support Islamization.

In Egypt the secular government of President Hosni Mubarak faced a growing threat from fundamentalists, often centering

22, but on the pretext of national security the election was cancelled by the government. The Islamists then took to arms: an early victim was President Muhammad Boudiaf, one of the original founders of the FLN, recently returned from 27 years in exile. Terrorist tactics, perpetrated by both rebels and the government, soon descended into the abyss: some 75,000 people have died in the

**HOLY WARRIOR** Initially the Mujaheddin ("fighters of the Holy War") in Afghanistan were lightly armed. They compensated for Soviet military superiority with a determination fused from Islam and national pride.

**ESCALATING FIREPOWER** By the late 1980s the Soviet army in Afghanistan was facing the threat of sophisticated rockets, supplied to the Mujaheddin by the U.S. and Britain as part of a continuing Cold War strategy.

on the revived Muslim Brotherhood. Sudden outbursts of violence, particularly against tourists, were intended to undermine the country's shaky economy, and hence the government itself.

In Algeria the fundamentalists, or Islamists, attempted another route to power—the ballot box. They formed a political party called the Islamic Salvation Front (FIS), which picked up on growing unrest over a stagnant economy, corruption, poor housing and rising food prices. The government of the National Liberation Front (FLN), which had been in power since independence from France in 1962, organized the first national elections, which took place in December 1991. The Islamists won the first vote by an overwhelming margin of 126 seats to troubles since 1991. The Algerian crisis also spread to France which suffered a series of bomb attacks, beginning in 1995.

Islam remains one of the world's most potent political forces. It was enough to defeat the Soviet Union in Afghanistan. Armed with religious fervor and light weapons supplied by the United States and Islamic nations, the Mujaheddin waged a relentless campaign against the Soviet forces following their invasion in 1979. In the end, despite their technical superiority, the Soviet government saw that they were fighting a war they could not win. They withdrew in 1989, leaving the puppet government of President Najibullah. A coalition of rebel forces eventually took Kabul in 1992. But in 1996 a new force of fundamentalist Muslims called the Taliban rose up and overran the capital to impose their strict interpretation of Islam. Music, dancing and television were banned. Women going out were obliged to wear the burka, which conceals them from

head to foot, and they were forbidden to work. Girls' schools were closed, leaving them with no chance to further their education in Islamic society. This puritan version of Islam makes the Shiism of Ayatollah Khomeini appear comparatively liberal.

**A FEARED FORCE** The Taliban took the city of Mazar-e-Sharif in August 1998 (above) on their way to securing complete domination of Afghanistan. They alienated Western sympathies with their extreme interpretation of Islamic law, severely limiting the freedom of women (below).

# COLLAPSE OF COMMUNISM

## AFTER SEVEN DECADES OF REPRESSION AND ECONOMIC TORPOR, THE SOVIET EDIFICE CAME CRASHING DOWN IN JUST SIX YEARS

The Soviet historian Konstantin Volkogonov, formerly a colonel-general in the propaganda department of the Soviet army, witnessed personally the shocking physical state of his nation's leader, Konstantin Chernenko: "In the summer of 1984 I heard him speak in the Great Hall of the Kremlin at an All-Army Conference of Komsomol Workers. Following the speeches and reports from the army's young political officers, Chernenko struggled to the podium. It was completely impossible to understand what he said in his 15 minute speech. He would stop every two or three minutes, wipe his forehead and take a puff from his inhaler. The audience sat in silence, their heads bowed . . . When it was all over we were invited into the St. George's Hall to be photographed with the General Secretary [Chernenko]. It took him 20 minutes to cover the 100 meters or so, stopping frequently to catch his breath. All the while, those accompanying him kept up some kind of conversation in order to give the impression that he had stopped to talk, and not from exhaustion. From time to time he would give a weak, agonized smile, turning his head to the right and left with difficulty, as if he was unsure where he was being

**LYING IN STATE** Brezhnev died in November 1982. His last decade as leader of the Soviet Union saw increasing economic stagnation.

taken, what was going on and what all these people in army uniform were saying to him."

Chernenko was the living symbol of the decay of the Soviet Union, an uninspired bureaucrat, the product of a moribund system, appointed by an aging coterie of peers in 1984 to lead the world's second most powerful nation. But having an incapacitated leader was something of a Soviet trend.

Leonid Brezhnev had been sick and senile for the last years of his 18 year leadership. After his death in November 1982 he was replaced by Yuri Andropov, at first welcomed by the West as youthful, enlightened and a lover of jazz. In fact, he was a dyed-in-the-wool Leninist, a former KGB chief, and at 68 was young only by comparison with most of his Politburo colleagues. Within three months of coming to power, Andropov suffered kidney failure and made his last public appearance in August 1983. The Soviet Union, however, had no political machinery to retire its leaders except by force: Andropov ruled from his sick bed until his death in February 1984. He was immediately replaced by Chernenko, then 72.

The country staggered on under this leadership, kept afloat by its centralized economy, massive bureaucracy, feared secret services and a systematic repression that anesthetized people

**TIME CHECK** Gorbachev and Reagan at their third summit, in Washington in December 1987. They signed the historic Intermediate-Range Nuclear Forces Treaty, agreeing to eliminate an entire category of nuclear weapons.

**PARTY MAN** Konstantin Chernenko, who was Soviet general secretary for 13 months, left virtually no mark on history.

trapped into a regime of low expectations. The dream of a socialist paradise, for which several generations had sacrificed their lives, seemed destined to remain a mirage. Alcoholism had reached epidemic proportions.

The economy had ground to a halt under the strain of maintaining the arms race, into

1980 Solidarity trade union formed in Poland

1981 Martial law in Poland crushes Solidarity

1982 Leonid Brezhnev dies

1985 Gorbachev comes to power in the U.S.S.R.

which the Soviet government was still pouring over a quarter of its revenue. But for all its military spending, the U.S.S.R. was mired in a hopeless war in Afghanistan, which week by week returned 30 or so young Soviet soldiers to their motherland in tin coffins. Even so, the U.S.S.R. still attempted to export revolution, assisting insurgency movements and revolutionary governments around the globe, in Vietnam, South Yemen, Syria, Nicaragua, Ethiopia, Somalia, Angola, Mozambique.

This was the regime that President Reagan labeled "the Evil Empire," as he turned down the thermostat yet further on the Cold War. In September 1983 superpower relations hit an all-time low when a South Korean Boeing 747 flying from New York to Seoul was shot down by Soviet fighters over the militarily sensitive region of Sakhalin Island, killing all 269 passengers and crew. The Kremlin was at first silent, then declared that the plane was spying and had refused to respond to warnings. The United States claimed it was simply off course.

Reagan increased the stakes by announcing the Strategic Defense Initiative (SDI), dubbed "Star Wars" in the press. The plan was to exploit American technological superiority to develop satellite weapons with laser beams ("Ronnie's Ray Guns") capable of intercepting hostile nuclear missiles close to their launch sites. It was vastly expensive and technically unproven. But the SDI had the effect of pushing the U.S.S.R. deeper into crisis. The military-industrial formula of socialism simply could not match this threat and make its sums add up.

## Gorbachev

Throughout the Andropov-Chernenko era a young and charismatic party official was waiting in the wings: Mikhail Gorbachev. Coming to power in March 1985, Gorbachev, a loyal Leninist, immediately hinted that radical change was needed. Soviet socialism was not working: it needed overhauling and reinvigorating. Initially, he was cautious, and in the first 18 months of his rule there was little outwardly to differentiate his policies from those of his predecessors. His main strategy was to introduce younger cadres into the hierarchy of government, but this alone proved an inadequate remedy: the Soviet institutions were deeply resistant to change. The West was cautious in its judgment, but was optimistic that Gorbachev might at last represent a new breed of Soviet leader. Just 54 years old, he was young; he had a ready smile, and a personable nature. For a Soviet leader he seemed uncharacteristically human.

High on Gorbachev's agenda was the need to reduce defense spending, and he put new energies into arms negotiation, backed by his smooth-mannered foreign minister, Eduard Shevardnadze. However, after the promising Strategic Arms Reduc-

## THE WAR IN AFGHANISTAN

Locked into the arid highlands of Central Asia, Afghanistan has been the graveyard of successive empires since ancient times. It played this role again in the 1980s: the war in Afghanistan is cited as a key cause of the Soviet Union's collapse.

By opting to invade in 1979, the U.S.S.R. plunged the world into a renewed Cold War after nearly a decade of détente, and brought upon itself a new phase of spiralling defense costs. Its enemy

**DRAGON SLAYERS** Mujaheddin guerrillas with a Soviet helicopter gunship they shot down.

in the field was a small but determined coalition of guerrillas called the Mujaheddin, inspired by God and armed with light weapons supplied by the U.S. and other Western nations. The Mujaheddin could move like mercury through rocky canyons, pinning the Soviet army down to the cities and fortified camps through repeated ambushes. The effectiveness of this campaign was underlined by a well-founded reputation for blood-curdling atrocity, to which the Soviet army responded with similar atrocities and acts of indiscriminate retribution, including the torching of whole villages.

When he came to power in 1985 Mikhail Gorbachev realized that it was imperative to disengage from Afghanistan. The Soviet army, caught up in a humiliating war that had now lasted as long as the Second World War, was becoming deeply demoralized. The Soviet government attempted an honorable solution by declaring a unilateral cease-fire in January 1987, but this was rebuffed by the Mujaheddin. It took Gorbachev a further two years to end the war: phased withdrawal began in May 1988 and the last Soviet soldier left on February 15, 1989. The Soviet army had lost 13,836 men, as well as its self-confidence and prestige. Afghanistan had lost over a million of its people.

**PRIVATE ENTERPRISE, PUBLIC EMBARRASSMENT**
A young West German, Matthias Rust, is the center of attention in Red Square after landing his Cessna light aircraft there in May 1987.

tion Talks (START) in Geneva in November 1985, progress was derailed at a summit meeting at Reykjavik in 1986. This broke up without agreement when President Ronald

Reagan refused to drop plans for the SDI.

The impression that the Soviet military was in crisis was underlined by an incident in May 1987, when a 19-year-old West German, Matthias Rust, with just 25 hours' flying experience, flew all the way to Moscow in a Cessna light aircraft. His escapade exposed the vulnerability of the defense system upon which so much of Soviet self-esteem rested. The Defense Minister, Marshal Sergei Solokov, was summarily dismissed and replaced by Dmitri Yazov, a close associate of Gorbachev.

It was clear to the United States that the Soviet Union was desperate to reduce its arms commitments. In December 1987, in a treaty signed in Washington, the United States and the Soviet Union made a major breakthrough by agreeing to cut their land-based intermediate nuclear missiles—essentially all Soviet SS20s and American Pershing IIs in Europe. Cuts in long-range nuclear weapons were announced after further START negotiations in Moscow in 1988.

### Glasnost and perestroika

Gorbachev soon realized that only radical change could steer the U.S.S.R. out of crisis. It needed complete restructuring, or *perestroika*, a buzzword that became current in 1987. This meant reforming Soviet institutions. In a radical deviation from the old centralized economy, a limited amount of free enterprise was permitted: farmers could sell surpluses privately and individuals could set up their own businesses. Inward foreign investment was encouraged: Russia's first McDonald's fast-food restaurant opened in Moscow in 1988.

Within the Communist Party, in place of appointments from above, multi-candidate elections and secret ballots were introduced in an embryonic form of democracy. In June 1988 the Supreme Soviet was replaced by the Congress of People's Deputies, two-thirds of whom were elected by popular vote. In this way, Gorbachev managed to remove many of the old

**A TASTE OF THE WEST** A yearning for consumer goods was a key motive for economic reform. Moscow's McDonald's, opened in 1988, was symbolic of opportunities to come.

hardliners who completely opposed reform.

Gorbachev also wanted Soviet institutions to be more transparent and accountable through a new kind of openness, or *glasnost*. This was one of the lessons of the nuclear accident at the Chernobyl power station in the Ukraine in April 1986: initially, the Soviet government adhered to its traditional posture of secretiveness, but it became increasingly clear to the outside world that the Kremlin was dealing inadequately with a disaster of international consequence. In the future, Gorbachev wanted to avoid this kind of embarrassment.

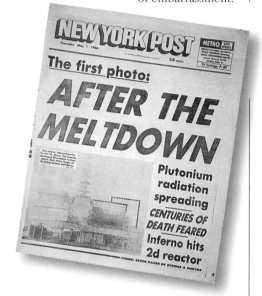

**NUCLEAR NIGHTMARE** News of the Chernobyl explosion quickly spread around the world. Although the Soviet authorities were initially inclined to be secretive, the scale of the disaster made that impossible.

*Glasnost* brought with it a new intellectual thaw. Dissidents were released, notably the physicist Andrei Sakharov and his wife Yelena Bonner: on their return to Moscow in December 1986 from internal exile in Gorky they were greeted by jubilant crowds. Historians and journalists were permitted greater freedoms and even encouraged to pursue the truth. Unfortunately, the truth often turned out to be unpalatable: the horror of the Stalinist era and the incompetences of more recent Soviet history were gradually dragged into the open. Soon communism itself came under the spotlight: many began to believe that it was not just the structures of socialism that were at fault, but the system itself.

Expectations were running high by 1987-8. The Soviet people were promised a better standard of living afforded by reduced defense spending and a more liberal economy. *Glasnost* offered unprecedented freedoms of thought, speech, expression and religion. But the dream was already turning sour. The shops remained empty, unemployment was rising, nationalistic sentiments in constituent republics of the Union were beginning to fan old antagonisms. Disgruntled workers went on strike, including coalminers in July 1989. While Gorbachev was lionized in the West as a reformer—seen attending international banquets with his fashion-conscious wife Raisa, chatting comfortably with old class enemies such as President Bush, Margaret Thatcher and even the Pope—his own people began to see that he could not deliver. In truth, no one could: Soviet communism had reached the end of the road.

## The Empire unravels

It was not in the Soviet Union itself, however, that communism first collapsed, but in its satellites in Eastern Europe. In Poland, always one of the most reluctant communist client states, the combined forces of worker revolt and Roman Catholicism had managed to pierce the system back in 1980, when government concessions to striking workers in the shipyards of Gdansk gave rise to the independent trade union Solidarity.

This proved too much for the Soviet government: in 1981 it rattled the saber of the Brezhnev Doctrine, which authorized military intervention in communist countries that threatened to deviate from the socialist path. The Polish government was replaced in February 1981 by a military regime led by General Wojciech Jaruzelski, the defense minister. An inscrutable party man in tinted glasses, Jaruzelski had the thankless task of holding off the Soviet bear: he succeeded, but only by instituting savage repression. After martial law was declared on December 13, 1981, Solidarity was outlawed. A measure of the repression was the death of the popular radical priest Father Jerzy Popieluszko at the hands of the security services; his body was discovered in a reservoir on October 30, 1984.

Gorbachev's appointment as the Soviet leader brought about a major shift in fortunes for Poland. Solidarity re-emerged from hiding in 1988. In 1989 Gorbachev declared that the Brezhnev Doctrine was dead: the U.S.S.R. would no longer intervene militarily

## MIKHAIL GORBACHEV

To superstitious Russians the seventh leader of the Soviet Union was a man of destiny: did not the strange birthmark on his head indicate that he was marked by fate? But what would he bring—Paradise or the Apocalypse? Mikhail Gorbachev certainly launched his leadership with a clear vision: he wanted to bring about the "perfection, improvement, acceleration, and finally the restructuring" of the communist system.

On the day he came to power, March 11, 1985, Gorbachev was virtually unknown within, or outside, the U.S.S.R. Born in 1931, the son of peasant farmers in the Stavropol region in the northern Caucasus, he had worked his way to Moscow via the youth organization Komsomol and leadership of his regional government. Coming to Moscow in 1978, he became Party Secretary of Agriculture. Once appointed General Secretary of the Communist Party, hence leader of the Soviet Union, Gorbachev acquired a popular following: he was admired for his dynamism and accessibility. Abroad, the British premier Margaret Thatcher declared that he was a man she could "do business with." He was afforded an extra note of glamour by his wife Raisa, his confidante throughout his career: traditionally the wives of Soviet leaders remained virtually anonymous.

But having taken the path of reform, Gorbachev rapidly found himself out of his depth. Foreign observers championed his daring as a reformer; in 1990 he was awarded the Nobel peace prize. But it was Soviet citizens who paid the cost in declining standards of living. Although Gorbachev survived the coup of August 1991, he was badly crippled. His role as President of the U.S.S.R. had become redundant by the time he resigned four months later. He spent most of the final decade of the century in obscurity.

Gorbachev's admirers credit him with ushering in the change from communism to capitalism and democracy, and making the transition easier than it might have been. Paradoxically, as a committed Communist Party member, this was precisely the outcome he was trying to avoid.

THE NEW FACE OF COMMUNISM  Smiling and personable, to the Western world Mikhail Gorbachev and his wife Raisa were the visible symbols of a new Soviet Union.

in East European states. Observers quipped that it had been replaced by the Sinatra Doctrine: "They can do it their way."

In May 1989 Hungary opened its borders with Austria, thus breaching the Iron Curtain. This was still a time of great uncertainty, and tens of thousands of East Germans grabbed the opportunity that presented itself. Under the guise of taking a vacation in communist Hungary, they poured across the open borders in their primitive and polluting Trabant cars to reach West Germany, where they were immediately granted citizenship.

Many of the East Germans who fled were professionals, and the country faced collapse. Nevertheless, its deeply conservative and repressive communist government clung to

## SOLIDARITY

Poland was where the collapse of the Soviet empire began. In 1980, during the Brezhnev era, workers in the massive Lenin Shipyards of Gdansk went on strike to protest against the persecution of trade union activists and massive rises in food prices as the Polish economy came close to collapse. In August 1980, 17,000 workers occupied the shipyards, which were then surrounded by a million well-wishers. The movement had the support of the Catholic Church, led by a Polish pope in Rome.

Under threat of wider national strikes, the Polish government acquiesced, and made a number of remarkable concessions in the Gdansk Agreement of 1980: it permitted free and independent trade unions, with the legal right to strike, and agreed to allow greater religious and political freedoms. In September 1980 the nationwide general trade union Solidarity (Solidarnosc) was formed under the chairmanship of one of the strike leaders, the electrician Lech Walesa. This was the first independent trade union in the Soviet world, and it soon had over 10 million members.

But the Polish leader General Jaruzelski was coming under pressure from Moscow to curb this dissent, and in December 1981 he declared martial law. Strikes were outlawed, and some 14,000 Solidarity members rounded up and imprisoned, including Walesa. He was released after almost a year, and continued to work for Solidarity, which operated underground after being banned in October 1982. To the fury of the Soviet and Polish authorities, he won the Nobel peace prize in 1983.

Conditions began to ease after Gorbachev came to power in the U.S.S.R. in 1985. In 1988 Jaruzelski sanctioned negotiations with Solidarity, despite the fact that it was still outlawed. In 1989, following a round-table conference with the government, Solidarity won back its legal status. In free elections held in June 1989, Solidarity's candidates won virtually all the seats for which it was entitled to canvas. The resulting government was a coalition between Solidarity and the communists.

Lech Walesa succeeded Jaruzelski as president in 1990, but his gruff, jocular and autocratic style—a cherished feature of the revolutionary atmosphere of the shipyards—sat less easily with the demands of the leader of a new state. He was replaced in 1995. Solidarity similarly lost much of its popular support as Poland struggled with the market economy, and it was former communists, now relabelled Social Democrats, who filled the resulting vacuum.

**THE FIREMAN** Often called upon to dampen the enthusiasm of his more radical colleagues, Lech Walesa called himself the fireman.

**VICTORY SALUTE** Solidarity supporters demonstrate their confidence in Lech Walesa's candidacy during his successful campaign to become Poland's president in 1990.

power. But pressure for reform was building by the day, encouraged by Mikhail Gorbachev who, during the 40th anniversary celebrations of the East German state in October 1989, declared that its government had to step up the pace of reforms. There were massive demonstrations in Leipzig on October 9 as 70,000 people joined together for "peace prayers." On October 18, after 18 years of rule, the premier Erich Honecker was replaced by the equally intransigent Egon Krenz. But as the Iron Curtain elsewhere

**POWER OF THE PEOPLE** The destruction of the Berlin Wall symbolized the seismic changes taking place in the Soviet bloc. Below right: Revellers on the Wall on New Year's Eve 1989. Background: A demonstration in Leningrad against the attempted coup in August 1991.

came down, East Germany could no longer hold its borders. Travel restrictions were lifted on November 4; on November 9 the checkpoints along the Berlin Wall were removed. Over the following weekend, amid scenes of jubilation that echoed around the world, the Berlin Wall was breached. Within days it had been dismantled by the hammers of thousands of people, and a new world order dawned.

Free elections in East Germany in March 1990 showed massive support for reunification with West Germany, a move blessed by Gorbachev himself. Thus on October 3, 1990, Germany became one nation again and embarked on a long struggle to repair the damage of 40 years of separation.

This pattern of liberation was echoed across Eastern Europe. In Czechoslovakia,

**SPRING IN NOVEMBER** Czech demonstrators took to the streets in largely peaceful protests in November 1989. The moving, night-time processions recalled the doomed Prague Spring of 1968, led by Alexander Dubcek.

after mass candlelit demonstrations against police brutality in Wenceslas Square in November 1989, the communist government was ousted in multi-party elections; on December 29 the dissident playwright Václav Havel—a leader of the opposition Civic Forum, who had spent years in jail for his beliefs—was voted in as president. Czechoslovakia's path to independence was so smooth that it was dubbed the "Velvet Revolution," but this term might be applied to the breakup of almost all the Soviet bloc, despite the fear of a violent backlash. Poland won its freedom in multi-party elections in the summer of 1989; Solidarity's leader Lech Walesa became president the following year. In Hungary, the national assembly approved of multi-party elections in October 1989.

Only in Romania was the collapse of the old regime bitter and bloody. The West had once regarded President Nicolae Ceausescu, in power since 1967, as something of a rebel for daring repeatedly to deviate from the Moscow line; in fact, he developed one of the most vicious and impoverished regimes of the Soviet bloc. The center of Bucharest was evacuated to create a vast palace and administrative complex, while his radical agro-industrial policies involved the destruction of villages. His drive to increase the national population was enforced by outlawing contraceptives and abortion; this meant that women had large families in an economy that was unable to sustain them. Many babies were born unwanted and abandoned to squalid orphanages.

Reforms in Eastern Europe sparked revolt in December 1989 in the Romanian city of Timisoara, where demonstrators clashed with security forces and hundreds were killed. But on December 21 the army joined the rebels and on Christmas Day soldiers stormed the presidential palace, seized Ceausescu and his wife Elena, then tried and executed them. In Romania, as also in neighboring Bulgaria, communist regimes lived on, however, albeit in modified guises.

## Back in the U.S.S.R.

Under the Conventional Forces in Europe Treaty of 1990, both the U.S.S.R. and NATO began to withdraw foreign troops from the old Iron Curtain, and the Warsaw Pact was wound up. The rapid

**SUMMARY JUSTICE** Nicolae Ceausescu and his wife were executed by a firing squad on Christmas Day 1989. Pictures of his dead body were broadcast around the world.

breakup of the Soviet empire was deeply disturbing for many Soviet citizens: another of the old certainties was crumbling. Furthermore, various of the U.S.S.R.'s own constituent republics now had regional governments elected with varying degrees of democracy, and were pressing for greater autonomy. The largest of these by far was Russia, an entity that had been barely spoken of since the 1917 Revolution. On May 29, 1990, its parliament of elected delegates chose Boris Yeltsin as president.

Yeltsin was one of the most dynamic

**MILITARY DILEMMA** During the attempted coup in 1991, many parts of the Red Army were sympathetic to the coup leaders, but the opposition of the people was irresistible.

reformers in the Soviet political arena. Originally a construction engineer from Sverdlovsk, he had been brought to Moscow by Gorbachev in 1985, where he made his mark as a daring critic of the old regime. As First Secretary of the Moscow City Committee he appeared genuinely to have the people's grievances at heart, sorting out many of the chronic iniquities of housing, welfare and party privileges. Already by 1987 he had become Gorbachev's chief rival and bugbear: Yeltsin ceaselessly pushed for reform and a more rapid adoption of the market economy. Gorbachev, as initiator of these trends, deeply resented the criticism, but he was fast losing popularity. During the May Day parade of 1990, traditionally a celebration of Soviet might and unity, Gorbachev was jeered and booed by the crowd. The dominoes continued to fall: Lithuania claimed independence on March 11, 1990; Georgia followed suit in April. Uzbekistan and the Russian Federation itself declared indepen-

# THREE DAYS IN AUGUST 1991

Gorbachev was enjoying a summer vacation in the presidential dacha in Foros, Crimea, on August 18, 1991, when he received an unscheduled visit by five senior politicians. They announced that they represented the "Committee for the State of Emergency" that had just been declared, and they requested Gorbachev to stand down in favor of his vice-president, Gennady Yanayev. It was clear that this was an attempt to seize power by the conservative rump of Gorbachev's own government. Gorbachev refused to cooperate, and so was placed under house arrest. The palace was surrounded by a cordon of troops.

The Soviet people knew that something was afoot when normal radio and television broadcasts were replaced by music and ballet—a familiar trick of the old regime. They were later officially informed that President Gorbachev had taken ill. In the meantime, however, many had tuned in to foreign news stations, such as the BBC World Service, where the truth was gradually revealed.

Boris Yeltsin, as President of the Russian Federation, stood firmly by Gorbachev. He went straight to the White House parliament building in central Moscow, which was now surrounded by tanks. Climbing onto one of these, he denounced the plotters' actions as a "cynical attempt at a right-wing coup," asked the people to show their disapproval through strikes and demonstrations, and encouraged the army to mutiny. Images of his courageous defiance were beamed around the world. It was Yeltsin's finest hour. He and his colleagues then holed up in the White House as thousands of supporters converged upon it. The coup leaders wavered. The army, although in a rebellious mood over its declining role in Soviet life, was reluctant to fire on fellow citizens.

It was soon clear that the Russian people, despite their dissatisfaction with the changes under Gorbachev's leadership, were not prepared to turn back the clock. On August 21, the army moved in on the White House, but it was a half-hearted attack; three people were killed in accidents, before the Defense Ministry ordered a retreat. The coup crumbled. Fourteen of its leaders were arrested and later served short prison sentences; one committed suicide.

Gorbachev returned to Moscow, but his power had been broken. Yeltsin rubbed salt into the wounds by obliging him to read out the list of the coup leaders before parliament. They included Valentin Pavlov, the prime minister; Vladimir Kryuchkov, the head of the KGB; Boris Pugo, the interior minister; Dmitri Yazov, the defense minister; and Anatoli Lukyanov, the speaker in the Soviet parliament. Most of them had been appointed by Gorbachev and were closely associated with him. Gorbachev never recovered his authority. The Soviet Union was formally disbanded on December 25, 1991.

**IN THE DOCK** Gorbachev may have expected a warm welcome from the Russian parliament after surviving the coup, but Yeltsin used the moment to imply Gorbachev's responsibility for the crisis.

**FALLEN IDOL** In Leninplatz, Berlin, a giant statue of Lenin, the father of Soviet communism, was dismantled and hauled away in November 1991.

dence in June. Gorbachev now vacillated and temporarily sided with the conservatives, ordering troops into Lithuania and Latvia, which provoked massive protest demonstrations in Moscow in January 1991. Gorbachev, meanwhile, continued to press forward with his foreign policy. On July 31, 1991, START agreements, signed by the Soviet leader and President George Bush in Moscow, cut all nuclear weapons by one-third.

Gorbachev and Yeltsin papered over their differences as the pressure on the Union mounted. Together they forged an agreement by which the U.S.S.R. would become a federation to be re-defined as the Union of Soviet Sovereign States. The treaty was due to be signed on August 20.

**NEW MAP** The breakup of the Soviet Union left the Russian Federation, plus 14 new countries—from Central Asia to the Caucasus to the Baltic region.

This was too much for conservative elements in Gorbachev's government. On August 18 they staged a coup, imprisoning Gorbachev in his presidential vacation retreat in the Crimea and sending the army into Moscow. The coup proved to be a damp squib: it failed to arouse popular support, the army was left in a quandary, and the moment was seized brilliantly by Boris Yeltsin, in the name of the reformers.

Gorbachev, looking humbled and in a state of shock, returned to Moscow, fatally indebted to Yeltsin. The failed coup had precisely the consequence it had aimed to prevent. Now 15 constituent republics rushed to announce their independence, including

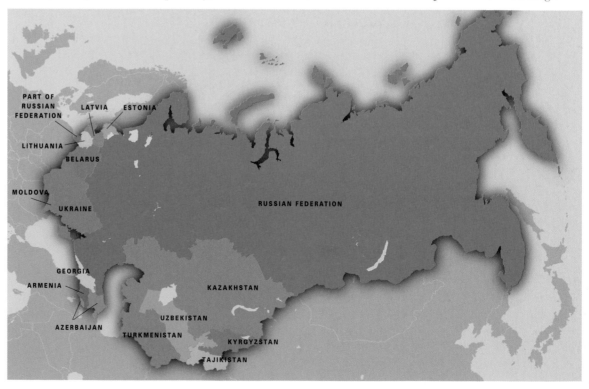

Belarus, Azerbaijan, Moldova and Estonia in August, Latvia and Armenia in September, Kazakhstan in October, Ukraine in December. As the year unfolded, the U.S.S.R. withered away. On September 5, 1991, it was effectively replaced by the Confederation of Independent States (CIS), which was joined by all the former Soviet republics except Georgia, Estonia, Latvia and Lithuania. Gorbachev, with no job left as president of the defunct U.S.S.R., resigned on December 25, 1991.

These events were greeted with a mixture of euphoria and anxiety. As statues of Lenin and other fallen Soviet heroes were toppled, cities recovered their pre-revolutionary names. Leningrad reverted to St. Petersburg, Sverdlovsk to Ekaterinburg. But the republics were now assailed by countless difficulties inherited from the Soviet empire. In many of them large minorities of

Russians found themselves resented and powerless. The ownership of Soviet military hardware, naval bases and nuclear arms remained in dispute. In 1991-4 Azerbaijan and Armenia came to blows over Nagorno-Karabakh, an Armenian enclave in Azeri territory. In Georgia, Russian troops had to intervene in a clash over Abkhazia. In Russia itself, the southern region of Chechnya attempted to break away; Russian troops were sent in on December 11, 1994, leading to a prolonged and bloody confrontation in which the capital, Grozny, was laid waste.

On October 4, 1993, Boris Yeltsin had to order troops into Moscow when opponents of his reforms staged an attempted coup. As tank troops loyal to Yeltsin fired on the White House parliament buildings, crack Spetnaz commandos flushed out armed resistance; 140 people were killed.

But the greatest concern was the economy. In spite of loans from

**COMMUNISM FED US** By early 1993 it was clear that capitalism and the market economy would offer no quick fixes. Russian women took to the streets to protest against rising food prices, nostalgic for the communist era, which at least had provided basic necessities.

the International Monetary Fund totaling $22 billion, and investment from Europe, America, and Japan, the legacy of the Soviet command economy proved obdurate. As the old industries ground to a standstill, miners, railway workers and the army went unpaid. Yeltsin could not find the formula for economic recovery among a population brought up to believe they would always be provided for. The joys of new freedoms of expression faded in the lines for bread and milk, while the black market flourished, the crime rate soared, and profiteers and the mafia swooped down on the pickings. By the end of the 1990s many Russians began to look back nostalgically to the Soviet era, years of the KGB and May Day parades, when the architecture of life was at least solid and predictable.

**THE PAIN OF SEPARATION** This grieving Chechnyan woman was just one of thousands of civilians who felt the brutal hand of military intervention as Russian forces put an end to Chechnya's bid for independence.

# THE BALKANS: UNFINISHED BUSINESS

## THE DISPARATE COLLECTION OF BALKAN STATES HAS LONG BEEN A COCKPIT OF STRIFE IN EUROPE, AND THE DISINTEGRATION OF YUGOSLAVIA ADDED TO THIS SAD RECORD

**S**arajevo, capital of Bosnia-Herzegovina, is remembered with trepidation as the scene of the assassination of Archduke Franz Ferdinand in 1914, which sparked the First World War. In 1929 Yugoslavia became the new name for a collection of nations: Serbia, Macedonia, Bosnia-Herzegovina, Slovenia and Croatia. After the Second World War, Marshal Tito held these nations together beneath an umbrella of strong-arm communist rule. He also kept his country non-aligned and outside the Soviet orbit. However, he acknowledged the fragility of the federation when he said: "I am a leader of one country which has two alphabets, three languages, four religions and five nationalities living in six republics surrounded by seven neighbors."

**SERBIAN AGGRESSION** Dubrovnik, on the coast of Croatia, was bombed in 1991 by the artillery of Serb-led forces, seeking better access to the sea.

**ARKAN'S EAGLES   Members of an ultra-nationalist militia, led by the Serb warlord "Commander Arkan," ready for action above Sarajevo.**

One of these neighbors, Albania, became a secretive state under the communist rule of Enver Hoxha, who developed links with Maoist China before cutting off Albania from the outside world in 1978.

At Tito's death in 1980 the unity of Yugoslavia came under strain. Communist governments managed to hold the nation together until the late 1980s when a wave of strikes, demonstrations and calls for autonomy had the effect of rekindling Serbian nationalism and the concept of a "Greater Serbia" dominating the region. The Serbian communist leader Slobodan Milosevic came to power in 1987 riding this nationalist tide. In 1990, as the constituent republics of Yugoslavia began to hold free elections, Milosevic chose to exert Serb ascendancy. In 1990 provincial autonomy was rescinded in Kosovo, an enclave that Serbians hold as their historic heartland, but where the majority were, in fact, of Albanian ethnic origin.

This was the writing on the wall for the republics with non-Serbian majorities, notably Slovenia and Croatia. On June 25, 1991, both declared their independence from Yugoslavia. This was resisted by the Yugoslavian government, which sent in the national army in support of Serbian minorities. In Slovenia, after brief military clashes, the Yugoslavian forces withdrew. The Croatian map was more complex, however, with its *krajina* (Serb) region containing enclaves of people who wanted to set up their own autonomous Serb republics. Military conflict lasted until January 1992, when a fragile peace was achieved through an American-brokered treaty.

Albania, meanwhile, had stumbled back into the free world five years after the death of Enver Hoxha in 1985. Multi-party elections were held in 1991, while boatloads of refugees, attempting to flee the threadbare conditions of their country, set sail for Italy.

In December 1991, Macedonia declared independence from Yugoslavia; in March 1992 Bosnia-Herzegovina followed suit. Bosnia had the most complex demographic map of all the republics, with large enclaves of Serbs interspersed among communities of Croatians and Muslims. A month after it declared its independence, civil war erupted between the Serbs on the one hand and the Croats and Muslims on the other. The Bosnian Serbs were backed by Milosevic and what remained of Yugoslavia—Serbia with Montenegro. They achieved initial successes and by 1993 had conquered 70 per-

cent of the territory, while the Muslims were pinned down mainly to the cities. Sarajevo was subjected to a gruelling three-year siege by Serb forces, during which shells exploded among bread lines and snipers picked off citizens attempting to reach their places of work.

Ethnic divisions now became polarized as whole communities were uprooted, deported, imprisoned and massacred. This process went by the newly coined euphemism "ethnic cleansing." There were atrocities on both sides. The world's press was filled with images of starving prisoners in concentration camps and stories of mass graves and systematic rape as a means of ethnic defilement.

In early 1995 a ceasefire brokered by former President Jimmy Carter collapsed as forces of Bosnian and Croatian Serbs, under General Ratko Mladic, made a last-ditch attempt to wrest territory from the Muslims. In August, NATO forces and a Croatian-Bosnian alliance took the initiative and pushed the Serbs out of much of the territory they had won. By then there were 2.3 million refugees across the region; 200,000 people had died or were missing. The warring parties were forced to the negotiating table, and in October a peace settlement was hammered out in Dayton, Ohio. Bosnia-Herzegovina became a nation-state consisting of two roughly equal parts, the Muslim-Croat Federation of Bosnia and Herzegovina, and the Serb Republika Srpska. A complex map was drawn up to mark out their areas of jurisdiction, to be imposed by 60,000 NATO-led troops.

But the lessons had not been learned. In 1998, trouble flared in Kosovo, where the Albanian majority of 1.5 million was straining under the dominance of a Serb minority. The Kosovo Liberation Army began a separatist campaign that was met by a massive Serbian military response, sending hundreds of thousands of refugees over the border into Albania. In March 1999, NATO unleashed an aerial bombing campaign against Serbia in support of the Kosovo Albanians. The result was to increase Serbian atrocities against the Kosovars. As NATO's power prevailed, the Serbs abandoned Kosovo and UN troops moved in to supervise the return of the refugees. But tensions remained high and, as the twentieth century came to a close, this corner of the Balkans was still not free from strife.

**CITY UNDER SIEGE   Sarajevo suffered widespread and arbitrary shelling from Bosnian-Serb forces throughout the siege, lasting from 1992 to 1995.**

# EUROPEAN INTEGRATION

## IN THE 1990S THE EUROPEAN UNION, WHICH BEGAN AS A TRADING COMMUNITY, BECAME A DYNAMIC FORCE ON THE WORLD STAGE

On September 20, 1988, Margaret Thatcher made her famous speech at the College of Europe in Bruges. "Working more closely together does not require power to be centralized in Brussels," she declared. "Europe will be stronger precisely because it has France as France, Spain as Spain, Britain as Britain, each with its own customs, traditions and identity." With characteristic forthrightness, she had pinpointed the great European dilemma of the age.

**VOTING IN DROVES** A protest by sheep farmers in Nice in 1997. Already feeling threatened by EC directives, the farmers opposed the reintroduction of wolves into the Mercantour national park.

Would increased European integration compromise nationality—one of the key factors in twentieth-century European history? At stake were national identity, national pride and sovereignty. Was this a price worth paying for the promise of greater political stability and combined economic might?

It was an argument that reverberated across Europe throughout the last three decades of the twentieth century—and it was important enough to cost Thatcher her job as British prime minister. In November 1990, the Conservative Party dropped her after an 11 year run in office, and replaced her with the chancellor of the exchequer, John Major, a more conciliatory figure. Nevertheless, Europe remained one of the

**LEADER NO MORE** Margaret Thatcher's opposition to closer European integration was one of the reasons why the Conservative Party replaced her in 1990.

thorniest problems throughout his six-year administration, too.

Major was not alone, however: all over Europe, politicians on the right and the left of the political spectrum loved or hated the European Union, and the general public likewise blew hot and cold. The fact was that during the 1980s, the European Community

had undergone a dramatic transformation: quite suddenly, it had developed into a mighty ship, and was now heading into uncharted waters.

## Butter mountains and wine lakes

At the beginning of the 1970s, the European Community (EC) still consisted of the six countries that had signed the 1957 Treaty of Rome: France, Germany, Belgium, Italy, the Netherlands and Luxembourg. In 1973, they were joined by three more countries, Denmark, Ireland and Britain.

Despite the hopes expressed in the Treaty of Rome that the EC would work toward political as well as economic integration, the Community was still spoken of mainly as a "Common Market," in which internal trade barriers and tariffs were minimized. In practice, however, economic recession made member states conscious of their national priorities, and protectionist barriers were introduced under a number of guises.

Meanwhile, currency fluctuations played havoc with trade. To combat this, the Exchange Rate Mechanism (ERM) was introduced in 1979, whereby the currencies of participating member states were pegged to an exchange band, and were underpinned by the European Monetary Fund. The European Currency Unit, called the Ecu, was also introduced, running parallel to national currencies.

The Common Agricultural Policy (CAP) was attracting widespread criticism. The system was designed to protect farmers from cheap imports through subsidies. These were replaced after 1979 by a system of price support that offered a minimum price for agricultural produce, and guaranteed to buy surpluses. Farmers were in effect being paid to produce large quantities of food that was not required. The result was vast stockpiles of surpluses, referred to by labels such as the "butter mountain," the "beef mountain" and the "wine lake." Such policies were embarrassing, wasteful and expensive.

Subsidies, regulations and quotas led to frustrations and resentment among farmers and the fishing industry, and resulted in frequent outbursts of protest, or "direct action," particularly in France. In August 1980, for instance, French fishermen blockaded the Channel ports, trapping thousands of British tourists. A decade later, French farmers physically inhibited the transport of cheaper

**UNINTENDED OUTCOME**
Franco's legacy of dictatorship was ended within three years of his death. Below: Right-wing Civil Guards, led by Lieutenant-Colonel Antonio Tejero, made an unsuccessful attempt to turn back the clock in February 1981 by storming the Spanish parliament.

## SPAIN AFTER FRANCO

When the Spanish dictator General Franco died in November 1975, age 82, leadership passed to his hand-picked successor, Juan Carlos, grandson of the last king, Alfonso XIII, who had abdicated in 1931. Franco had assumed that, as king, Juan Carlos would toe the Francoist line, but Juan Carlos proved to be his own man. Treading a path between Francoist conservatism and the need for modernization, in 1976 he appointed Adolfo Suárez as prime minister.

Suárez was a reformist, and, at the age of 43, represented a new generation. In 1976 Spain's parliament, the Cortez, voted to legalize opposition political parties and trade unions. In 1977, in the first general election since 1936, Suárez was confirmed as prime

minister, at the head of his Democratic Center Party (UCD). The newly legitimized Spanish Socialist Workers' Party (PSOE) became the official opposition. In 1977, Spain applied to join the EC and NATO. Greater autonomy was granted to the regions, with the exception of the Basque country, which was still plagued by the separatist terrorism of ETA. During his four-year term of office Suárez faced increasing dissent within the UCD, and a dramatic rise in ETA violence. He resigned in January 1981, and was replaced by Leopoldo Calvo Sotelo. The following month a right-wing backlash erupted in the shape of Lieutenant-Colonel Antonio Tejero, who stormed the Congress of Deputies with 200 armed Civil Guards. He held Sotelo hostage, along with his cabinet and 350 members of parliament. King Juan Carlos spoke directly to army chiefs who might have been tempted to support Tejero, and the coup collapsed.

Spain joined NATO in May 1982. In elections in October that year the nation voted for the PSOE led by Felipe González. He took Spain into the EC in 1986. González was in power until 1996, when he was defeated by José María Aznar López, leader of the center-right Popular Party. By then, Spain had joined the European nations on equal terms.

**A NEW BLOSSOMING** The Barcelona Olympics of 1992 were a celebration of sports and of the new, revitalized Spain.

1985 Jacques Delors becomes president of the EC; Schengen Agreement on border formalities is signed

1986 Spain and Portugal join the EC

1991 The Maastricht conference agrees to the Treaty on European Union

1994 The Channel Tunnel opens

1995 Jacques Santer becomes president of the EC; Austria, Sweden and Finland join the EU

1996 BSE causes a crisis in the British beef industry

1999 The euro is introduced in 11 EU countries

## JACQUES DELORS: A FORCE FOR UNITY

If there was one person to be credited with the creation of a modern, unified Europe, it might be Jacques Delors. He was president of the European Commission from 1985 to 1995, during a period of critical and dynamic change. When he took over, the EC had begun to stagnate. By the time he left, it was driven by a new vision of unity, galvanized by the real prospect of a single currency. He was instrumental in bringing the Maastricht Treaty to fruition.

Jacques Delors was born in Paris in 1925. He spent the early part of his career with the Banque de France, then as an academic. He served as adviser on social affairs to the Gaullist government of Jacques Chaban-Delmas in 1969-72 before switching to the socialists in the mid 1970s. He was elected an MEP in 1979, and became minister of economics and finance under President Mitterrand in 1981. He left the government to take up his appointment as president of the European Commission in 1985.

Delors essentially played the role of a technocrat, but he also displayed a sure footing in economic realities and knew their impact on the political sphere. In addition, he was a Catholic with a social conscience, which chimed with the center-left and center-right politics in which the new Europe was being forged. If he was criticized for pushing European Union too hard and too fast, it was because he had a vision of what an integrated Europe—burying its differences in a seamless political and economic union—might achieve.

His insistence on driving Europe forward while circumstances were favorable made Delors something of a bogeyman among the Euroskeptics. In a famously vitriolic headline the British *Sun* newspaper declared: "Up Yours, Delors!" It could be seen as a backhanded compliment to his influence and stature. Elsewhere he was dubbed with the tamer sobriquet "Monsieur Europe."

**VISION OF A NEW EUROPE** Jacques Delors brought a new energy and focus to his role as president of the European Commission, with the result that much was achieved during his ten-year term of office.

British lamb into their country: the resulting "lamb war" led to ugly scenes as truckloads of lamb carcasses, and even some live animals, were torched and a number of drivers beaten.

### Maastricht

By the mid 1980s, changes were afoot, aided by improved economic conditions, and the advent of center-left (social democrat) and center-right (Christian democrat) governments that espoused a combination of free-market economics and a sense of social welfare. Two key players in this development were François Mitterrand and Helmut Kohl.

Mitterrand, leader of the French Socialist Party, was the surprise winner of the 1981 presidential election that ousted the conservative Valéry Giscard d'Estaing. Mitterrand's new government attempted to introduce a range of radical reforms, such as nationalizing the banks and key industries, fixing a minimum wage and increasing some social benefits. After electoral setbacks in 1986, Mitterrand's tactics became more pragmatic and free-market oriented, and in 1988 he won a second seven-year term in office.

Kohl, head of the German Christian Democratic Union (CDU), was able to stitch together a majority coalition with the Bavarian Christian Social Union (CSU) and the Free Democratic Party (FDP) to become chancellor of Germany in 1982. A towering figure, both physically and politically, he remained a dominant force in European affairs until his defeat by the socialist Gerhard Schröder in 1998.

Although from different bands of the political spectrum, Kohl and Mitterrand shared a common ambition for the EC: they wanted to see it strengthened and revitalized. Kohl was motivated by the prospect of a stable market in which Germany could thrive, and a political consensus across Western Europe that would afford security against East Germany and the Soviet bloc on his doorstep. Mitterrand shared the old French suspicion of Germany's economic might and ambitions: Germany's commitment to Europe therefore had to be encouraged and matched with equal commitment.

Their viewpoint was shared by another key European figure of the late 1980s, Jacques Delors, Mitterrand's former finance minister, who became president of the European Commission in 1985. Delors was

RE-DRAWING THE MAP  While the Soviet bloc was collapsing in the 1990s, the European Community expanded to 15 member states.

determined to push the EC toward a new era. It was continuing to grow: Greece joined in 1981, Portugal and Spain in 1986, thus forming the "Twelve" that were symbolized by the twelve stars of the European flag.

The focus of the Intergovernmental Conference in Luxembourg in late 1985 was the concept of a "single Europe." If the right structures could be found, and consensus achieved, the member states could head down the path toward European Monetary Union, and greater political union, involving increased power to the European parliament and integrated social, defense and foreign policies. At the end of this process lay the possibility of creating "a United States of Europe," as Kohl later put it.

European Monetary Union (EMU) was one of the most controversial plans: a single currency for the EC governed by a Central European Bank. The reasoning behind this proposal was that a single market would always be prey to currency fluctuations and inherent instability, as long as national currencies existed.

Opponents argued that national currencies granted flexibility, and could sensitively reflect the differences in local economic conditions. Also, they were a symbol of national sovereignty.

In 1985, two commissions were set up to look at ways to achieve these reforms. Their conclusions were drawn up in more than 300 pieces of legislation that would form the basis of the Treaty on European Union. Once the proposals had been circulated, the details had to be discussed. This took place at a summit of the heads of state in December 1991, in the city of Maastricht.

The deliberations by now had a new urgency: the parameters of the world were changing with the collapse of communism in eastern Europe and the U.S.S.R. It was all the more vital for Europe to come together and show a common purpose. Those leading the push toward an integrated Europe, notably Helmut Kohl and Jacques Delors, saw the need to act fast as a rare historical window of opportunity presented itself.

Most of the Treaty recommendations were accepted: the single currency would be introduced in 1999—but only in countries that met the "convergence criteria," which demanded pre-agreed standards of exchange-rate stability and levels of inflation and government debt. The EC would be superseded by the European Union (EU). Across Europe, national barriers would be eliminated: there would be free movement of goods, capital, services and EU citizens.

Britain, led by John Major, rallied a minority voice of dissent at Maastricht. One sticking point was the introduction of the "social chapter," a raft of moderate social reforms that, to Major's Conservative government, smacked of "socialism by the back door"; another sticking point was the single currency. Major negotiated a separate position on both of these: Britain would delay joining the single currency until a later date—an option also taken up by Denmark. It also "opted out" of the social chapter. The buzzword was "subsidiarity": Britain insisted that national bodies (subsidiary to the overarching European bodies) should retain the right to deal with all matters within their competence.

Britain's negotiating position reflected a constant concern of many—voiced also in France, Germany and Denmark—that the European Union was becoming too powerful and too centralized, at the expense of national governments and institutions. To the mass of newly coined euro-words—eurocheque, eurocrat, euro-lounge, eurotrash—was added the term euroskeptic, applied to all those who expressed reservations about the European project. They ranged from those who approved of the concept of a trading community along the lines of the Common Market, but resented the ever-increasing powers of Brussels, to those who wanted to disengage from the

KEY PARTNERSHIP  President François Mitterrand of France and Chancellor Helmut Kohl of Germany drove forward the radical agenda for increased European integration.

European Union completely. The hesitancy of many Europeans was exhibited in the national referenda that took place after Maastricht, in preparation for its ratification in 1993. In Denmark the electorate voted "no" in 1992 by a slim margin (50.7 percent against). Since all 12 nations had to ratify Maastricht, its future was on the line. In a second referendum in 1993, the Danes narrowly approved, with a 58 percent majority. In France only 51 percent voted "yes."

Britain did not hold a referendum: it was argued that the case had been put to the people in the general election of 1992, and it was up to parliament to make the decision. The Conservative government won the vote for ratification in July 1993 by a margin of just three votes. However, other events overshadowed this. Britain had joined the Exchange Rate Mechanism (ERM) in October 1990, but at an unsustainably high rate. The pound was soon considered overvalued, and became the target of massive speculation on the international exchanges, a fate that simultaneously befell the Italian lira. In a single day, September 16, 1992, British interest rates were raised from 10 percent to 12 percent, and then to 15 percent before the chancellor, Norman Lamont, withdrew Britain from the ERM. This sterling crisis is estimated to have cost Britain $22.5 billion. Italy was likewise forced to leave the ERM and let the lira float. It seemed to be a lesson in the dangers of inflexible centralized banking systems.

### Expanding horizons

The Maastricht Treaty was formally ratified in October 1993 and came into operation on November 1. Notwithstanding the slim majorities in favor of the treaty, the EU had been given a fillip. The single market now contained 375 million people. Some 60 percent of member states' trade now took place within it, as opposed to 40 percent in the 1980s. Foreign multinationals were lining up with inward investment in the hope of getting a foot in the door.

The EU's political initiatives proved rather less successful than its economic ones. There had been some hope that the EU would be able to construct a common foreign policy, but its lack of consensus over the

## BIOTECHNOLOGY

One issue of concern for the EU is biotechnology. If the benefits of individual genes can be identified, they can be isolated and inserted into the DNA sequences of other organisms to form improvements. In medicine, this means identifying the gene that exposes an individual to disease, notably hereditary diseases such as muscular dystrophy and some forms of cancer. This gene can then be replaced or manipulated early on to prevent the disease from developing. The international Human Genome Project promises to map the entire human genetic sequence in the early years of the 21st century. In theory, it will then be possible to map every individual's DNA, identify his or her health risks, and prescribe tailor-made medicines.

Before this occurs, genetic engineering is likely to have a more widespread impact through agriculture. By altering and transferring the genes of plants and animals, it is possible to import such properties as higher yields, pest resistance and enhanced flavor. Tomatoes, for instance, have been modified with fish genes to make them frost-resistant. Plants and animals could also be used to produce vaccines for human medicine. No one can yet predict the full consequences of releasing genetically modified organisms (GMOs) into the environment. For example, it is possible to alter the genes of soy beans so that they resist pesticides, but what if the gene in question transfers through cross-pollination, producing pesticide-resistant weeds?

Genetic engineering in medicine could also produce unforeseen, possibly disastrous consequences. And genetic mapping of individuals has serious implications for civil liberties: who will possess such information and control its use? Meanwhile, the commercial aspects of the science remain controversial: pharmaceutical companies, investing millions in genetic research, want to patent the genes that they have identified—but should any life form be patented?

Since the mid 1980s, the EU Commission has attempted to address these problems through a series of research and monitoring programs. On the one hand, it has to heed the concerns of individuals and nations about GMOs, and reassure them that its regulations regarding "biosafety" are watertight. On the other, it must provide a constructive environment for the development of what could be one of the most important scientific breakthroughs in human history.

**BIOTECH VEG** Some strains of tomato have been genetically modified, and pressure is growing for clear labeling to give the consumer the choice.

violent disintegration of Yugoslavia—and its failure to impose a solution there—showed that this would be difficult to achieve.

Similarly, the concept of a European defense force proved elusive—although by October 1998 even Britain was arguing for a common European defense policy, if not yet a European army. In the event, NATO effectively assumed this role, and accounted for almost all the EU area. But the American connection, and old anxieties about the United States-British axis, still made the French reluctant partners, while Austria remained neutral.

The EU was enlarged in 1995, as Austria, Sweden and Finland joined, bringing the number of members up to 15. Various voices called for further expansion. Turkey had applied to join in 1987, but was consistently

denied, despite membership in NATO. Poland and Hungary applied in 1994; Romania, Bulgaria, Estonia, Lithuania, Latvia, Slovakia, in 1995; Slovenia and the Czech Republic in 1996. All had to accept interim trade agreements as the wheels of the EU slowly turned. In two referenda in Norway, in 1971 and 1994, the Norwegians voted "no" to joining. Switzerland, fearing that membership would compromise its neutrality, similarly rejected the proposition.

Meanwhile, national borders within the EU melted away. In March 1995, Germany, Belgium, France, the Netherlands and Luxembourg (signatories to the 1985 Schengen Agreement on lifting border restrictions), plus Spain and Portugal, agreed to suspend passport controls for EU nationals.

As Europe was coalescing, regions previously toying with autonomy or separatism—such as Brittany, Flanders, Catalonia and

**EUROLAND CURRENCY** From January 1999, the currencies of 11 EU countries were pegged to the euro. The old currencies will be replaced by new euro coins and notes in 2002.

performing its role as the EU civil service, charged with seeing that policy and directives were uniformly carried out.

The politics of member states always threatened to disrupt the smooth running of the supranational European organizations. After 1990, Germany had to contend with reunification: the modernization of East Germany was costing over half the country's annual budget by 1993, creating a recession.

Italy experienced deep turmoil in the early 1990s as its entire political class came under the spotlight of the magistrate-led "Clean Hands" campaign to eradicate corruption. The media magnate Silvio Berlusconi rose rapidly to power with his right-of-center Forza Italia Party. Forming a coalition called the Freedom Alliance with the right-wing Northern League and National Alliance, he became prime minister in March 1994—but within nine months his administration also fell foul of the anticorruption drive and he was forced to resign.

Despite its new link with Europe in the form of the Channel Tunnel, which began operations in 1994, Britain still exasperated its EU partners. Also in 1994, Major's government decided to obstruct the appointment of Jacques Delors's successor. France and Germany favored the Belgian prime minister, Jean-Luc Dehaene. Britain, fearing this would give too much power to the Franco-German axis, vetoed this appointment and the EU had to accept a compromise candidate, the prime minister of Luxembourg, Jacques Santer.

The EU's frustrations with

Britain came to a head during the BSE crisis, which erupted in 1996 when the EU banned all export of British beef throughout the world. After a decade of obfuscation by its Ministry of Agriculture, the British Government announced that the brain disease BSE in cattle could possibly be linked to the fatal Creutzfeldt-Jakob disease. Faced with the devastation of its beef and dairy industry, Britain began calling on Europe to extract compensation for farmers and an easing of export restrictions. But Britain's negotiating position had become compromised by its record as a reluctant European, and was not to improve until the election of the new Labor government led by Tony Blair in 1997.

Even more divisive was the question of the single currency—a project that Margaret Thatcher had dismissed as "cloud cuckoo land." In 1998, it was announced that 11 countries had met the convergence criteria. Only Greece had failed to match up to requirements; Britain, Denmark and Sweden opted to stay out of the "first wave." Never before had a currency been created without a central government to oversee it. In 1995, it had been baptized the euro. On January 1, 1999, the euro was introduced alongside the Deutschmark, the French and Belgian and Luxembourgeois franc, the Dutch guilder, the Italian lira, the Irish punt, the Spanish peseta, the Austrian schilling, the Finnish mark and the Portuguese escudo. And in 2002 it will replace these national currencies.

**NEW BROOM** Optimism that Silvio Berlusconi, elected in March 1994, would bring much-needed reforms to the Italian political establishment was short-lived.

Scotland—began to see that they could realign themselves within the embrace of Europe. Hence, on the one hand, the European project promoted globalism; on the other, it fostered a revitalized regionalism.

## Local difficulties

Within the EU, the gradual transfer of power from national governments to European institutions was the subject of heated debate. Direct elections to the European Parliament in Strasbourg had been introduced in 1979, and gradually this body was carving out a greater role for itself, but nonetheless it remained subsidiary to national governments, and to the Council of the European Union—the collective heads of state. The Commission, headed by the president and 20 commissioners appointed by national governments, remained aloof,

# POLICING THE WORLD

## THE CHANGING SHAPE OF INTERNATIONAL POLITICS STRENGTHENED THE HAND OF THE UNITED NATIONS AS THE WORLD'S PEACEKEEPER

With the collapse of communism and the end of the Cold War in the early 1990s, many people began to speak optimistically of a new world order, a world in which aggressive and iniquitous governments could be brought to book by the collective will of the international community. The agency best placed to see through this new agenda was the United Nations—directed by the Peruvian Javier Pérez de Cuellar, UN secretary-general from 1982 to 1991, and by the Egyptian Boutros Boutros-Gali from 1992 to 1996.

The United States, now the primary superpower, took up the challenge of leading this new world order. During the previous two decades, however, it had not always seen eye to eye with the UN, despite the fact that the organization's headquarters were in New York. The UN had achieved considerable success and respect in many areas of its global range of concerns—economic development, health, the environment, human rights, care for refugees. Its agencies, which include the UN International Children's Emergency Fund (UNICEF), the UN Educational, Scientific and Cultural Organization (UNESCO), and the World Health Organization (WHO), had made a considerable impact, matched only by the growing importance of international non-governmental organizations (NGOs), such as CARE, Save the Children and Oxfam. The United States, however, was critical of the UN's performance in its central role of peacekeeping: the UN had become bogged down in Israel (where it had been present since 1948), in Cyprus (since 1964), and in the buffer zone in southern Lebanon (since 1978). More serious differences with the

**INTERNATIONAL CARE** Mothers in Kenya await inoculation for their newborn babies, as part of a wide-ranging program of preventive medicine orchestrated by the World Health Organization (WHO).

United States had arisen over the UN's opposition to American intervention in Vietnam, and in its critical stance over many of America's foreign confrontations arising from the Cold War.

### U.S. intervention

During the 1980s, the United States simply took a unilateral approach wherever and whenever it felt its own interests were threatened, particularly in its backyard of Central America and the Caribbean. This occurred in the tiny independent—formerly British—island of Grenada, in the southern Caribbean, which became increasingly socialist after the coup that toppled the government of Sir Eric Gairy in 1979. The new prime minister was Maurice Bishop, leader of the New Jewel Movement. To the United State's alarm, he turned to the Soviet Union and Cuba for aid, and the Cubans began building a large airstrip on the island that could have strategic military implications. In October 1983, Maurice Bishop was ousted by a Leninist faction of his People's Revolutionary Army, and he and 40 colleagues were executed. Citing the need to protect 600 American medical students on the island, the United States decided to

send in an intervention force of 1,900 troops, backed by contingents from neighboring East Caribbean islands. Operation *Urgent Fury* restored order, then gradually withdrew over the next two years.

American involvement in Central America was altogether more complex, especially in Nicaragua. In 1979, the Nicaraguan president, Anastasio Somoza Debayle, was forced into exile. His family had led a deeply corrupt and dictatorial government for 43 years, largely supported by the United States. His unpopularity and abuses of human rights became too much even for the Americans, and in 1979 they withdrew support, which left the rebel Sandinistas with the upper hand. Named after César Augusto Sandino, a Liberal politician murdered by the Somoza dynasty in 1934, the Sandinistas had been fighting a gruelling guerrilla campaign to oust Somoza and his cronies since 1962. Although not communist, they were left-leaning. Once in power they pursued an increasingly socialist agenda and

threatened to expropriate American businesses. When the United States suspended aid in 1981, the Sandinista government turned to the U.S.S.R. for help. A rump of Somoza supporters meanwhile formed a guerrilla army and called themselves the Contras. The civil war intensified.

## The Iran-Contra Affair

The government of Ronald Reagan, ever fearful of the spread of communism in Central America, was inclined to support the Contras. But as the Contras' atrocities reached the world's attention, Congress voted to suspend aid and CIA support to them. Responsibility for liaising with the Contras now passed from the CIA to the National Security Council (NSC) in Washington, and specifically to its deputy director, Lieutenant-Colonel Oliver North.

Meanwhile, a number of American citizens had been taken hostage in Lebanon by Iranian-backed Shiite Muslim terrorists. Iran's relations with America remained virtually non-existent following the hostage crisis of 1979-81, but Iran was now trapped in a costly war with

**HERO AND VILLAIN** Lieutenant-Colonel Oliver North was at the center of the Iran-Contra scandal in 1986-7. Although operating illegally, he won sympathy at home for his patriotism and anti-communist stance.

**ISLAND INTERVENTION** In 1983, U.S. and Caribbean troops mounted an intervention force to restore order in Grenada following a violent military coup.

Iraq and desperately needed modern arms. Congress had banned any sales of arms to Iran. Despite this, the NSC began covert negotiations with the Iranians, who offered to mediate for the release of hostages in Lebanon in return for the sale of arms. The NSC thereby set up an illicit trading structure to sell anti-tank and anti-aircraft missiles to the Iranians. The arrangement also contravened the American policy of not bargaining with terrorists. Furthermore, in another illegal operation, the NSC decided secretly to divert a proportion of the profits from the Iranian arms sales to the Contras in Nicaragua.

The scam was exposed in October 1986, after an American cargo plane was shot down in southern Nicaragua, and a surviving crew member confessed to being on a mission sponsored by the CIA. At this point, Oliver North began shredding incriminating documents. The plot was gradually revealed before a Joint Congressional Panel between May 5 and August 6, 1987, in a series of televised hearings that gripped the United States. Oliver North became the object of fascination: a decorated Vietnam veteran playing a high-risk game with terrorists, he claimed that his motives were patriotic and anti-communist, and that he had acted illegally in the interests of America. It became

**2000**

1986 Iran-Contra scandal exposed

1988 UN brokers end to war in Afghanistan and Iran-Iraq

1989 U.S. intervenes in Panama

1991 Iraq evicted from Kuwait in the Gulf War

1992 Boutros Boutros-Gali becomes UN secretary-general; UN begins peacekeeping mission in Yugoslavia; U.S. and UN intervene in Somalia

1994 UN fails to intervene in Rwandan massacres; U.S. intervenes in Haiti

1997 Kofi Annan becomes UN secretary-general

clear that the White House knew about the operation, although it was never proved that Reagan authorized it. The public, however, was dismayed at the degree to which government agencies were willing to bypass stated policy and bend the law, and measures were taken to improve accountability.

The United States continued to take unilateral action. One of the most blatant examples of this was the surprise air raid on Libya on April 15, 1986. It was ordered by President Reagan as a punishment for Libya's state-sponsored terrorism, and aided by the decision of Margaret Thatcher, then prime minister, to allow the Americans to refuel in Britain en route to Libya. Some 130 Libyans were killed, including President Gaddafi's adopted daughter.

In May 1989, Panama collapsed into turmoil as its leader, General Manuel Noriega, lost an election and then declared it void, triggering widespread demonstrations that were met with bloody suppression. Noriega's continuing role as strongman of Panama was unpalatable to America on two counts. First, America was due to give the Canal Zone to Panama in the year 2000, and needed reassurance that this vital strategic link was controlled by a stable government. Second, Noriega was known to be involved in the lucrative trade in illegal narcotics. Following a failed coup in October, on December 21, American troops invaded from the Canal Zone with the purpose of arresting Noriega. Some 200 civilians, 19 American soldiers and 59 Panamanian soldiers died, but to the embarrassment of the American military, Noriega himself eluded capture for two weeks. In 1992, he was convicted in Miami of cocaine trafficking and money laundering.

## The Gulf War

By the late 1980s, the UN had scored three notable successes, which brought about a

**THE LONG VIGIL** An American tank patrols the Kuwaiti border after the Gulf War. The U.S. kept forces in the area to maintain pressure on Iraq to comply with its truce commitments to destroy its weapons of mass destruction.

revision in America's attitude toward it. In 1988, it forged the peace treaty to end the devastating Iran-Iraq war, negotiated a withdrawal of Soviet troops from Afghanistan and persuaded South Africa to grant independence to Namibia. The UN had shown its mettle. Furthermore, as the Cold War came to a close, there was a mood of cooperation among the five permanent members of the UN Security Council: the United States, the U.S.S.R., Britain, France and China. As never before, the UN seemed like the body best suited to shouldering the responsibility of policing the world. But it was about to face its greatest test.

Despite the colossal losses incurred in his war against Iran, Iraq's belligerent president, Saddam

*DESERT STORM* To oust Iraq from Kuwait, the U.S.-led coalition forces took full advantage of their superior fire power, attacking military and infrastructure targets with computer-directed missiles (main picture) and from the air. Above: Kuwaiti oil wells burn as U.S. troops advance toward the border with Iraq.

Hussein, continued to buy arms and bolster his army after the peace treaty of 1988. A measure of his ambitions was his Supergun project, intercepted by British customs officers in 1990. With a range of over 400 miles, the gun—had it been completed—would have been capable of hurling missiles at Israel. He demonstrated his readiness to use chemical and biological weapons in 1988, when his forces dropped bombs filled with poison gas on Halabjah and other rebellious Kurdish villages in northeastern Iraq, killing over 6,000 people and maiming scores of survivors. Saddam still clearly posed a dangerous threat to the international community, as well as to his own people.

By 1990, Iraq was in deep financial trouble, saddled with massive debts, particularly to its neighbor, oil-rich Kuwait, which had helped to fund the war with Iran. During the summer of 1990, Saddam moved his forces to the border with Kuwait, and on August 2 they invaded. Kuwait was quickly overrun, and Saddam announced that it had become the 19th province of Iraq.

He had miscalculated the world's reaction. No country could tolerate this disregard for international borders. Furthermore, Kuwait's oilfields were of economic interest to the industrialized world, and the international community feared further attacks on the oil-rich nations of the Arabian Gulf.

Saudi Arabia appealed to the world for protection.

The UN and America spoke with a common purpose: Iraq had to leave Kuwait. The UN Security Council imposed a worldwide trading ban on Iraq. On November 29,

after Saddam's usual prevarication, he was given a deadline of January 15, 1991, to withdraw. Meanwhile, a massive military force was assembled in Saudi Arabia. Led by the United States, it was joined by ground forces, warships and warplanes from France, Britain, Saudi Arabia, Syria, Egypt and others—a coalition of 28 countries building an army of 700,000. This was an unprecedented achievement for the UN. Israel, in the direct firing line, was persuaded to remain neutral in the dispute. Jordan was the only neighboring Arab country to voice active support for Saddam; Algeria, Sudan, Tunisia, Yemen and the PLO also backed Iraq.

Saddam chose to ignore the deadline. Two days after its expiration, Operation *Desert Storm* was launched, under the direction of General "Stormin'" Norman Schwarzkopf in Saudi Arabia and General Colin Powell in Washington. For 39 days the coalition forces attacked Iraq, using hi-tech weaponry and missiles to take out anti-aircraft weapons, military installations, communications centers, power stations, bridges and roads. Iraq's response was to launch Scud missiles at Israel, killing four civilians, and at an airbase in Saudi Arabia, killing around twenty-eight Americans. Many of its Scuds were successfully taken out by new Patriot missile systems, but the coalition forces retained a residual fear that these warheads might contain biological or chemical weapons.

This was the first war fought on live television, and Saddam used Western journalists still in Iraq as a conduit for his side of the story, focusing on the collateral damage in which ordinary citizens—possibly totalling 100,000-200,000—were killed. The coalition,

however, accused him of cynically placing strategic sites among ordinary people, so they could form a human shield.

With its infrastructure pulverized, Iraq now depended on the fighting spirit of its million-strong army. But its soldiers were already demoralized, exhausted by a month of air attacks, and leaving in droves. On February 24, General Schwarzkopf sent in the ground troops. The Iraqi armed forces folded, but as they retreated, they torched the Kuwaiti oil wells, an act of vandalism that triggered one of the century's worst ecological disasters. After just 100 hours, the coalition forces had driven 120 miles into Iraq. Operation *Desert Storm* had achieved its goal. Saddam Hussein capitulated. His country had lost up to 100,000 men; the international coalition had lost 300.

At this point the Shiite Muslims in Iraq—representing 60 percent of the Iraqi population, but politically dispossessed—rose up to topple Saddam from power. But Saddam had retained the trust of his elite Republican Guard, and in crushing their own people they could now score the victory that they had so abjectly failed to achieve in Kuwait. The Shiite rebellion was savagely put down. The Marsh Arabs, living since ancient times in the delta of the Tigris and Euphrates, were subjected to particularly harsh repression, including deliberate drainage of the marshes to destroy their traditional way of life. The Kurds also rebelled and were similarly treated, but Saddam's vengeance was mitigated by the imposition of a UN-enforced air exclusion zone over their homelands.

### The lawman's tarnished badge

The UN and the United States won a decisive victory in the Gulf War, but they were unwilling to root out the cause of the war—Saddam himself. They could have conquered

## SADDAM HUSSEIN—RULING THROUGH FEAR

In the early 1990s, a UN special report on Saddam Hussein's regime in Iraq concluded that its atrocities were so grave and of such a massive nature that since the Second World War few parallels can be found. The death toll is indictment enough: 370,000 dead in the Iran-Iraq war; 200,000 Kurds killed since the start of his rule; 100,000 dead in the Gulf War. Iraq, it seems, is caught in the nightmare of a regime run by a lethal but cunning psychopath.

Born in 1937 in Tikrit, into a Sunni family of melon-farmers, Saddam joined the opposition Ba'ath socialist party at the age of 19. At age 22, he was wounded in his unsuccessful attempt to assassinate the prime minister, Abdul Karim Kassem. He fled to Cairo, where he won the favor of President Nasser. He returned to Iraq after the Ba'athists seized power in 1963, but went underground in the violent period that ensued. In 1968, Ba'athists under Ahmad Hassan al-Bakr once again seized power, and Saddam now became a leading figure in the regime. Al-Bakr resigned in 1979, and Saddam took over as president. Ten days after taking power there was an attempted coup. Saddam had the leaders rounded up and executed. He had soon assumed the roles of president, prime minister, chairman of the Revolutionary Command Council and head of the armed forces: he had become an all-powerful dictator. He had grand ambitions to make Iraq the leader of the Arab World: "The glory of the Arabs stems from the glory of Iraq," he declared.

Saddam demanded absolute loyalty; his opponents were dealt with ruthlessly. The cement of his regime was terror. On one occasion he personally shot dead a general who brought him unwelcome advice. Countless other political colleagues and military leaders were executed on suspicion of posing a threat to him, and Saddam often requested his colleagues to carry out such executions in order to deepen their terror and to create a complicity of guilt.

Saddam's rule of terror was maintained among his people by a similarly ruthless secret police, able to detect and crush any dissent. Merciless punishment for criticism was meted out not only on the critics, but also their families. But this politics of fear was combined with a well-orchestrated personality cult and strong appeals to nationalistic pride. Saddam won the loyalty of many Iraqis, who did not in general hold him personally responsible for the nation's suffering as a result of his two disastrous wars and crippling UN trade sanctions. Rather, by repeatedly tweaking the American tail, Saddam became a hero to many of his own people and many in the Arab world beyond, a symbol, albeit imperfect, of defiance.

Iraq, but this would then have given them the responsibility of setting it back on its feet. Saddam remained in power, and persisted in obstructing UN weapons' inspectors sent to monitor the demolition of his weapons of mass destruction, a condition of the truce. The Iraqi people had to endure years of hardship as the UN-sanctioned trade embargo remained in force.

In 1992, the deteriorating situation in Somalia called for intervention. Somalia had been in decline since the withdrawal of Soviet support in 1977. When President Siyaad Barre was ousted in 1991, the country broke up into warring factions and widespread banditry, which disrupted the fragile agricultural economy. Concurrently, Somalia suffered a two-year drought, taking 1.5 million people to the brink of starvation, and sending thousands of refugees over the borders into neighboring countries. Aid agencies tried to bring relief food supplies to the starving, but were obstructed by militiamen.

Faced with a humanitarian disaster, America decided to intervene, and won UN backing to mount Operation *Restore Hope*. In December 1992, a force of 30,000 American soldiers landed in Somalia to protect the food supplies. This proved hazardous in the volatile atmosphere created by the armed factions. A UN-sponsored ceasefire in January 1993 collapsed in February as rival Somalis clashed in Mogadishu; the American forces' attempts to intervene met with resistance, notably from the warlord General Muhammad Farah Aydid. Another ceasefire was called in March, and in May America's force was partially replaced by a reduced multinational force (UNISOM II). The following month, 24 Pakistani soldiers were killed by Aydid's forces, but UN efforts to arrest Aydid were thwarted. Amid accusations of abuses by UN soldiers, four journalists were killed by protesters, and in October, 18 American soldiers were killed in battle.

The anarchy in Somalia seemed beyond repair. Having achieved a modicum of order, the UN forces withdrew in early 1995, behind the cover of 1,800 marines. This debacle was a major setback for the new world order, and henceforth the U.S. was much more wary of direct intervention.

It did, however, have some success closer to home. The impoverished Caribbean state of Haiti had been ruled by the Duvalier family since 1957, first by François Papa Doc

**TRAGIC LESSON** To the international community, it seemed simple enough to bring succor to the starving in Somalia in 1992, by pushing aside the warlords who were obstructing relief work. It proved a thankless and unsatisfactory task.

Duvalier, until 1971, and then by his son Jean-Claude (Baby Doc). Ruthless and avaricious dictators, they controlled their people through a feared and reviled security apparatus called the Tontons Macoutes. In 1986, popular unrest forced Baby Doc into exile, and he was replaced by a series of chaotic military regimes. Presidential elections in December 1990 gave victory to Jean-Bertrand Aristide. A Catholic priest and tireless humanitarian who had survived numerous attempts on his life, he held out the prospect of bringing stability and justice to his beleaguered country. But in September 1991, he was ousted by a right-wing military coup supported by the Tontons Macoutes. Donor countries suspended aid, and in the resulting economic collapse, violent repression and assassination of political opponents, tens of thousands of Haitians fled in boats toward America.

America called for urgent action to stem the flow of refugees. In July 1993, the UN

# THE RWANDA TRAGEDY

No one knows how many died in the frenzy of killing that took place in Rwanda during ten weeks in mid 1994. Estimates put it at more than half a million people, most of them Tutsis. Although in the minority, the Tutsis had been nurtured by the colonial authorities as the ruling elite, and dominated the government after the country gained independence from Belgium in 1962. They were overthrown by the Hutus in 1966, following a seven-year civil war in which up to 100,000 Tutsis died and 150,000 fled into neighboring countries. The Tutsis in exile formed the Rwandese Patriotic Front (FPR), which after 1990 began an effective guerrilla campaign inside Rwanda. Under peace accords signed in 1993, the Hutu president of Rwanda, Juvenal Habyarimana, agreed to lead a mixed-race transitional government. All the while, however, Habyarimana had cultivated a fanatical Hutu militia called the Interahamwe ("those who kill as one"). When given the signal, they would rise up and rid Rwanda of all Tutsis, and any moderate Hutus, once and for all.

That signal came on April 7, 1994, but not from Habyarimana. The previous day he had been killed when his plane crashed, probably shot down by members of the presidential guard who could not accept his power-sharing. The Interahamwe now launched their preplanned massacre, using lists of Tutsis and moderate Hutus drawn up in advance. The exhortation to slaughter was spread by radio, and thousands of Hutus responded. The world was stunned at the viciousness of this genocide, which scythed down men, women and children alike. Most were killed by knives and machetes, apparently to save ammunition. More people were killed by hand in Rwanda than died in the detonation of the atomic bombs at Hiroshima and Nagasaki.

Two million Tutsis—a quarter of Rwanda's population—fled to neighboring Burundi, Tanzania, Uganda and Zaire. The UN evacuated most of its personnel, and the United States refused to intervene. In May, a UN force of 5,500 troops volunteered by African countries materialized. The French, with a record of policing Central Africa, sent in troops in late June with UN approval, but were distrusted by the Tutsis and left in mid August. The Tutsi FPR made rapid advances and by July had conquered most of the country. Now the Hutus, and the Interahamwe, were fleeing over the border into the refugee camps. Inter-tribal violence flared up in the camps, along with malnutrition and disease. By 1995, a new Tutsi-led government began restoring stability. The UN set up a war-crimes court to try the principal perpetrators of the genocide, while 47,000 Hutus suspected of murder were held in prison. Those in camps abroad began to return, and Hutus and Tutsis attempted to rebuild their lives, but in constant fear of reprisals.

**TRAIL OF MISERY** Rwanda suffered not only genocidal massacres, but widespread displacement as hundreds of thousands of traumatized people from both sides of the conflict fled over the borders, seeking safety in ill-equipped refugee camps.

## THE WAR ON DRUGS

By the mid 1990s, the single most prosperous business sector in the world was the trade in illegal narcotics, estimated to be worth about $500 billion. Three UN agencies were spending $80 million a year to fight the drug trade, but they were outgunned by the colossal sums of money going into the business. Narcotics seizures in America alone were valued at about ten times the UN budget to combat the trade.

The real problem was the boundless market, particularly in America. During the era of liberal youth culture in the late 1960s and 1970s, drug-taking became fashionable, and was justified for its mind-altering effects. By 1974, over half of Americans between the age of 18 and 25, and a quarter of 12- to 17-year-olds, had experimented with drugs, mainly marijuana. During the 1980s, cocaine use increased dramatically, reaching a quarter of 18- to 25-year-olds. It was particularly prevalent among the middle class, who argued that cocaine was harmless. The arrival of the highly addictive cocaine-derivative crack in 1988 demonstrated the fallacy of this assumption.

**SOMETHING FISHY  A U.S. Drug Enforcement Administration agent displays cocaine worth $28 million seized in a shipment of anchovies from Argentina.**

Not only were narcotics illegal in almost all countries where they were consumed; they also spawned a criminal underclass, ranging from those who trafficked in drugs or laundered their money to those who had to steal in order to maintain habits of addiction, particularly to heroin. The United States, European countries and the UN strove to reduce the problem by hitting the sources of the drugs. The supply lines led back to a number of Third World countries, where growers could operate beyond the reach of the law, often behind the shield of corrupt government officials or guerrilla armies, who shared in the profits. The old Chinese trade in opium shifted to the remote highland areas of Burma, Thailand and Laos, the so-called Golden Triangle, while poppies were also grown in the far north of Pakistan (the Golden Crescent). Marijuana or hashish was grown in Jamaica, Colombia, Brazil, Nigeria, America, Nepal, Pakistan, Afghanistan and Morocco; cocaine came from Bolivia, Peru and particularly Colombia. In addition, Western nations produced new manufactured narcotics such as Ecstasy, which became popular in the late 1980s.

International campaigns against drugs, instigated by America and the UN, involved such tactics as spraying drug crops from the air, destroying processing laboratories, and burning tons of narcotics seized in transit. However, this often resulted in the destitution of peasant farmers who had no other crop that approached the lucrativeness of narcotics; their plight provided fertile ground for left-wing activism, of the kind the United States feared almost more than the criminal drug trade. Many poorer countries, pressed to carry out drug-enforcement policies, argued that the real way to stamp out the trade was to tackle the demand for narcotics among the wealthy nations that finance the trade in the first place.

**EASY PICKINGS  In grower countries such as Pakistan, opium can bring far greater wealth to farmers, and to a whole chain of middlemen, than any other crop.**

Security Council thrashed out an agreement under which the military would withdraw and restore Aristide as the legitimate president. But when a UN force arrived to implement the agreement in October, it was forced by angry crowds to make a humiliating retreat. In July 1994, America was sanctioned by the UN to invade; however, a last-ditch mission led by former president Jimmy Carter and General Colin Powell persuaded the military government to step down peaceably. In September 1994, 20,000 troops landed unopposed. Aristide was returned to power in October 1994, and in January 1995 a multinational UN force arrived to relieve the 6,000 American troops still on the island. They held the volatile peace through to the end of Aristide's term in office and replacement by his chosen successor, René Préval, in 1996.

The United States had less success in influencing events in Central America. Following a ceasefire in the civil war in Nicaragua in 1987, free elections in 1990 saw the removal of the Sandinistas in favor of the moderate leader of the National Opposition Union, Violeta Chamorro, but the country was soon reeling under renewed battles between the Sandinistas and the Contras. An agreement sponsored by the UN brought a 12 year civil war in El Salvador to a close in 1992; two years later a UN Truth Commission reported that senior army officers had been responsible for the murder of thousands of citizens, but no legal action was taken. Guatemala had been torn apart by civil war between the government and left-wing rebels since a U.S.-backed coup in 1954; an estimated 100,000 had died in the fighting. In 1995, a UN mission found widespread cases of torture and killings. A fragile ceasefire was finally forged in 1996.

By the late 1990s, a lesson had been learned: the new world order could be applied when both the problem and the solution were cut and dried—but few of the world's troubles are so straightforward.

# THE LEGACY OF CONFLICT

## AMONG CONTINUING CONFLICTS SHONE BEACONS OF PEACE, ACHIEVED BY DETERMINED NEGOTIATION AND THE WILL FOR RECONCILIATION

A lesson drawn from the ancient Hindu epic, the *Ramayana*, is that the problems of the world are never completely resolved; they just go through cycles—and occasionally catastrophic ones. Humans cannot hope to halt this cycle, but they can influence the way in which it proceeds.

India itself went through troubled times in the 1980s and 1990s. In the early 1980s, the second administration of Indira Gandhi faced an increasing threat from Sikh separatists, who wanted to create an independent state of Khalistan (Land of the Pure) out of the Punjab, and were prepared to use violent terror tactics to achieve this. Over several months in early 1984, armed extremists took over the Sikhs' holiest shrine, the Golden Temple in Amritsar. On June 6, Indira Gandhi sent in the Indian army to remove them by force. Operation *Blue Star* was a success, in that the separatists were removed, but it made a martyr out of the leader Sant Jarnail Singh Bhindranwale and cost the lives of 712 other Sikhs and 90 national soldiers. This act of aggression caused indignation among the Sikh population.

The Sikhs had traditionally played a key role in the Indian army; Indira Gandhi's bodyguards were Sikhs. Against advice, she did not replace them, declaring that she trusted them. But she had misunderstood the depth of resentment felt by all Sikhs over Operation *Blue Star*. On October 31, 1984, as she walked across her garden to a meeting, her bodyguards drew their guns and assassinated her. She was succeeded by her son Rajiv, age 40. As Rajiv lit his mother's funeral pyre, anti-Sikh riots erupted across India, and at least 1,000 people died. In June 1985, an Air India flight from Toronto to London disappeared over the Atlantic with 329 people on board: Sikh extremists were suspected of sabotage, and one suspect later confessed.

Meanwhile, Sri Lanka had been plunged into civil war. The conflict stemmed from the ethnic divide, between the mainly Buddhist Sinhalese, who represented 70 percent of the population, and the mainly Muslim Tamils. After independence from

**TIGER CUBS** The Tamil Tigers recruit supporters at an early age. The government has failed to oust them from their strongholds, such as the Jaffna peninsula in the north of Sri Lanka.

Britain in 1948, the two communities shared power, but later Sinhalese-dominated governments aggravated tensions with the Tamil minority. After 1983, separatist guerrillas known as the Tamil Tigers began a campaign of violence to carve out an autonomous homeland on the north and east. In 1987 India, concerned at possible repercussions among its own Tamil population in the south, persuaded the Sri Lankan government to allow it to send peacekeeping forces to the island to impose a ceasefire on the Tamils; they caused much resentment, however, and were forced to withdraw in 1990.

In May 1991, Rajiv Gandhi was attending a political rally in the city of Madras when he was as-

**LETHAL VENGEANCE** Indira Gandhi's body was cremated in traditional Hindu fashion. She had paid the ultimate penalty for misjudging the loyalties of her Sikh bodyguards.

sassinated by a female suicide bomber, presumed to be a Tamil sympathizer. So it was that his 20-year-old son lit his father's funeral pyre, just as Rajiv had lit his mother's seven years before.

### Going nuclear

India, meanwhile, was witnessing the rapid growth of Hindu nationalist politics, exploiting the 83 percent majority held by Hindus over other religious groups across the nation. The vehemence of this movement, and its appeal to crowd instincts, was witnessed at the destruction of the Muslim mosque at Ayodhya in 1992.

The main Hindu nationalist organization was the Bharatiya Janata Party (BJP), which made ground in local elections in 1995. It joined forces with the more extreme Hindu Shiv Sena Party, which took control of Maharashtra state and altered the name of the capital to Mumbai, after the Hindu goddess Mumbhadevi. After national elections in May 1996, the BJP was able to form a coalition government under its leader Atal Behari Vajpayee,

but this lasted just 13 days, giving way to a coalition representing the poor and untouchables (the lowest caste in Indian society). A BJP-dominated coalition returned to power in 1998. The dreams of secular government cherished by the founding fathers of modern India, Gandhi and Nehru, were evaporating, and with them the fortunes of the Congress Party to which they had belonged.

To shore up its support and appeal to nationalism, the BJP sanctioned the testing of five atomic bombs under the northwestern desert in May 1998. It claimed that these tests were conducted to face off any threat from China, but they caused greater consternation to Pakistan. India and Pakistan had a long-running border dispute, notably over Kashmir, where Muslim separatists had been fighting an insurgency campaign since 1989. Pakistan responded in June with its own atomic tests.

The world beyond was at a loss over how to respond. President Clinton was currently attempting to steer the Comprehensive Test Ban Treaty through Congress: designed to prevent the proliferation of nuclear weapons, it had been signed by 149 countries, but had also to be ratified by the 44 considered capable of producing nuclear weapons. The French and British ratified it in 1998, but it looked as though the Indians and Pakistanis were taking a leaf out of the French book: test first (as the French had done, despite protests, in the Mururoa atoll in the South Pacific in 1995), then sign.

### Old sores

In some parts of the world, political strife seemed sim-

**HINDUS INFLAMED** A Hindu mob invaded the Muslim mosque at Ayodhya on December 6, 1992, and tore it down, claiming that the site was sacred to the god Rama. The resulting violence claimed some 800 lives.

ply to stagnate. The Myanmar (formerly Burma) military government held elections in 1990. Aung San Suu Kyi and her National League for Democracy were the victors by an overwhelming margin, but the military promptly annulled the elections. Suu Kyi was held under house arrest from 1989 to 1995, and her movements have been severely curtailed since. For her patient pressure for nonviolent change, she was awarded the Nobel peace prize in 1991.

The 1996 Nobel peace prize went to Bishop Carlos Belo and Jose Ramos-Horta, for their campaign to free East Timor from Indonesian rule. Since the annexation of the mainly Christian half of the island in 1975, an estimated 25 percent of the population has died through violent repression and neglect. After the fall of President Suharto in 1998, President Habibie announced in 1999 that a referendum would be held on autonomy for East Timor.

The Camp David Accords of 1978 had

**PASSIVE RESISTANCE** The Burmese military government has held the opposition leader Aung San Suu Kyi under house arrest almost permanently since 1989.

brought peace between Egypt and Israel, but the Palestinians, especially those in the occupied West Bank and Gaza, still harbored deep resentment toward Israel. In December 1987, large numbers of Palestinian citizens, many of them women and children, rose up in a prolonged revolt called the *Intifada* ("shaking off"). The Israelis were hard pressed to quell this unrest, which was fought mainly with gas bombs and stones. Over 1,000 Palestinians were killed, a quarter of them under 16 years old. An Islamic paramilitary movement called Hamas, committed to overthrowing the Israeli rule of Palestine, also emerged at this time to wage a savage campaign of violence, often perpetrated by suicide bombers.

As the Intifada continued into the 1990s, it transpired that secret negotiations had been going on between the Israeli government and the PLO, brokered by the Norwegians. Under the Washington Declaration of September 1993, Israel agreed to grant limited self-rule to the Gaza Strip and parts of the West Bank. A Palestinian Authority was set up, led by

Yasser Arafat as president. The ultimate goal was a peace accord to be agreed to by December 1998.

It represented a significant compromise for both the PLO and the Israelis. Yasser Arafat, the Israeli prime minister Yitzhak Rabin, and the foreign minister, Shimon Peres, were awarded the Nobel peace prize in 1994. But the agreement was condemned by extremists on both sides. In February 1994, in the West Bank town of Hebron, Baruch Goldstein, a Jewish settler recently arrived from America, opened fire in a crowded mosque, killing 30, before being killed himself when he ran out of ammunition. Hamas continued its terror campaign: in October 1994, a suicide bomber killed 21 on a bus in Tel Aviv. In November 1995, Yitzhak Rabin was shot dead by a young Jewish radical, Yigal Amir. "I acted alone on God's orders and have no regrets," he proclaimed. This assassination deeply shocked the nation: Jews did not kill Jews.

The peace process nonetheless went ahead, if falteringly. After the election of the

right-wing Benjamin Netanyahu in June 1996, progress seemed under threat, but new agreements were thrashed out, in talks overseen by President Bill Clinton in Washington in October 1998.

## Repression and rebellion

Two West African countries were gripped by violent turmoil in the 1990s. In 1996, Ahmed Tejan Kabbah was elected president in Sierra Leone, a nation ravaged since 1991 by warring factions. One year later he was ousted by one of the warlords, Johnny Paul Karoma, whose followers then went on the rampage, cutting off the hands of anyone who had voted in the last election. In the end, Nigeria intervened to restore Kabbah, who was also assisted by arms shipments from Britain—made in spite of UN sanctions that Britain itself had helped to draw up.

Nigeria also brokered a peaceful end to Liberia's civil war, which had raged since President Tolbert was killed in 1980. For these two for-

**NEGOTIATING TABLE** In the Wye River Agreement brokered by President Clinton in October 1998, Israel's Benjamin Netanyahu and Yasser Arafat, the Palestinian leader, signed a pact whereby Israel would withdraw from parts of the West Bank.

**2000**

1987 The *Intifada* uprising begins in Palestine

1990 Nelson Mandela released from prison

1993 The Palestinians win limited self-rule

1994 Nelson Mandela is elected president of South Africa

1995 Yitzhak Rabin is assassinated

1997 President Mobutu is ousted in Zaire

1998 The Good Friday Agreement brings prospects of peace in Northern Ireland

**MISSING** In the refugee crisis following the massacres in Rwanda in 1994, 27,000 children became separated from their families. UNICEF attempted to reunite some of them by exhibiting photographs in eastern Zaire.

eign interventions, Nigeria acquired some international credit. But the dictatorship of General Sani Abacha, president of Nigeria since 1993, was widely condemned. Nigeria had some of the world's richest oilfields, but a corrupt elite squandered their benefits while the vast majority of people remained in poverty. Abacha, while promising a return to democracy, pushed his nation ever farther from it. Opposition parties were banned, the Press gagged, and critics were imprisoned and murdered. The Social Democratic Party leader Moshood Abiola won an election in 1993, but this was annulled. In June 1994 he was arrested, and was kept in prison until his sudden death in 1998.

Abacha also waged war on the Ogoni tribe, who complained that oil exploitation in their homelands was causing an ecological disaster. After the murder of four Ogoni leaders, the Ogoni writer and human rights activist Ken Saro-Wiwa was arrested, tried and executed despite international protests. Nigeria was then expelled from the Commonwealth. Abacha died in 1998, at the age of 54. He was succeeded by the chief of the defense staff, Abdusalam Abubakar, who similarly promised a return to civilian rule.

Following the massacres in Rwanda in 1994, and the influx of millions of refugees, eastern Zaire became a cauldron of discontent. In 1997, a rebel army, the Alliance of Democratic Forces for the Liberation of Congo, rose up against the despotic regime of President Mobutu. The rebel forces, led by Laurent Kabila, swept into Kinshasa and Mobutu resigned, dying from cancer that same year. Kabila renamed Zaire the Democratic Republic of Congo. The optimism surrounding his victory soon dissipated, however. In 1998, a new wave of rebels swept in from the eastern highlands. These

were mainly Tutsis, supported by Uganda and Rwanda. They reached the outskirts of Kinshasa, before Angola and Zimbabwe intervened on behalf of Kabila and forced them back. The Democratic Republic of Congo became a power vacuum, ripe for partition by surrounding nations.

### The end of apartheid

Not all stories coming out of Africa were bad. By the late 1980s, South Africa was in deep crisis, suffering economically from international sanctions imposed to bring about an end to apartheid, and demoralized by its isolation in sports and culture. When the die-hard conservative P.W. Botha stepped down as state president in 1989, his place was taken by F.W. de Klerk, a moderate reformer who knew that something had to give. De Klerk undertook a series of initiatives to dismantle apartheid, scrapping many of its petty laws. In 1990, he lifted the 30 year ban on the African National Congress (ANC), the most vocal and active organization opposing apartheid, and ended the state of emergency that had been in force since 1985. He also freed the ANC's most famous prisoner, Nelson Mandela. The last of the apartheid laws was scrapped in February 1991. The international community responded by lifting sanctions. A series of talks began between the National Party government and the ANC, resulting in a decision to hold free, all-race, multi-party elections. F.W. de Klerk had effectively negotiated away white supremacy, for in one-person, one-vote elections the ANC would clearly win.

On election day, April 27, 1994, millions of black South Africans voted in national elections for the first time in their lives. The result was an overwhelming victory for the ANC, with 62.6 percent of the vote. Nelson Mandela became president, leading a government of national unity. The following years proved difficult, with rising crime rates and growing despondency among whites,

**FIRST-TIME VOTER   A Zulu casts his vote in South Africa's first fully democratic elections.**

but, given the inequalities arising from decades of apartheid, the transition was relatively peaceful.

The achievement of a peaceful transition in South Africa was an inspiration to other nations riven by sectarian divides. In the late 1980s, Northern Ireland was trapped in a seemingly endless cycle of terrorist violence. It was clear to John Major, the British prime minister, that Britain could not hope to suppress the IRA by force, and it was clear to the Sinn Fein leaders that the IRA would never remove the British from Northern

Ireland by military means. As a way out of the impasse, John Hume, leader of the Social Democrat and Labor Party (SDLP), a nonviolent Catholic party, began negotiations with Gerry Adams and other leaders of Sinn Fein. The British Government likewise held secret talks with Sinn Fein.

On December 15, 1993, John Major and the Irish prime minister Albert Reynolds proclaimed the Downing Street Declaration: this set out a plan for peace talks between London and Dublin and representatives from Northern Ireland including Sinn Fein, if the IRA could be persuaded to renounce violence. The IRA eventually announced a ceasefire on August 31, 1994; the main loyalist groups followed suit on October 13. Official negotiations now took place, and Gerry Adams, the leader of Sinn Fein, was fêted by President Clinton at the White House at a St. Patrick's Day celebration in March 1995. The talks, however, ran into the sand, and Sinn Fein

## NELSON MANDELA—DEFEATING APARTHEID

In 1990, after 27 years in jail as a political prisoner, Nelson Mandela, now a white-haired man of 71, appeared before the public and declared: "I greet you in the name of peace, democracy and freedom for all."

Born in 1918, Mandela trained as a lawyer and set up the first black-only legal practice in Johannesburg during the 1940s. Confronting the injustices of institutionalized segregation daily, he joined the African National Congress (ANC), which at that time preached nonviolent protest. After the Sharpeville Massacre of 1960, and the banning of the ANC, Mandela formed Spear of the Nation, which adopted guerrilla tactics. In 1962 he was arrested and tried. Facing the death sentence for advocating sabotage, he made a declaration from the dock: "During my lifetime I have dedicated myself to the struggle of the African people. I have fought against white domination, I have fought against black domination. I have cherished the ideal of a democratic and free society in which all persons live together in harmony and with equal opportunities. It is an ideal which I hope to live for and to achieve. But, if need be, it is an ideal for which I am prepared to die." He was sent to Robben Island, a penal settlement for political prisoners.

In 1989 a new state president, F.W. de Klerk, softened the government line on apartheid, and on February 11, 1990, Mandela was released. The legitimized ANC and the government agreed on a procedure for the transition to democracy and majority rule. Mandela and F.W. de Klerk were awarded the Nobel peace prize in 1993. In the election in 1994 the ANC gained power, and Mandela, as its leader, became president.

**INSPIRATIONAL LEADER   Mandela won international acclaim through his blend of honesty and affability and his lack of vindictiveness even after 27 years in prison.**

CONTINUING CARNAGE  On August 15, 1998, with the Good Friday Agreement not yet six months old, a bomb exploded in a busy street in Omagh, Northern Ireland, killing 28 people.

abandoned them in June. Then, on February 9, 1996, the IRA signaled the end of their 17 month ceasefire by detonating a huge bomb in London's Docklands, killing two. A bomb in June that year devastated the center of Manchester, injuring 228.

Talks resumed after the Labor Party, led by Prime Minister Tony Blair, came to power in May 1997. Sinn Fein was again drawn in from the cold. After negotiations with all parties, involving the intervention of President Clinton, a solution was hammered out and announced on Good Friday, April 10, 1998. Under the Good Friday Agreement, a 108 seat elected Northern Ireland Assembly would run the day-to-day affairs of the province, while the British-Irish Council and a cross-border body would help to bind the United Kingdom and the Irish Republic into the agreement. The Irish government agreed to release its constitutional claim to Northern Ireland, and the British Government would have to allow all Ireland to unite if the people of the North voted for it.

A referendum held in both parts of Ireland in May 1998 showed approval for the agreement by 94 percent of the votes, although the turnout was just 56 percent. In June elections, the members of the new assembly were chosen. David Trimble, leader of the Ulster Unionists, became first minister. After nearly 30 years of turmoil in which 3,249 people had been killed, there was a real prospect of peace.

Those who predicted that peace could never be so easily won had their prejudices confirmed during a demonstration in August by 5,000 Protestant Orangemen, who had been banned from making a traditional march down the Catholic Gavaghy Road at Drumcree. During a tense stand-off with the military, a bomb was pushed through the door of a Catholic home in a predominantly Protestant area of Ballymoney, and three young boys died. In August, a huge bomb exploded in Omagh, killing 28. A breakaway republican movement called the Real IRA claimed responsibility.

In October 1998, David Trimble and John Hume were awarded the Nobel peace prize. One year after the Good Friday Agreement, however, the establishment of a devolved Northern Ireland Assembly still hung in the balance, as the Unionists refused to share power with Sinn Fein, backed, as they saw it, by the threat of IRA guns.

## THE MOTHERS OF THE DISAPPEARED

Every Thursday a group of women gathers in the Plaza de Mayo in central Buenos Aires and parades in a circle within sight of the presidential palace, as they have done since 1977. On their heads they wear white kerchiefs, each embroidered with the names of their children, and the date on which they disappeared.

In 1976, a military dictatorship led by General Jorge Videla seized power in Argentina. The country was racked by political turmoil, and the violent campaign of the left-wing Montoneros guerrillas. The generals cracked down hard on all opposition, especially the university students and young professionals who expressed any sympathy for the Left. Their critics called it the dirty war. At least 15,000 people (some say 30,000) disappeared—imprisoned, tortured, summarily executed or assassinated by death squads. Faced with silence about the fate of their children, the mothers began their dignified protest. It transpired that young children of the junta's victims had been handed out for adoption to the police and the military.

The desire of the Mothers of the Disappeared for the truth was dealt a blow in 1990 when President Carlos Menem, in the interests of political stability, pardoned the generals and they were released from prison. However, in 1998 a judge ruled that this should not include crimes against children, and General Jorge Videla was rearrested to stand trial.

CONSCIENCE OF THE NATION  Mothers demand to know the fate of their children and their grandchildren.

### Democracy in South America

By the late 1990s, there was only one country in Latin America that was not a democracy: Cuba. Although some of these democracies teetered on the edge of domestic turmoil and military intervention, this nonetheless represented a remarkable turnaround from the 1970s and 1980s. Democracy had come to Argentina in 1983, Brazil in 1985, Chile and Paraguay in 1989, Nicaragua and Panama in 1990, and Uruguay in 1995.

In Argentina the military dictatorship had gone from bad to worse after General Jorge Videla left office in 1981 to give way to Major-General Roberto Viola. After nine months, he was ousted by hardliners and replaced by General Leopoldo Galtieri, who in 1982 undertook the ill-judged military adventure of seizing the Falkland Islands. The British responded with force, and three days after the Argentine army's defeat, Galtieri resigned. His successor paved the way for free elections, which took place on October 30, 1983, and civilian rule resumed, albeit amid the economic and political chaos inherited from the generals. The military leaders were subsequently tried, and many of them were given life sentences, but they were released under an amnesty introduced by President Carlos Menem in 1990.

In Chile the rule of General Pinochet came to a close in 1989, when he introduced free elections. These were won by Patricio Aylwyn, of the Christian Democratic Party, who took office in 1990. The military, however, remained a potent force, and Pinochet created a role for himself as senator for life. This was considered an acceptable compromise by many in return for stability, democracy and the burgeoning economy. However, Pinochet's record of human rights abuses still rankled with those who had borne the brunt of it: after the violent removal of President Allende, some 3,200 people had died, and 1,100 had disappeared. For this reason, General Pinochet was detained in a London hospital in October 1998, following a request by a Spanish magistrate to have him extradited to face allegations about the disappearances of Spanish nationals in Chile during his rule. It caused a major diplomatic incident, and raised questions over the degree to which dictators should be made to answer for the abuses of their regimes.

The specter of left-wing terrorism in South America did not disappear. In 1992, the leader of the Shining Path guerrilla movement in Peru, Abimael Guzmán, was captured, but the Shining Path continued to terrorize rural villages. On December 17, 1996, 20 members of the Maoist Túpac Amaru Revolutionary Movement seized the Japanese embassy in Lima in an attempt to secure the release of political prisoners. They took hostage hundreds of dignitaries attending celebrations in honor of Emperor Akihito's birthday. President Alberto Fujimori refused to negotiate, and brought the siege to a dramatic conclusion in April 1997, when armed forces released the remaining 72 hostages, with just one casualty. As ever, there was another side to the story. In May, 1996, Amnesty International had published a report claiming that the Peruvian government had unjustly imprisoned thousands of suspected terrorists.

## CONFLICT IN KOSOVO

America's intervention in Kosovo in 1999 generated much controversy and media attention. From March to June 1999, the United States and its military allies in the North Atlantic Treaty Organization (NATO) fought a war over an area about the size of greater Los Angeles. Though this area was small, the political implications of the bombing were extensive. NATO had never attempted war on its own, so the Kosovo conflict tested the alliance militarily for the first time. This conflict was also one of the first wars inspired, at least in theory, by humanitarian motives as much as by strategic or geopolitical considerations. There were no oilfields to defend in Kosovo, as in Kuwait in 1991 during the Persian Gulf War. NATO launched its bombing campaign in defense of Kosovo's ethnic Albanian population, which was being brutalized by Serbian police, paramilitaries, and Federal Republic of Yugoslavia (FRY) army troops.

NATO's air campaign began after the collapse of negotiations over Kosovo with president Slobodan Milosevic. For more than a decade, tensions had been building in Kosovo, where the ethnic Albanian majority was subject to discrimination and mistreatment. Milosevic ordered a fierce counteroffensive against an

**CASUALTIES OF WAR** An ethnic Albanian sits next to 23 bodies of ethnic Albanians shot in the village of Racak (above). Serb forces move with their tanks en route to Pec in the western part of Kosovo. The Serb forces are withdrawing following the threat of a NATO attack (right).

armed Kosovo Albanian resistance movement, the Kosovo Liberation Army (KLA), which was fighting for independence. Thousands of Kosovar Albanians

were driven from their homes or killed. Diplomats from the U.S. and Europe foresaw a massive humanitarian crisis that could destabilize all of southeastern Europe. With Russian assistance, a peace plan was drawn up that called for the deployment of a large international peacekeeping force in Kosovo. When Milosevic rejected the peace plan, NATO launched its attack.

Meanwhile, Milosevic ordered his security forces to sweep across Kosovo, uprooting the ethnic Albanian population in an attempt to wipe out the rebels. Hundreds of thousands of civilians were driven from their homes, their villages burned or looted. Whether the U.S. should have intervened in this conflict or not has elicited serious debate. Many feared the U.S. was acting as a "global policeman," while others doubted that a NATO intervention could stop any ongoing civil war.

# THE NEW MILLENNIUM

## AS THE NEW MILLENNIUM DAWNS, IS THE WORLD HEADING FOR TECHNOLOGICAL HEAVEN OR GLOBAL DYSFUNCTION?

The approach of the end of the twentieth century was greeted with mounting excitement, fueled by the global media that had itself been such a feature of the century. But the end of the century also marked the beginning of a new millennium. As technology raced ahead at unprecedented speed, opening up countless new horizons—some inviting, others disturbing—would this be a major turning point in history?

The economic prospects did not look so rosy. Instead of a bright, brave new world, in 1997 Professor John Gray of the London School of Economics forecast "a tragic epoch, in which anarchic forces and shrinking world resources drag sovereign states into ever more dangerous rivalries." The problem, as he saw it, was the spread of unregulated, laissez-faire market economies—the kind that had been in fashion during the 1980s and 1990s. But market efficacy was promoted at the expense of social concerns. Those countries that built

welfare safety nets into their economies could not compete against economies that had not burdened themselves with state responsibility for looking after people. In other words, the endless striving for market efficiency would inevitably have a social cost, which would end in unrest.

This scenario began to look all too possible as the world economy began to unravel in 1997, but the problems arose in the very places that had been hailed as models for developing nations—the "Tiger economies." In May that year, Thailand's economy began to falter; by July the Thai currency, the baht, had lost 18 percent of its value on the foreign exchanges. Investors began to pull out their money; the Philippines floated the peso. The International Monetary Fund (IMF) began an unprecedented series of loans to help bail out the faltering economies, with $17.2 billion to Thailand and $1.1 billion to the Philippines. In August Indonesia floated the rupiah, and the Malaysian ringgit and the Singapore dollar came under severe pressure. In October, the IMF stepped in to rescue Indonesia with a $23 billion package, but this could not prevent 16 Indonesian banks collapsing in November. Japan—the world's second-largest economy—was also caught in the tailspin. The banks, whose value was propped up by shares, headed for bankruptcy as share prices tumbled. In December South Korea had to negotiate an IMF loan of $57 billion.

The collapse seemed unstoppable. In Indonesia, government cutbacks, rising prices and the bankruptcy of savings funds led to widespread rioting in March 1998. Much of

**DESPONDENCY** Throughout 1998, traders at the Tokyo Stock Exchange watched their stock values drop away, before prices began to bottom out at the end of the year.

## VISION OF A BLEAK WORLD

Science fiction began more than 100 years ago with Jules Verne's *Twenty Thousand Leagues Under the Sea* (1870). Since then, it has grown with the century. Its fascination rests in the mixture of imaginative and readable plots, and fantasy coupled with plausibility. Extrapolations of technological advances play a central role; whether or not these deliver progress or happiness is a key issue.

One of the most celebrated science-fiction movies is *Blade Runner*

**DYSFUNCTIONAL FUTURE** *Blade Runner* portrays a technologically advanced but decaying urban world.

(1982), directed by Ridley Scott, and based on the novel by Philip K. Dick, *Do Androids Dream of Electric Sheep?* Harrison Ford plays the role of Rick Deckard, a blade runner (police officer) in Los Angeles in the year 2019. The human race has expanded into space, and uses human-like robots called "replicants" to reach distant colonies. After a mutiny by replicants, all are to be recalled and dismantled—but some have hijacked a spacecraft. It is Deckard's job to hunt them down across Los Angeles, which, for all its technological wizardry, is a bleak and decaying environment. At the heart of the film are questions that were causing concern as the 20th century closed: as more functions are handed over to machines, at what point do we risk losing control to them? And could technological progress lead to meaninglessness and despair?

this was directed at the country's ethnic Chinese community, who controlled large sectors of the economy, and also at the family of President Suharto, who owned controlling interests in industries, essential amenities such as water, and financial services. Suharto was forced out of office in

**PROTEST IN INDONESIA** Spearheading the rebellion against President Suharto in 1998 were 3,000 students who occupied the parliament buildings for a week.

May, 31 years after seizing power, and replaced by Bucharuddin Habibie.

By now the "Asian flu" had spread; the buzzword was "contagion." Russia was the next domino in the line. It needed a $22.2 billion rescue loan in July 1998, and a further $4.8 billion in August as the rouble was devalued. Soldiers and industrial and public-sector workers across the country went

unpaid for months. Russians began to despair of the market economy and democracy. As its coffers began to run low, the IMF came in for criticism for making hasty loans that had been squandered by corrupt or inept governments.

Brazil, with the largest economy in South America, but propped up by short-term loans, now suffered a rapid flight of capital. Even with interest rates raised to 50 percent, millions were being withdrawn from Brazilian banks every day. By September 1998, its foreign debt had reached $260 billion. Suddenly, the new millennium looked far less appealing than it had in 1996. But the millennium is just a date—a date on the

**HANGING ON** President Suharto addresses the Indonesian parliament in March 1998, in the midst of financial turmoil. Two months later he was forced out of office.

Christian calendar marking the birth of Christ, which in any case is now believed to have taken place in 4 BC. It is not a turning point that economic cycles would respect.

## Blasts from the past

Nonetheless, the millennium provided cause for reflection, a search for patterns in the past. As the international stock markets tumbled in 1998, there was talk of a 1929 type crash and an ensuing recession lasting a decade, like the Great Depression. And at the sudden death of Princess Diana in 1997, Britain experienced an outpouring of grief that recalled the funeral of Queen Victoria at the beginning of the century.

In July 1998 the remains of Tsar Nicholas II, his wife Alexandra and three of their

1997 Thailand's economy falters; Princess Diana dies

1998 The Tsar is reburied; Anti-American bombs explode in Nairobi and Dar es Salaam

1999 World population reaches 6 billion

2000 Chaos is threatened by the "millennium bug"

## THE DEATH OF A PRINCESS

In the first week of September 1997, flowers were stacked waist high around Kensington Palace in memory of Diana, Princess of Wales, killed days before in a car accident. The Princess had become an icon of her age. Married in 1981,

**OUTLAWING LANDMINES** One of Princess Diana's last and best-publicized campaigns was for a worldwide ban on landmines.

at the age of 20, to Prince Charles, the heir to the British throne, she had produced two sons and grown in beauty with maturity.

Yet what seemed like a charmed life was clouded by misery: divorced parents in childhood, an unfaithful husband, eating disorders, separation and loneliness—all before a press hungry for photographs and scandal. Reviled by many in the establishment, she was revered by thousands who had experienced her common touch in her public engagements and through her charity work. She embraced with affection the sick, the malnourished and the distraught. Above all, she went public about her vulnerability.

Her death came at a moment when she appeared to have found happiness with Dodi Fayed, son of Egyptian tycoon Mohammed Fayed. Their car, chased by photographers, crashed into a pillar in a Paris underpass.

Like her life, Diana's funeral was exposed to the full glare of the media, watched on television around the world.

daughters (the bodies of Alexei and Marie have never been traced) were carried in coffins draped with the imperial flag and laid to rest in the Peter and Paul Fortress in St. Petersburg—producing distant echoes of pre-Revolutionary Russia. Only after the collapse of communism in 1990 could this have been possible—and even in 1998 the Russian state, still not officially accepting the Romanov family's murder, referred to their remains simply as the noncommittal "Ekaterinburg bodies."

Other sinister events, such as the rise of neo-Nazism and anti-Semitism, especially in the countries of eastern Europe, recalled

**EIGHTY YEARS LATER** The reburial of the bodies of the Russian imperial family, assassinated in 1918, caused mixed emotions in a nation struggling to fathom its communist legacy.

dark eras of the past, not yet buried. In May 1998, a synagogue in Moscow was bombed. In July 1998, neo-Nazis from Germany attacked French police in an organized attempt to disrupt the World Cup soccer competition.

The ghost of the 1918 Spanish flu epidemic was raised in 1997. Flu viruses constantly mutate, creating new forms to which, sometimes, humans have little resistance. The 1918 epidemic spread rapidly around the world and killed over 20 million people. Virologists are

**SOLEMN FAREWELL** A note on a wreath on Princess Diana's coffin spelled out the human story behind the public one. It read: "Mummy."

permanently on the lookout for new and lethal mutations, and one was detected in Hong Kong in May of 1997. It stemmed from the large chicken population, which had been decimated by a flu virus, and several human deaths had occurred. It was decided that all of Hong Kong's chickens should be exterminated—a policy that was much derided at the time, but which may in fact have saved the lives of millions of people.

## Into the future

We cannot always look over our shoulders as time passes. New generations come to deal with new circumstances, which do not always have reverberations from the past. Many countries are now ruled by people who were born after the Second World War, postwar "baby boomers," such as President Bill Clinton (born in 1946), and British Prime Minister Tony Blair (born in 1953), bringing with them new, changed perspectives. They face some issues that are entirely new, without precedent. In the mid 1990s, computer experts alerted the world to a potential catastrophe: the "millennium bug." Because computers used only two digits to signal the year (the last two), they would interpret the year 2000 as 1900, and all time-based calculations would be erroneously restructured accordingly. This had major implications for all computer systems, in banks, hospitals, reservations offices, pension funds and so on—indeed, a complete collapse of the global network of computers threatened the world. Fighting the "millennium bug" involved intricate and expensive adjustments, costing the world close to $600 billion between 1996 and the year 2000.

The computer is unquestionably destined to play a key role in the new century. Voice recognition by computers, and the ability of programs to decipher handwriting, may well have a significant impact and will certainly reduce the role played by the keyboard. If it is possible for computers to interpret the human voice accurately, it should also be possible to make other machines respond to voiced instructions, such as video recorders, washing machines, thermostats, even equipment designed to lock doors and close curtains. The car of the future is likely to be computer-programmed, perhaps assisted by

**TRANSATLANTIC CONNECTIONS  President Clinton and Prime Minister Blair maintained a mutual support that was called on in dealing with Northern Ireland and Iraq.**

global satellite navigation systems, dispensing with the need to have a driver at all. With a projected increase in cars to a global total of 1 billion by the year 2021, this may be the only feasible way of negotiating the busy streets. Humans will be replaced by computer-operated robots on factory assembly lines, certainly in the wealthier industrial nations. Digital broadcasting, meanwhile, will deliver into the home a vast array of information, communications and entertainment, increasingly tailored to personal requirements. Global media networks are also likely to homogenize the world.

Computer chips embedded under the skin could take the place of identity cards and passports. Of course, this would have major implications for the liberty of the individual. The issue of government control, and the fear of "Big Brother," remains a central concern in democracies as information is standardized and centralized.

Weapons are destined to become increasingly "smart"—clinical for the user but deadly to the recipient. In August 1998, terrorist bombs were detonated near the American embassies in Nairobi and Dar es Salaam.

**IMPEACHMENT  On December 19, 1998, President Clinton was impeached for perjury and obstruction of justice over his affair with the White House intern Monica Lewinsky. The articles of impeachment were rejected by the Senate on February 12, 1999.**

They were believed to be the work of groups organized by a millionaire Saudi Arabian called Osama bin Laden, who harbored a deep-seated hatred for all things American. In response, President Clinton ordered a missile attack on two targets: a chemical factory in Sudan, said to be a source of poison gas, and bin Laden's bases in Afghanistan. Both places were reached by computer-programmed and guided Tomahawk missiles, with little risk to United States military personnel—except in revenge attacks. This remote-control form of destruction could represent the war of the future. Indeed, at the time of the attack, the targets seemed so remote and so swiftly dealt with that most of the world's press soon returned once more to a concurrent story—Bill Clinton's sexual affair with the young White House intern Monica Lewinsky.

At some time in the not-too-distant future, computers will become intelligent—able to use programmed information to make judgments and decisions. At this point, human-like robots may be developed to do tedious work, such as housework or mowing the lawn, thus permitting people greater leisure time. Like the "replicants" in the movie *Blade Runner*, robots may also be able to take spacecraft to distant stars while human passengers remain suspended in a form of hibernation. Some more outrageous predictions even suggest that humans may become obsolete and redundant in a robotic world striving for perfect order and organization.

Medicine, meanwhile, will have moved forward in leaps and bounds, with the benefits of biotechnology producing new drugs and even replacement limbs. The average

**STEERING INTO THE FUTURE** The Sirius in-car navigation system provides warning of a traffic jam (red line). Computers may be able to do the work of drivers within two decades.

human life span is projected to grow from a worldwide average of 62 for men and 65 for women in 1998 to 73 for men and 78 for women in 2045—although some projections suggest figures of around 140 by that time. Over the next 50 years, the number of people over 65 will rise to over 15 percent of the world population, two and a half times the current percentage.

But will such projections ever come to pass in a world that may simply grind to a halt under the weight of massively expanding populations? At the time of the 1918 flu epidemic there were an estimated 1.6 billion people in the world. By 1999, that figure had grown to 6 billion—and the last billion had been added in just 12 years. By the year 2050, according to UN estimates, there will be 9.4 billion people in the world. Are there enough resources to feed and support these numbers, let alone to grant them the kind of rights and material comforts

**REMOTE-CONTROL MEDICINE** A medical technician simulates robot-aided brain surgery.

that the industrialized world deems to be essential for dignified existence?

To produce such material comforts, the world will need to keep consuming energy, pumping carbon dioxide and other "greenhouse gases" into the atmosphere. The Earth is already warming up: world temperatures are rising, and the ice caps are melting, causing sea levels to rise and flood coastal settlements. The jury is still out as to whether this warming is caused by the greenhouse effect, or by long-term weather cycles as we emerge from the last mini ice age. If it is the former, the prospects of remedial action look grim, particularly in a world of unregulated market economies, where commercial efficiency tends to take precedence over environmental considerations.

Is the future bright, or gloomy? On the one hand, the human race appears to have the technological potential to impose perfect control and acquire all human comforts—which in itself may have nightmarish implications. On the other hand, population growth, pollution and weapons of mass destruction threaten total breakdown.

In June 1998, the British theoretical physicist Stephen Hawking addressed a meeting of the White House Millennium Council, using computer-assisted speech to overcome the severe disabilities of degenerative neuromuscular disease. He opened his lecture by complaining that visions of the world tended to

show a place where "science, technology, and the organization of society, are supposed to have achieved a level of near perfection." He continued: "I want to question this picture and ask if we will ever reach a final steady state of science and technology. At no time in the 10,000 years or so since the last Ice Age has the human race been in a state of constant knowledge and fixed technology."

In 1900, the idea of putting a man on the Moon seemed like pure science fiction, yet it was achieved 69 years later. In 1970, few people believe that interlinked computers would be used in millions of homes around the world, yet this had happened a quarter of a century later. The pace of change in technology is constantly accelerating. By 2025, the world will probably contain countless life-changing inventions that none of us had dreamed of in the year 2000.

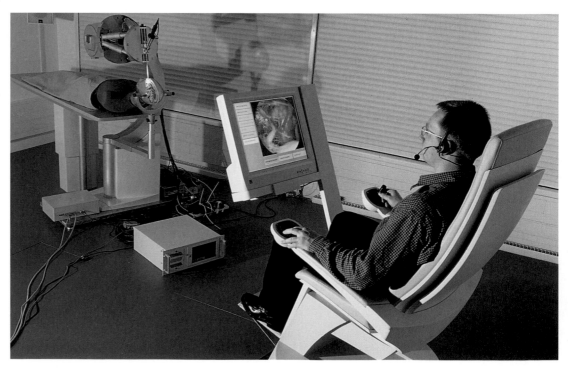

# TIMECHART

## 1970

### JANUARY

**1** The **age of majority** and voting age in Britain is reduced from 21 to 18.

**15** Nigeria accepts the unconditional surrender of **Biafra**, following a brutal war of attrition.

**23** The first 747 **jumbo jet** crosses the Atlantic to land at Heathrow, heralding a new era of mass air travel.

### FEBRUARY

**11** A nine-year war against the **Kurds** ends as Iraq grants them autonomy.

**18** In Cambodia, Prince Norodom Sihanouk is overthrown by **General Lon Nol**. Sihanouk joins the communist rebels, the Khmer Rouge.

**25** The abstract expressionist painter **Mark Rothko** commits suicide, at the age of 66.

### APRIL

**17** The three **Apollo 13** astronauts return safely to Earth following an on-board explosion in space.

### MAY

**4** Four students, protesting against the invasion of Cambodia, are killed at **Kent State University**, Ohio.

### JUNE

**19** The Conservative leader **Edward Heath** becomes British prime minister after a surprise victory over the Labor Party led by Harold Wilson.

### JULY

**27** The revue *Oh! Calcutta* challenges British censorship laws by presenting nude ballet on stage.

### SEPTEMBER

**12** Palestinian terrorists destroy three **hijacked airliners** in Jordan, then release their last hostages in exchange for seven imprisoned colleagues.

**18** Rock guitarist **Jimi Hendrix** dies, age 27.

**28 Gamal Abdel Nasser**, president of Egypt since 1956, dies, age 52. He is succeeded by the vice-president, Anwar Sadat.

### OCTOBER

**5 Salvador Allende** becomes president of Chile, the first communist to be democratically elected as head of state.

**8** Germaine Greer publishes her controversial feminist book, *The Female Eunuch*.

**9** The Soviet writer **Alexandr Solzhenitsyn** is awarded the Nobel prize for literature, but dares not travel to Stockholm to receive it.

**10 Fiji** becomes independent, from Britain.

**18** In Canada, the body of Pierre Laporte, the Quebec minister of labor, is found, the victim of kidnap by the separatist **Front de Libération du Québec**.

**19** Test drilling proves that the **North Sea** contains major reserves of accessible oil and natural gas.

### NOVEMBER

**9** Former president of France **Charles de Gaulle** dies, age 79.

**12 Hafez al-Assad** becomes president of Syria after the military wing of the Ba'ath Party seizes power.

**27** Britain's first **Gay Liberation Front** demonstration takes place in London.

## 1971

### JANUARY

**14** An **Angry Brigade** bomb explodes in the home of the British secretary of state for employment.

**15** The **Aswan High Dam** in Egypt is inaugurated after 11 years of construction.

**24** General **Idi Amin** becomes president of Uganda after leading a military coup to oust Milton Obote.

### FEBRUARY

**9** The first British soldier is killed in **Northern Ireland** since the troubles began in 1969.

**15** Britain introduces its new **decimal currency**.

### MARCH

**25** West Pakistan launches an attack on Dhaka, capital of **East Pakistan**, in an attempt to suppress violent demonstrations for independence. Two million refugees flee into neighboring India.

**29** Lieutenant William Calley is sentenced to life imprisonment for his part in the **My Lai massacre** in Vietnam in 1968.

**ELIMINATED  Lin Biao was a potential successor to Mao Zedong until he was killed in a plane crash.**
**Background: The first jumbo jet comes in to land at Heathrow on its inaugural passenger flight.**

### APRIL

**6** The Russian-born composer **Igor Stravinsky** dies, age 88.

**21 Papa Doc Duvalier**, dictator of Haiti, dies at 63 and is replaced by his son, Jean-Claude (Baby Doc).

**Hot pants** become the latest fashion in a trend toward revealing clothing.

China invites the U.S. and other Western nations to take part in a table-tennis tournament, signaling a willingness to break out of its isolation through **ping-pong diplomacy**.

### MAY

**20** Video cassette recorders for domestic use go on sale in Britain.

### JUNE

**30** Three **Soviet cosmonauts die** during their return journey from the Salyut space laboratory.

### JULY

**3 Jim Morrison**, charismatic singer for The Doors, dies in Paris, age 27.

**26** Riot police are called onto beaches in the French Riviera to try to suppress **topless bathing**.

**31** Astronauts on the *Apollo 14* mission explore the Moon's surface using a **Moon Rover** vehicle.

**Henry Kissinger**, assistant national security adviser to President Nixon, travels in secret to China to open the path toward rapprochement.

### AUGUST

**9** The British introduce **internment without trial** in Northern Ireland.

### SEPTEMBER

**11 Nikita Khrushchev**, Soviet premier 1958-64, dies at 77.

**13 Lin Biao**, once groomed to be the successor to Mao Zedong, dies mysteriously in a plane crash, allegedly while fleeing to the Soviet Union.

**24** Britain expels 90 Soviet diplomats accused of **spying**.

### OCTOBER

**13** The hit musical *Jesus Christ Superstar*, by Andrew Lloyd Webber and Tim Rice, has its opening night in New York City.

### DECEMBER

**17** After a two-week campaign by invasion forces from India, West Pakistan capitulates and East Pakistan becomes independent **Bangladesh**.

Intel introduces a **silicon chip** containing 2,300 transistors. It is considered the first commercially viable microprocessor.

Urban violence is the theme of several of the year's most noted movies, among which are *The French Connection* and Stanley Kubrick's *A Clockwork Orange*.

# 1972

## JANUARY

**1** Austrian diplomat **Kurt Waldheim** becomes secretary-general of the UN, replacing U Thant of Burma.

**22** Britain, Denmark, and Ireland sign the Treaty of Rome, in preparation for joining the **European Community**.

**LEGEND** Pablo Picasso was one of the great innovators of 20th-century art. He first made his mark with Cubism back in 1907.

**30** On **Bloody Sunday** in Northern Ireland, 13 Catholic demonstrators are killed by British paratroopers.

## FEBRUARY

**21** President Richard Nixon begins his week-long official **visit to China**, considered a major step in superpower realignment and détente.

## MARCH

**25** The British Government decides to suspend Northern Ireland's assembly at **Stormont** and assumes direct rule over the province.

## MAY

**29** The first **SALT agreement**, restricting anti-ballistic missile sites and freezing the growth of

intercontinental ballistic missiles, is signed by President Nixon and the Soviet leader Leonid Brezhnev in Moscow.

**30** Three terrorists from the Japanese **Red Army** kill 25 with machine guns and grenades at Tel Aviv airport.

## JUNE

**16** Five burglars are caught in an attempt to raid the Democratic Party election headquarters in the **Watergate** complex in Washington DC. It transpires that they have connections with the White House.

## AUGUST

**6** President Idi Amin announces that some 50,000 **Ugandan Asians** holding British passports will be expelled from Uganda.

**12** The last U.S. ground combat **troops leave Vietnam**.

## SEPTEMBER

**5** Palestinian terrorists seize 10 Israeli hostages during the **Olympic Games in Munich**, Germany. Nine hostages are killed during a bungled attempt to rescue them at a nearby airfield.

## NOVEMBER

**7 Richard Nixon** is re-elected president by a landslide.

## DECEMBER

**7** *Apollo 17* performs the **last manned Moon landing** of the century.

**17** The massive **Christmas bombing campaign** of North Vietnam by the U.S. air force brings widespread condemnation.

**23** An **earthquake in Managua**, Nicaragua, kills 6,000.

**26 Harry S Truman**, president from 1945-53, dies, age 88.

**29** The survivors of a **plane crash in the Andes** in October admit that they ate the remains of dead fellow passengers in order to survive.

Hollywood icon **Marlon Brando** stars in the much acclaimed mafia history *The Godfather*, then surprises the film-going public with his role in

the sexually explicit *Last Tango in Paris*, directed by Bernardo Bertolucci.

**David Bowie** produces *The Rise and Fall of Ziggy Stardust and the Spiders from Mars*, representing the more intellectual arm of glam rock. Less publicized is *Catch a Fire*, the first album by **Bob Marley** and the Wailers with Island Records, which launches reggae on the world market.

Texas Instruments produces the **first pocket calculator**; and *Pong*, the **first electronic video game**, is launched.

# 1973

## JANUARY

**21 Lyndon B. Johnson**, president from 1963-9, dies, age 64.

**23** A **ceasefire agreement** between the U.S. and North Vietnam is signed in Paris.

## APRIL

**8** The Spanish artist **Pablo Picasso** dies at 91.

## MAY

**4** The **Sears Tower** in Chicago is topped out, becoming the world's tallest building at 1,454 feet, taking the title from the World Trade Center in New York, which was dedicated just one month before.

**8** Sioux members of the American Indian Movement end their 72 day siege of **Wounded Knee** in South Dakota.

**14** The U.S. space station **Skylab** is launched.

## JUNE

**4** A prototype of the **Soviet supersonic airliner** Tupolev TU-144 crashes at the Paris airshow.

## JULY

**17** It is revealed that President Nixon has taped all his conversations in the Oval Office, and therefore has evidence about his role in the **Watergate scandal**.

**19 Bruce Lee**, the Chinese-American star of the hugely popular

kung-fu movies, such as *Enter the Dragon* (1973), dies, age 32.

## SEPTEMBER

**2 J.R.R. Tolkien**, British author of *The Lord of the Rings*, dies, age 81.

**11 President Allende** of Chile dies in a military coup led by General Augusto Pinochet.

**28** The British poet **W.H. Auden** dies at 66.

## OCTOBER

**6** Syria and Egypt launch a surprise attack on Israel during the Jewish festival of **Yom Kippur**, but are repulsed after initial successes.

**10** The U.S. vice president, **Spiro Agnew**, resigns in the face of charges of extortion, bribery and tax fraud when governor of Maryland. He is replaced by Gerald Ford.

**17** The Organization of the Petroleum Exporting Countries (OPEC) raises crude oil prices by 70 percent and places an **oil embargo** on the U.S. and other countries that have assisted Israel. This marks the start of the oil crisis, triggering a world recession.

**20** In the so-called **Saturday Night Massacre**, Nixon forces the resignation of his attorney general, his deputy attorney general and a special prosecutor as the Watergate scandal envelopes the White House.

**22** The great Spanish cellist **Pablo Casals** dies at 96.

**26** President Nixon places **U.S. forces on worldwide alert** in response to the threat of intervention by the U.S.S.R. on behalf of Arabs in the war against Israel.

## NOVEMBER

**11** After extensive **shuttle diplomacy** by the U.S. secretary of state, Henry Kissinger, Israel and Egypt sign a ceasefire agreement.

**25** Right-wing **Greek generals** overthrow the government of Colonel George Papadopoulos.

## DECEMBER

Universal Product Codes, or **bar codes,** are patented in the U.S.

# 1974

## JANUARY

**6** In Britain, **professional soccer** is played on a Sunday for the first time.

## FEBRUARY

**14** The dissident Soviet writer **Alexandr Solzhenitsyn** is exiled to West Germany.

## MARCH

**5** The Labor Party leader **Harold Wilson** becomes British prime minister for the third time, after forming a coalition with the Liberals.

**9** The **Japanese soldier** Lieutenant Hiroo Onoda surrenders in the Philippines, unaware for nearly 30 years that the war had ended.

**10** Police are called to the University of Delaware to put a stop to the new fad of **streaking**.

Chinese farmers in Xi'an stumble upon the clay soldiers that form the 2,000-year-old **terracotta army**.

## APRIL

**2 Georges Pompidou**, president of France, dies at 62, while in office.

**25** In a **coup in Portugal**, the right-wing regime of Marcello Caetano is overthrown by leftist military officers.

## MAY

**6** The respected German chancellor **Willy Brandt** is forced to resign after it is revealed that one of his close aides is an East German spy.

**19 Valéry Giscard d'Estaing** is elected president of France.

## JUNE

**17** An **IRA bomb** wrecks the 877-year-old Westminster Hall, next to the British parliament.

## JULY

**1 Juan Perón**, president of Argentina, dies at 78. His wife Isabel takes his place.

**20** Turkey invades northern **Cyprus** as guarantor of the rights of Turkish Cypriots, following an attempt to grab power by a group seeking the unification of Cyprus and Greece.

## AUGUST

**8 President Nixon resigns** over the Watergate scandal. He is replaced by vice president Gerald Ford.

## OCTOBER

**29 Muhammad Ali** regains the world heavyweight boxing title in a fight against George Foreman.

## DECEMBER

**10** The Russian writer **Alexandr Solzhenitsyn** collects his 1970 Nobel prize for literature.

# 1975

## MARCH

**25 King Faisal** of Saudi Arabia is assassinated in his palace in Riyadh by a mentally disturbed nephew.

## APRIL

**13 Lebanon** slides into civil war after 27 Palestinians are killed on a bus by Christian militiamen.

**17** The **Khmer Rouge** captures the Cambodian capital Phnom Penh and two years of terror begin.

**OIL CRISIS** Gas ration books were issued in Britain in November 1973, though in the end never used. From December 1973 to May 1974 the maximum speed limit was reduced to 50 mph. Background: The shooting by British soldiers of 13 Catholics on January 30, 1972, led to a rapid escalation of the conflict.

**30** North Vietnamese troops capture **Saigon**, and rename it Ho Chi Minh City.

## MAY

**16** Junko Tabei of Japan is the **first woman** to climb Mount Everest.

## JUNE

**5** The **Suez Canal** reopens for the first time since the Arab-Israeli War of 1967.

## JULY

**5** Tennis player **Arthur Ashe** becomes the first black player to win Wimbledon.

**17** U.S. astronauts and Soviet cosmonauts meet in space in the first **Apollo-Soyuz link-up**.

## AUGUST

**1** The **Helsinki Accords** are signed by most East and West European countries, plus the U.S. and Canada. Signatories agree to respect the integrity of existing borders, and the human rights of their citizens.

**WAR IN CYPRUS** Greek Cypriots celebrate the capture of a Turkish stronghold, but Turkey gains control of the northern third of the island.

## SEPTEMBER

**28** In Spain, Franco's government executes five **Basque separatists**.

## OCTOBER

**9** The Soviet physicist and leading dissident **Andrei Sakharov** is awarded the Nobel peace prize.

## NOVEMBER

**11** The governor-general of Australia sacks the Labor prime minister, **Gough Whitlam**, causing outcries over the exercise of his power.

**20** Spain's dictator **General Franco** dies at 82. King Juan Carlos replaces him as head of state.

## DECEMBER

**21** A pro-Palestinian terrorist squad led by **Carlos the Jackal** captures 70 delegates at an OPEC conference in Vienna. The hostages are released on payment of a $20 million ransom.

# 1976

## JANUARY

**8** The death of the moderate Chinese premier **Zhou Enlai**, age 78, is used as an alibi for demonstrations against radicals associated with Mao.

**12** The British crime novelist **Agatha Christie** dies at 85.

**21** The Anglo-French supersonic airliner **Concorde** begins commercial passenger flights.

## FEBRUARY

The Marxist MPLA faction gains the upper hand in **Angola** with the aid of 15,000 Cuban troops.

**ANTI-FASHION**
Elaborate spiky hairdos, requiring careful maintenance, are part of the shock tactics of Punk style.

## MARCH

**16** The British prime minister, **Harold Wilson**, resigns. His place is taken by James Callaghan.

**24 Isabel Perón** is ousted as president of Argentina by a military junta led by General Jorge Videla.

## MAY

**9** The German urban terrorist **Ulrike Meinhof** is found dead in her prison cell in Stuttgart, apparently after committing suicide.

## JUNE

**16** Attempts by the apartheid government of Transvaal to enforce the use of Afrikaans in schools gives rise to riots in the Black township of **Soweto**, near Johannesburg.

**28** The **Seychelles** become independent from Britain.

## JULY

**3** In a **raid on Entebbe**, Uganda, Israeli commandos rescue 106 Jewish hijack victims held by Palestinian and West German terrorists.

**4** The U.S. celebrates the **bicentenary** of the Declaration of Independence.

**20** The U.S. space probe Viking I sends back pictures from the **surface of Mars**.

## AUGUST

The **Montreal Olympic Games** in Canada are boycotted by 22 African nations in protest at a New Zealand rugby tour to South Africa.

## SEPTEMBER

**9 Chairman Mao** dies at 82. His widow Jiang Qing and others in her Gang of Four attempt to seize power, but are arrested in October.

## NOVEMBER

**2** Gerald Ford is defeated in the presidential elections and replaced by Democrat candidate **Jimmy Carter**.

**27** In London, 30,000 demonstrators march for peace in Northern Ireland, led by the founders of the **Ulster Peace Movement**, Betty Williams and Mairead Corrigan.

## DECEMBER

**4** The British composer **Benjamin Britten** dies at 63.

Alex Haley's historical novel *Roots* contributes to a trend in re-evaluating Black American history. The *Hite Report on Female Sexuality* is published, treating the subject with unprecedented frankness.

# 1977

## JANUARY

**7** Human rights activists in Czechoslovakia publish **Charter 77**, pressing for respect for the human

rights provisions laid out in the Helsinki Accords of 1975.

**21** President Jimmy Carter grants a pardon to all those who evaded the **draft** during the Vietnam War.

## MARCH

**28** The world's **worst air disaster** occurs when two jumbo jets collide at Tenerife airport in the Canary Islands, killing 583.

## APRIL

**28** Andreas Baader and members of the **Baader-Meinhof** gang of German terrorists are jailed for life.

## MAY

**17 Menachem Begin** is elected prime minister of Israel.

## JUNE

**7** Britons celebrate the **Silver Jubilee** (25th anniversary) of the accession of Queen Elizabeth II.

**15** Spain holds its first general election for 41 years, and **Adolfo Suarez** is returned as prime minister.

## JULY

**5** President Zulfikar Ali Bhutto of Pakistan is ousted in a military coup led by **General Zia ul-Haq**.

**22 Deng Xiao-ping** is restored to power in China as deputy premier.

## AUGUST

**16** The king of rock 'n' roll, **Elvis Presley**, dies at 42.

## SEPTEMBER

**12 Steve Biko**, anti-apartheid activist, dies at 30 while under arrest in South Africa.

**17** The Greek-born opera singer **Maria Callas** dies at 53.

## OCTOBER

**10** The 1976 Nobel peace prize is awarded to **Betty Williams and Mairead Corrigan**, founders of the Ulster Peace Movement.

**18** Hostages on an airliner hijacked to **Mogadishu**, Somalia, by

pro-Palestinian terrorists are released by a German anti-terrorist squad.

**19** German terrorists **Andreas Baader and Gudrun Ensslin**, whose release was demanded by the Mogadishu hijackers, commit suicide.

**IN FROM THE COLD** The Chinese leader Deng Xiao-ping, age 71, returned to power within a year of Mao's death, heralding a period of economic reform.

## NOVEMBER

**19** President **Anwar Sadat** of Egypt becomes the first Arab leader to visit Jerusalem.

## DECEMBER

**4** President Jean-Bedel Bokassa crowns himself emperor of the **Central African Empire** in a ceremony of distasteful extravagance.

**10** The 1977 Nobel peace prize is awarded to **Amnesty International**.

**25** The British film comedian **Charlie Chaplin** dies at 88.

The first Vietnamese **boat people** are picked up in the South China Sea.

In the year that Apple produces the first **Personal Computer** (PC), the public is more fascinated by a puzzle called **Rubik's Cube**.

Two blockbuster movies dominate the silver screen, *Star Wars* and *Close Encounters of the Third Kind*, while the hugely successful *Saturday Night Fever* reflects the current vogue for disco dancing.

# 1978

## JANUARY

**29** Sweden is the first country to ban **aerosol sprays**, in order to protect the ozone layer.

## FEBRUARY

**15 Muhammad Ali** loses his heavyweight boxing title to Leon Spinks.

## MARCH

**14** Israel launches an invasion into **southern Lebanon**, targeting Palestinian camps.

**16** In Italy, six gunmen of the **Red Brigades** kidnap former prime minister Aldo Moro.

## APRIL

**27 President Muhammad Daud** of Afghanistan is killed in a coup by pro-Soviet army officers.

## MAY

**9** The body of the murdered former prime minister of Italy, **Aldo Moro**, is found.

## JULY

**7** The Czech-born tennis star **Martina Navratilova** wins Wimbledon for the first time.

**14** The Soviet human rights activist **Anatoly Shcharansky** is sentenced to 13 years' hard labor.

**26** The first **test-tube baby** is born in England.

## AUGUST

**22 Jomo Kenyatta**, president of Kenya, dies at 89. His is succeeded by Daniel Arap Moi.

## SEPTEMBER

**8** In riots in Tehran at the end of Ramadan 100 demonstrators die on **Black Friday**, and push the Shah into imposing martial law.

**15** The Bulgarian defector Georgi Markov dies in London after a secret agent at a bus stop injects a **poison pellet** into his thigh from the tip of an umbrella.

**FIRST OF MANY** Martina Navratilova wins Wimbledon for the first time in 1978, age 21, then goes on to win the singles trophy a record nine times.

**18** A peace treaty between Israel and Egypt is agreed to by President Anwar Sadat and Prime Minister Menachem Begin at **Camp David**, Maryland.

**30 Pope John Paul** dies after just 33 days in office.

## OCTOBER

**6** Under pressure from the Shah of Iran, Iraq expels **Ayatollah Khomeini**, who sets up his headquarters in Paris.

**16** Karol Wojtyla, Archbishop of Kraków in Poland, becomes **Pope John Paul II**, the first non-Italian pope for over 400 years.

## NOVEMBER

**29** The preacher Jim Jones presides over the suicide of 913 members of his People's Temple in **Jonestown**, Guyana.

## DECEMBER

**25** Vietnam begins its **invasion into Cambodia**.

# 1979

## JANUARY

**8** The Vietnamese army captures **Phnom Penh**, forcing the Khmer

Rouge regime into the borderland jungles. The extent of the Cambodian tragedy under the Khmer Rouge begins to be revealed.

**16** Facing unsuppressible turmoil organized by Islamic clerics led by Ayatollah Khomeini, the **Shah of Iran** and his family flee into exile.

Britain is hit by a tide of labor unrest which is dubbed the **Winter of Discontent**.

## FEBRUARY

**1 Ayatollah Khomeini** is greeted by ecstatic crowds as he arrives in Tehran from exile in Paris.

**17** China begins a series of punitive raids into **northern Vietnam**.

**22 St. Lucia** becomes independent from Britain.

## MARCH

**12** Maurice Bishop, age 33, seizes power in **Grenada**, ousting the prime minister, Sir Eric Gairy.

**29 President Idi Amin** flees as the Uganda Liberation Front advances on Kampala.

**31** The nuclear power station at **Three Mile Island**, Pennsylvania, comes close to meltdown, but disaster is averted.

## APRIL

**4 Zulfikar Ali Bhutto**, former president of Pakistan, is hanged for murder, despite international protests.

## MAY

**4 Margaret Thatcher**, leader of the Conservative Party, becomes the first female prime minister of Britain.

## JUNE

**2** Pope John Paul II visits **Warsaw,** the first visit by a pope to a communist country.

**THE POLISH POPE** The election of a Polish Pope, John Paul II, gives hope to Roman Catholics behind the Iron Curtain. Background: Concorde begins commercial flights.

**11 John Wayne**, Hollywood movie star, dies at 72.

**18** The **SALT II** arms limitation agreement is signed in Vienna by President Carter and Leonid Brezhnev, but is never ratified by the U.S. Senate.

## JULY

**20** The corrupt dictator **President Anastasio Somoza** of Nicaragua flees after a decade of civil war waged by Sandinista guerrillas.

## AUGUST

**27 Lord Louis Mountbatten**, cousin to the British Queen, is killed by an IRA bomb.

## NOVEMBER

**4** Iranian students and Revolutionary Guards storm the **U.S. embassy in Tehran** and take its staff hostage. This hostage crisis lasts over a year.

**21** In London, **Anthony Blunt**, Keeper of the Queen's Pictures, is revealed to be a Soviet spy.

## DECEMBER

**10 Mother Teresa of Calcutta** is awarded the Nobel peace prize for her work among the poor.

**21** The **Rhodesian government** agrees to a ceasefire in the civil war and to cede to black majority rule.

**24** The Soviet army invades **Afghanistan** to prop up the pro-Soviet military government.

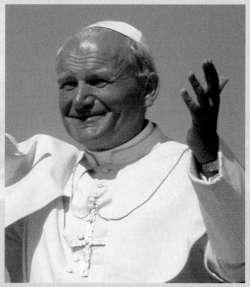

# 1980

## JANUARY

**22** Soviet dissident **Andrei Sakharov** is sent into internal exile in Gorky.

## MARCH

**4 Robert Mugabe** is elected prime minister of Rhodesia, now renamed Zimbabwe.

**24 Archbishop Oscar Romero** of El Salvador is gunned down by a

**FIRST ELECTIONS** After 15 years of brutal civil war costing 27,000 lives, elections in Rhodesia offer a more equitable and stable future.

right-wing paramilitary death squad while saying Mass.

**31** Athlete **Jesse Owens** dies at 66.

## APRIL

**15** French philosopher **Jean-Paul Sartre** dies at 74.

**25 Operation Eagle Claw**, mounted by the U.S. military to release U.S. embassy hostages in Tehran, turns into a debacle as helicopters fail in the Iranian desert.

**29** British film-maker **Alfred Hitchcock** dies at 88.

## MAY

**4 Marshal Tito** of Yugoslavia dies at 87.

**5** A squad of British SAS troops storms the **Iranian embassy in London** to release hostages held for nearly a week by five gunmen.

**17** Eighteen people die in **race riots** in Miami when an all-white jury acquits a white policeman accused of killing a black businessman.

**18 Mount St. Helens** in Washington erupts, killing seven, causing widespread devastation and affecting the world's weather.

## JUNE

**23 Sanjay Gandhi**, son and political heir of the Indian prime minister, Indira Gandhi, dies in a plane crash.

## JULY

**19** The **Olympic Games in Moscow** are boycotted by the U.S. and many other nations in protest of the Soviet invasion of Afghanistan.

**27** The exiled **Shah of Iran** dies in Cairo at 60.

## AUGUST

**2** In **Bologna**, Italy, 85 people are killed in the train station when a bomb is detonated by neo-fascists attempting to disrupt the trial of fellow terrorists.

**30** Polish shipyard workers win concessions from their government under the **Gdansk Agreement**.

## SEPTEMBER

**17** The former dictator of Nicaragua **Anastasio Somoza** is assassinated.

**21** Protests against the proposed siting of U.S. cruise missiles at the U.S. air base at **Greenham Common** in England lead to the establishment of the Women's Peace Camp.

**22** The trade union **Solidarity** is set up in Poland to represent workers across the country.

**23** Iraq invades southern Iran, triggering the **Iran-Iraq War**.

## OCTOBER

**11** Some 20,000 are killed in two **earthquakes in Algeria**.

## NOVEMBER

**4 Ronald Reagan** wins the presidential election.

**13** British Airways is sold as part of the Conservative government's innovative policy of **privatization**.

The episode of **Dallas** revealing who shot JR is watched by 41 million viewers in America, and by 125 million viewers worldwide.

## DECEMBER

**8** The former Beatle **John Lennon** is shot dead, age 40, by a deranged fan in New York City.

**19** The World Health Organization declares that **smallpox** has been eradicated.

# 1981

## JANUARY

**16** The **space shuttle Columbia** makes its maiden flight, the first mission by a re-usable spacecraft.

**21** The **U.S. hostages** from the embassy in Tehran are released on the day that President Carter hands over power to Ronald Reagan.

**25** Mao's widow **Jiang Qing** is sentenced to death, later commuted to life imprisonment.

## FEBRUARY

**9** Under pressure from Moscow, the Polish government is replaced by a hardline military regime led by **General Wojciech Jaruzelski**.

**23 Civil Guards in Spain** make an unsuccessful attempt to mount a coup by storming the parliament building and holding government leaders and deputies hostage.

**ROYAL WEDDING** The marriage of Prince Charles to Lady Diana Spencer is celebrated as a triumph of style and protocol.

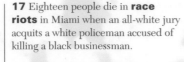

## MARCH

**26** In Britain, the **Social Democratic Party** is launched by four former Labor cabinet ministers: Shirley Williams, Roy Jenkins, David Owen and William Rodgers.

**30** President Reagan survives an **assassination attempt** when shot in Washington by John Hinckley.

## APRIL

**10 Brixton** in South London erupts in three days and nights of rioting as the black community reacts to a heavy-handed police operation against street crime.

## MAY

**5 Bobby Sands** becomes the first of ten IRA prisoners in Northern Ireland to die from a hunger strike.

**10 François Mitterrand**, leader of the Socialist Party, becomes president of France.

**23** Peter Sutcliffe, the so-called **Yorkshire Ripper**, is convicted of 13 murders committed since 1975.

## JUNE

**8** Israeli jets launch a surprise attack on a **nuclear reactor** being built in Iraq, to prevent the danger of Iraq developing nuclear weapons.

## JULY

**7** Sandra Day O'Connor becomes the **first woman judge** to be appointed to the Supreme Court.

**23** The International Whaling Commission votes for a complete **ban on commercial whaling** by 1985.

**29** Prince Charles, heir to the British throne, marries 20-year-old **Lady Diana Spencer**.

## OCTOBER

**6 President Anwar Sadat** of Egypt is assassinated at a military parade in Cairo.

## DECEMBER

**13** General Jaruzelski imposes **martial law in Poland**, and 14,000 Solidarity activists are arrested.

# 1982

## JANUARY

**1** Javier Pérez de Cuellar of Peru becomes UN secretary-general.

## FEBRUARY

**17** Robert Mugabe, prime minister of Zimbabwe, dismisses his one-time ally **Joshua Nkomo** from government in a bitter split.

## APRIL

**2** Argentine forces seize the **Falkland Islands** and claim them

**FALKLANDS STRUGGLE** The air attack on the British landing ships *Sir Galahad* and *Sir Tristram* at Fitzroy on June 8, 1982, caused 56 deaths and widespread injury.
Background: Mount St. Helens erupts after four months of warning rumblings.

for Argentina. Britain prepares a military task force to retrieve them.

## MAY

**18** The Reverend **Sun Myung Moon**, leader of the Unification Church of World Christianity, is found guilty of tax fraud and sent to prison.

## JUNE

**11** Israel launches a full-scale **invasion of Lebanon**.

**14** British troops retake the **Falkland Islands** from Argentina, following a three-week campaign.

**21** Princess Diana gives birth to **Prince William**, second in line to the British throne.

## JULY

**20** In London, **IRA bombs** blow up a mounted detachment of the Blues and Royals regiment in Hyde Park, and military bandsmen in Regents Park, killing eight.

**23** The Vatican banker **Roberto Calvi**, linked to the P-2 Masonic lodge under investigation in Italy, is found hanging from Blackfriars Bridge, London, after an apparent suicide.

## AUGUST

**30** Under military pressure from Israel, **PLO leaders** are forced to abandon Beirut as their headquarters.

## SEPTEMBER

**17** Christian militia massacre Palestinian refugees in the **Sabra and Chatila** camps, apparently in revenge for the assassination of the president-elect Bashir Gemayel.

## OCTOBER

**1** **Helmut Kohl** of the Christian Democratic Union replaces Helmut Schmidt as chancellor of West Germany.

**8** The trade union **Solidarity** is formally banned in Poland.

**28** Spain's socialist party wins a general election and **Felipe González** becomes prime minister.

## NOVEMBER

**10** The veteran Soviet premier **Leonid Brehznev** dies at 76 and is replaced by the hard-line former head of the KGB, Yuri Andropov.

**11** The new **Vietnam Memorial**, bearing the names of the 58,183 U.S. dead, becomes the focus of attention at Veterans' Day in Washington DC.

## DECEMBER

**2** A patient in Salt Lake City receives the **first artificial heart**, and survives for more than three months.

KIDNAP VICTIM An inquiry concludes that Shergar, winner of the 1981 Derby by a record 10 lengths, was the victim of a bungled kidnap by the IRA.

Science fiction movies prove popular with the release of Steven Spielberg's ***ET: The Extraterrestrial***, and the more pessimistic ***Blade Runner***, directed by Ridley Scott.

# 1983

## JANUARY

**19** South Africa reimposes direct rule on **Namibia**.

## FEBRUARY

**9** The champion racehorse **Shergar** is kidnapped in Ireland, and a ransom demanded. The horse is never recovered.

## MARCH

**23** President Reagan announces the Strategic Defense Initiative or **Star Wars** program.

## JUNE

**9** Margaret Thatcher, Conservative prime minister, wins a **second term**.

**24** The astronaut Sally Ride, on board the Shuttle *Challenger*, becomes the **first U.S. woman in space**.

## JULY

**25** The **Tamil Tigers** begin their separatist campaign, bringing civil war to Sri Lanka.

## AUGUST

**21** Opposition leader **Begnino Aquino**, age 50, is assassinated as he arrives back in the Philippines after a decade in prison and exile.

## SEPTEMBER

**1** A **South Korean jumbo jet** is shot down by Soviet warplanes after entering a militarily sensitive area of the eastern Soviet Union. All 269 passengers and crew are killed.

**15** Menachem Begin resigns as prime minister of Israel, and is replaced by **Yitzhak Shamir**.

**26** Australia takes the **America's Cup** sailing trophy from the U.S. for the first time in the competition's history.

## OCTOBER

**5** **Lech Walesa**, leader of the banned Polish trade union Solidarity, is awarded the Nobel peace prize.

**23** In Beirut, suicide bombers of the **Islamic Jihad** blow up the barracks of the U.S. marines, killing 241, and French barracks, killing 58.

**27** U.S. troops invade the Caribbean island of **Grenada** following the overthrow and execution of Maurice Bishop by left-wing military officers.

**30** Civilian democracy is restored in Argentina with the election of **Raúl Alfonsín**.

## NOVEMBER

**14** **Turkish Cypriots** declare unilateral independence, partitioning the island, a move declared illegal in a UN resolution.

## DECEMBER

**17** An IRA car bomb planted outside **Harrods** department store in London kills six.

# 1984

## JANUARY

**23** Apple Computer of California launches the user-friendly **Macintosh PC**, with icons and pull-down menus.

## FEBRUARY

**13** The Soviet leader Yuri Andropov, incapacitated by illness for most of his tenure, dies at 68 and is replaced by **Konstantin Chernenko**.

**14** British ice-dancing champions **Christopher Dean and Jayne Torvill** win gold with their performance to Ravel's *Bolero* at the Winter Olympics at Sarajevo, Yugoslavia.

**29 Pierre Trudeau**, Canadian Liberal Party leader, resigns as prime minister of Canada.

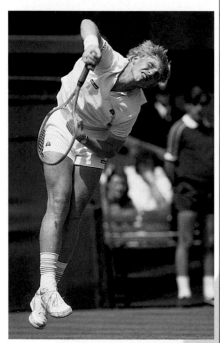

**YOUNG TALENT** At 17, Boris Becker is the youngest champion in the history of the men's tournament when he wins Wimbledon for the first time in 1985.

## MARCH

**6** The **Green Party** wins its first seat in the West German parliament.

**12** The **miners' strike** begins in Britain, and is taken up by Thatcher's Conservative government as a battle

between its free-market policies and trade union power. The strike is eventually called off in March 1985.

## APRIL

**1** The soul singer **Marvin Gaye**, age 44, is shot dead by his father.

## MAY

**6** The Soviet Union announces its **boycott** of the Olympic Games to be held in Los Angeles, in retaliation for the U.S. boycott of the 1980 Moscow Olympics.

## JUNE

**6** More than 800 are killed as Indian troops storm the sacred **Golden Temple in Amritsar** to flush out armed Sikh extremists.

## JULY

**18** A gunman shoots dead 20 people at a **McDonald's** restaurant at San Ysidro, California.

## AUGUST

**8** The **Los Angeles Olympics** close, celebrating the triumph of athlete Carl Lewis, who won four medals, echoing the achievements of Jesse Owens in 1936.

**21** A million Filipinos mark the anniversary of Benigno Aquino's assassination with **demonstrations in Manila** against President Marcos.

## SEPTEMBER

**20** A **suicide bomber** from Islamic Jihad attacks the U.S. embassy in Beirut, killing 40.

**26** Britain signs an agreement with China to hand back **Hong Kong** when the lease on the New Territories runs out in 1997.

## OCTOBER

**12** Four die and many narrowly escape with their lives when an IRA bomb explodes at the **Grand Hotel in Brighton**, where leaders of the British Government are staying for the Conservative Party conference.

**30** The body of the dissident Polish priest **Father Jerzy Popieluszko**, murdered by government agents, is found in a reservoir.

**31 Indira Gandhi**, prime minister of India, age 66, is assassinated by her Sikh bodyguards in revenge for the assault on the Golden Temple in June.

## NOVEMBER

**6 Ronald Reagan** is re-elected as president with a landslide victory.

## DECEMBER

**4** Some 2,000 are killed, and tens of thousands are injured, by a poison gas leak from the American-owned Union Carbide pesticide factory in **Bhopal**, central India.

**14** Rock musicians led by Boomtown Rats singer Bob Geldof raise $12 million for the starving in Ethiopia with a hit single, **"Do They Know It's Christmas?"**

# 1985

## JANUARY

**1 Jacques Delors** becomes president of the European Commission.

## FEBRUARY

**18** South African police clash with protesters as they attempt to remove **100,000 squatters** from Cape Flats, north of Cape Town, to homelands such as Transkei and Ciskei.

## MARCH

**1** Twelve years of military rule end in Uruguay as **Julio Sanguinetti** takes office as elected president.

**11** The Soviet leader Konstantin Chernenko dies at 74 and is replaced by the young and dynamic **Mikhail Gorbachev**.

## APRIL

**11 Enver Hoxha**, isolationist communist dictator of Albania, dies at 76.

## MAY

**25** Hundreds die as Syrian-backed Shiite militiamen launch an assault on **Palestinian camps in Beirut** in an attempt to disarm PLO supporters.

**29** Forty-one Italian and Belgian supporters are killed when rioting soccer fans cause a wall to collapse at

**Heysel Stadium**, Brussels, at the final of the European Champions' Cup between Liverpool and Juventus of Turin.

## JUNE

**23** An **Air India jumbo jet** with 329 people on board explodes over the Atlantic, believed to be the work of Sikh extremists.

## JULY

**7** The 17-year-old German **Boris Becker** wins the Wimbledon men's championship.

**10** The *Rainbow Warrior*, the Greenpeace flagship used to disrupt French nuclear testing in the South Pacific, is blown up and sunk by French secret agents in Auckland harbor, New Zealand, killing a Portuguese photographer.

**13** Rock musicians led by Bob Geldof hold the **Live Aid Concerts** in London and Philadelphia and raise $90 million for the victims of famine in Ethiopia.

## SEPTEMBER

**1** The wreck of the *Titanic* is discovered on the bed of the Atlantic Ocean.

**13** The World Health Organization announces that **AIDS** has reached epidemic proportions.

**20** An **earthquake in Mexico City** kills 7,000.

## OCTOBER

**2** The Hollywood film star **Rock Hudson** dies of AIDS, age 59.

**7** PLO terrorists hijack the Italian cruise liner *Achille Lauro*, demanding the release of 50 prisoners in Israel. They kill a handicapped Jewish passenger before reaching a negotiated settlement on October 9.

**10** Actor-director **Orson Welles** dies at 70.

## NOVEMBER

**13** A **mudslide** resulting from the eruption of the Nevado del Ruiz volcano in Colombia claims 25,000 lives.

# 1986

## JANUARY

**1** Spain and Portugal join the **European Community**.

**28** The **Shuttle *Challenger*** explodes shortly after liftoff from Cape Canaveral, killing all seven crew.

## FEBRUARY

**7 Baby Doc Duvalier**, president of Haiti, is forced into exile.

**20** The **Soviet space station** Mir is launched.

**25 President Ferdinand Marcos** of the Philippines is forced to flee Manila. Corazon Aquino, widow of Benigno Aquino, becomes president.

## APRIL

**15** U.S. warplanes make a surprise **bombing raid on Libya** to discourage state-sponsored terrorism.

**26** The **Chernobyl** nuclear power station in the Ukraine explodes, causing widespread radiation and up to 125,000 deaths.

## JUNE

**8** Despite accusations of a Nazi past, the former secretary-general of the UN, **Kurt Waldheim**, is elected president of Austria.

## JULY

**4** After undergoing extensive restoration, the **Statue of Liberty** in New York celebrates its centenary on Independence Day.

**TOO LITTLE TOO LATE**
A radiation warning at Chernobyl was scant protection against the massive pollution released by the explosion in the nuclear power station. Background: Torvill and Dean received maximum points for artistic impression for the ice dancing to *Bolero* that won them Olympic gold.

## AUGUST

**25** A **poison gas cloud** from Lake Nyos, Cameroon, kills 1,200.

## OCTOBER

**12** The **START** arms reduction talks between the U.S.S.R. and the U.S. in Reykjavik, Iceland, founder after President Reagan refuses to give up his Star Wars initiative.

**27** The British stock market is deregulated in a series of wide-ranging reforms known as the **Big Bang**.

## NOVEMBER

**22** The boxer **Mike Tyson** takes the WBC heavyweight title at 20, the youngest world champion on record.

## DECEMBER

**23** Jubilant crowds greet the Soviet dissidents **Andrei Sakharov** and his wife Yelena Bonner on their return to Moscow following their release from internal exile.

# 1987

## JANUARY

**20 Terry Waite**, the special envoy of the Archbishop of Canterbury, is kidnapped while attempting to negotiate the release of Western hostages held in Lebanon.

## FEBRUARY

**21 Andy Warhol**, a leader of Pop Art in the 1960s, dies at 58.

## MARCH

**6** The British car and passenger ferry, the ***Herald of Free Enterprise***, capsizes off Zeebrugge, Belgium, and 193 people are drowned.

## MAY

**5** In Washington, the Congressional hearings begin in which the **Iran-Contra scandal** is exposed through the testimony of Lieutenant-Colonel Oliver North and others.

## JUNE

**11 Margaret Thatcher** becomes the first British prime minister this century to win three elections in a row.

**22** Hollywood actor and dancer **Fred Astaire** dies at 88.

## JULY

**30** 150,000 Shiite Muslims from Iran riot during the annual **pilgrimage to Mecca**, resulting in 275 deaths.

## AUGUST

**17** Former Nazi leader **Rudolf Hess** commits suicide, age 93, in Spandau prison, Berlin.

**HORROR AT SEA** The *Herald of Free Enterprise* capsized shortly after leaving harbor on what should have been a routine car-ferry crossing.

## SEPTEMBER

**16** In Montreal, Canada, an international conference of 70 nations pledges to reduce the use of **chlorofluorocarbons** to help protect the ozone layer.

## OCTOBER

**15 Black Thursday** in New York marks the start of a week on the world stock markets when stocks lose around $500 billion in value.

## NOVEMBER

**11** A bomb detonated by the IRA kills 11 people at a Remembrance Day ceremony at **Enniskillen** in Northern Ireland.

**KIDNAP OF A PEACEMAKER** Terry Waite was known as a fearless humanitarian negotiator in Africa and the Middle East before being kidnapped himself.

**13** A rapist in Bristol, England, becomes the first criminal to be convicted through DNA analysis or **genetic fingerprinting**.

## DECEMBER

**8** Mikhail Gorbachev and President Reagan agree to cut **intermediate nuclear missiles** in Europe.

**12** The ***Intifada*** revolt by Palestinians in Israel begins.

**16** At the conclusion of a marathon mass-trial of **mafia** suspects in Palermo, Sicily, 338 are convicted.

# 1988

## JANUARY

**26** At the start of celebrations marking the **bicentennial** of the founding of modern Australia, a fleet of tall ships sails into Sydney Harbor on Australia Day.

## MARCH

**7** A British SAS squad shoots dead three members of an IRA active service unit in **Gibraltar**.

**16** Saddam Hussein authorizes the use of **poison gas** to kill over 6,000 Kurdish villagers in northeastern Iraq.

## MAY

**31** During a visit to Moscow, President Reagan praises Gorbachev's policies of **glasnost** and **perestroika**.

## JULY

**3** An Iranian airliner carrying 290 passengers is shot down over the Gulf by the U.S. naval ship **USS Vincennes**, which mistook it for an incoming enemy aircraft.

## SEPTEMBER

**8** A UN sponsored truce brings the eight-year **Iran-Iraq War** to a close.

## OCTOBER

**1 Mikhail Gorbachev** is elected to the post of president of the U.S.S.R.

**13** Carbon dating shows that the **Turin Shroud** is a medieval fake.

## NOVEMBER

**8 George Bush**, vice president to Ronald Reagan, is elected Reagan's successor as president.

## DECEMBER

**2** Civilian rule is restored to Pakistan under **Benazir Bhutto**, daughter of the executed Zulfikar Ali Bhutto. She is the first woman head-of-state of a Muslim country.

**9** An **earthquake in Armenia** claims over 50,000 lives.

**21** A Pan Am jumbo jet flying from London to New York is destroyed by a

**SURREALIST** Spanish Surrealist painter Salvador Dali was famous for his eccentricity. Background: Iraqi military hardware litters the desert in February 1991, after Allied forces retake the border town of Khafji in the campaign to liberate Kuwait.

bomb over the Scottish village of **Lockerbie**, killing all 259 passengers and crew, plus 11 people on the ground.

**22** UN negotiations win independence for **Namibia** from South Africa.

**Francisco Chico Mendes**, Brazilian rubber-tapper leader and environmentalist campaigning to protect Amazonia, is assassinated.

# 1989

## JANUARY

**23** The Spanish Surrealist painter **Salvador Dali** dies at 84.

## FEBRUARY

**2** In South Africa, P.W. Botha steps down as leader of the ruling National Party, and is replaced by **F.W. de Klerk**.

**14** The novel **The Satanic Verses** is condemned by Ayatollah Khomeini as blasphemous, and a *fatwa* is imposed on its author, Salman Rushdie. An Iranian religious group offers a $1 million reward for Rushdie's death.

**15** The last Soviet soldiers are withdrawn from **Afghanistan**.

## MARCH

**24** The **Exxon Valdez** oil tanker runs aground in Alaska, spilling nearly 11 million gallons of oil.

## APRIL

**15** Ninety-six soccer fans die in the crush of the overcrowded stadium of **Hillsborough** in Sheffield, England, at a cup-tie match between Liverpool and Nottingham Forest.

**17** The Polish government lifts the ban on the trade union **Solidarity**.

**21 GameBoy** is introduced by the Japanese Nintendo company.

## MAY

**2** Hungary draws back the **Iron Curtain** by opening its borders with neighboring Austria.

## JUNE

**3 Ayatollah Khomeini**, leader of Iran, dies at 87.

**4** Hundreds of protesters are killed as the Chinese authorities order the army into **Tiananmen Square** in Beijing to break up a two-month demonstration calling for democratic reforms.

**4 Free elections** in Poland give a huge majority to Solidarity candidates. Tadeusz Mazowiecki becomes the Soviet bloc's first non-communist premier.

## AUGUST

**25** The space probe *Voyager 2* sends back photographs of the **surface of Neptune**.

## SEPTEMBER

**10** Hungary permits East Germans to cross its border to the West, triggering a **mass exodus**. East Germans also

clamor for asylum at the West German embassy in Prague.

**26** Vietnam withdraws from **Cambodia** after an occupation lasting nearly 11 years.

## OCTOBER

**5** The **Dalai Lama** is awarded the Nobel peace prize for his nonviolent struggle for the liberation of Tibet.

**18** The hard-line East German leader **Erich Honecker** resigns after 18 years in power.

**23** With the promise of multiparty elections, a new republic is declared in **Hungary** on the anniversary of the 1956 uprising.

## NOVEMBER

**9** Checkpoints along the **Berlin Wall** are removed. Thousands of East Germans pour into West Berlin.

**24** Protesters against the communist government in Prague celebrate the return of **Alexander Dubcek**, architect of the 1968 Prague Spring.

## DECEMBER

**10** A non-communist government takes power in **Czechoslovakia**.

**14** The military government of General Pinochet in Chile steps down in favor of the democratically elected government of **Patricio Aylwyn**.

**25** In Romania, opposition forces arrest and try **President Nicolae Ceausescu** and his wife Elena, then execute them.

**BLOWN OUT OF THE SKY** The wreck of the Pan Am Boeing 747 lies scattered over the ground at Lockerbie, Scotland. First Iranian, then Libyan terrorists are suspected.

# 1990

## FEBRUARY

**2** The South African president F.W. de Klerk lifts the 30-year ban on the **ANC**.

**11 Nelson Mandela**, the veteran ANC activist, is released from prison in South Africa after 27 years' detention.

## MARCH

**11 Lithuania** declares independence, and is met with heavy-handed

**FREEDOM FOR A NATION** Nelson Mandela and his wife Winnie celebrate his release from prison.

intervention and an economic blockade by the Soviet Union.

**21 Namibia** becomes independent of South Africa.

## APRIL

**25** The **Hubble Space Telescope** is launched.

## MAY

**27** Elections in Burma are won by the opposition party led by **Aung San Suu Kyi**, but the results are annulled by the military government.

**29 Boris Yeltsin** is made president of Russia by the elected parliament.

## JUNE

**11** The **Russian Federation** declares independence from the Soviet Union.

**22** An **earthquake** in northern Iran kills up to 40,000.

## JULY

**8** West Germany beats Argentina 1:0 in the **World Cup** soccer finals in Rome. It is the third time Germany has won the World Cup.

## AUGUST

**2** Iraq invades **Kuwait** and Saddam Hussein announces that it has become a province of Iraq.

**8 Benazir Bhutto** is dismissed as prime minister of Pakistan.

**24** In Beirut, Irish hostage **Brian Keenan** is freed.

## SEPTEMBER

**8** French farmers burn British imported lamb in the **lamb war**.

## OCTOBER

**3** East and West **Germany** reunite as one country.

**8** The British Government takes sterling into the European **Exchange Rate Mechanism** (ERM).

## NOVEMBER

**27** In Britain, Margaret Thatcher is replaced as leader of the Conservative Party and prime minister by **John Major**.

**29** As international coalition forces led by the U.S. build up in Saudi Arabia, the UN announces that **Iraq** must leave Kuwait by January 15, 1991, or face the consequences.

## DECEMBER

**9 Slobodan Milosevic** is elected president of Serbia. In Poland, Solidarity leader Lech Walesa becomes president.

# 1991

## JANUARY

**17** Two days after the expiration of Iraq's deadline to leave Kuwait, **Operation Desert Storm** begins with 39 days of bombardment of Iraq.

## FEBRUARY

**24** Ground troops led by the U.S. liberate **Kuwait**, and the Iraqi army is defeated after four days of fighting.

## MARCH

**14** The convictions of the **Birmingham Six**, jailed in 1974 for an IRA pub bombing, are overturned.

## APRIL

**3** British author **Graham Greene** dies at 86.

## MAY

**21 Rajiv Gandhi**, prime minister of India, age 46, is assassinated by a suicide bomber in Madras.

## JUNE

**25** Following multi-party elections, **Slovenia and Croatia** declare independence from Yugoslavia.

## JULY

**31 START** agreements signed by Presidents Bush and Gorbachev cut all long-range nuclear weapons by a third.

**POCKET-SIZED FUN** GameBoy, the electronic game machine created by Nintendo, is launched in 1989. Interchangeable games cartridges could be inserted into the console.

**FLYING HOME** John McCarthy returns home after being held captive in Beirut for more than five years.

## AUGUST

**8** Beirut hostage **John McCarthy** is released after over five years in captivity.

## SEPTEMBER

**6** The Soviet Union grants independence to **Lithuania, Latvia and Estonia**.

## OCTOBER

**26** The historic Croatian port of **Dubrovnik** comes under attack by Serb forces as the war over Croatia's bid for independence intensifies.

## NOVEMBER

**8** The basketball star **Earvin "Magic" Johnson** announces that he has AIDS.

**18 Terry Waite**, the last British hostage in Beirut, is released after nearly five years in captivity.

## DECEMBER

**4 Terry Andersen**, the last U.S. hostage in Beirut, is released after five years in captivity.

**10** At a summit meeting in **Maastricht**, European Community leaders negotiate the details of the Treaty on European Union.

**25 President Gorbachev** resigns as head of state of the U.S.S.R., and the U.S.S.R. officially ceases to exist.

# 1992

## JANUARY

**1 Boutros Boutros-Gali** of Egypt becomes secretary-general of the UN.

## MARCH

**1** The non-Serb population of **Bosnia-Herzegovina** votes for independence from Yugoslavia.

**14** The **Earth Summit** in Rio de Janeiro, called to discuss the Earth's ecology, ends with limited progress.

## APRIL

**9** In an election in Britain **John Major** is reaffirmed as prime minister.

**9 Manuel Noriega**, former president of Panama, is convicted in Miami of cocaine trafficking and money laundering.

**29** Violent **race riots** erupt in Los Angeles when white police are acquitted over the beating of a black motorist, despite the fact that the deed was recorded on video.

## JUNE

**23 Yitzhak Rabin**, leader of the Labor Party, is elected prime minister

REVERSAL OF FORTUNE Manuel Noriega was president of Panama for six years before he was arrested by U.S. troops and put on trial for drug trafficking.

of Israel, bolstering the hopes of those who support the peace process.

**29 Muhammad Boudiaf**, president of Algeria, is assassinated, age 73. Militant Islamists are suspected.

## JULY

**9 Chris Patten** takes up his post as Britain's last governor of Hong Kong.

## AUGUST

**9** The **Olympic Games in Barcelona**, Spain, come to a close. It is the first Games in two decades not to be affected by political boycotts or incidents.

## SEPTEMBER

**16** Britain is forced to withdraw from the European **Exchange Rate Mechanism**.

## NOVEMBER

**3** Democrat **Bill Clinton** is elected president.

**11** The Anglican Church accepts the **ordination of women** as priests.

## DECEMBER

**3** Two people are killed when a bomb planted by Algerian extremists explodes in the **Paris Métro.**

**6** Militant Hindus storm and destroy a Muslim mosque standing on a sacred Hindu site in **Ayodhya**, in northern India.

**9** The U.S. sends 30,000 troops into war-torn **Somalia** to secure the country's supply lines so that aid can reach famine victims.

# 1993

## JANUARY

**1** Czechoslovakia divides into two nations, the Czech Republic and Slovakia, in a peaceable arrangement dubbed the **Velvet Divorce**.

## FEBRUARY

**26** Arab terrorists detonate a car bomb in the garage of the **World Trade Center**, New York, killing six people and causing injury to 1,000 others.

## MARCH

**10** A gynecologist is murdered in Florida as the campaign by **anti-abortionists** becomes increasingly violent.

## APRIL

**19** Authorities attempt to end a 51 day siege by the Branch Davidian cult at a ranch in **Waco**, Texas, but 82 members of the cult die in the resulting blaze.

## MAY

**18** In a second **referendum** the Danes narrowly vote to ratify the Maastricht Treaty.

## JUNE

**13 Tansu Ciller** becomes the first woman premier of Turkey.

**23** In Nigeria the opposition leader **Moshood Abiola** wins an election, but the result is annulled by the military government, plunging the country into turmoil and civil war.

## JULY

**31 King Baudouin** of the Belgians dies at 62.

## SEPTEMBER

**13** The Washington Declaration or **Oslo Accords** establish limited

SPAIN BLOSSOMS The Barcelona Olympics are launched with a spectacular opening ceremony. Background: A bomb at the Federal Building in Oklahoma kills 168 people.

self-rule for the Palestinians in the Gaza Strip and parts of the West Bank.

## OCTOBER

**1** The **Human Genome Project** is launched to map the entire genetic structure of the human race.

**15** The Nobel peace prize is awarded to **Nelson Mandela and F.W. de Klerk** for dismantling apartheid.

## NOVEMBER

**1** The ratified **Maastricht Treaty** comes into force, paving the way toward a more integrated Europe.

## DECEMBER

**15** The **Downing Street Declaration** sets out a new peace initiative for Northern Ireland.

**22** In Australia, the **Native Title Bill** grants Aborigines the right to claim ancestral lands.

# 1994

## JANUARY

**18** An **earthquake in Los Angeles** kills 34.

## FEBRUARY

**5** A mortar bomb kills 65 in a crowded market in **Sarajevo**.

**25** A lone **Jewish gunman** kills 30 Muslims in a mosque in Hebron.

## APRIL

**6** Hutu militia in Rwanda begin a preplanned **massacre of the Tutsi minority**.

**27** South African voters give an overwhelming majority to the ANC, and **Nelson Mandela** becomes president.

## MAY

**1** The Brazilian Formula One driver **Ayrton Senna** is killed, age 34, on the circuit at Imola, Italy.

**6** The **Channel Tunnel** is opened.

## JUNE

**3** The West Indian cricketer **Brian Lara** scores a record 501 runs in a first-class match against Durham.

**12** The body of Nicole Simpson is found at her home in Los Angeles, leading to the trial of her husband, **O.J. Simpson**.

**25 Jacques Santer**, prime minister of Luxembourg, becomes president of the European Commission.

## JULY

**8 Kim Il Sung**, the authoritarian leader of North Korea, dies at 82. His son Kim Jong II is later confirmed as his successor.

## AUGUST

**14** The international terrorist **Carlos the Jackal** is captured in Sudan and taken to France for trial.

**31** The IRA announces a **ceasefire**, a condition of taking part in talks to find a solution to Northern Ireland's troubles.

## SEPTEMBER

**19** The U.S. sends 20,000 troops to **Haiti** to restore the elected government of Jean-Bertrand Aristide.

**28** The car ferry *Estonia* sinks quickly in cold seas off Finland, and 912 people drown.

## OCTOBER

**4** Fifty-three members of the **Order of the Solar Temple** die in Canada and Switzerland, in an apparent mass suicide.

## NOVEMBER

**8** The **UN War Crimes Tribunal** in The Hague begins hearings concerning the former Yugoslavia.

**27 Norway** votes for a second time not to join the European Union.

## DECEMBER

**11** Russian troops are sent into the breakaway region of **Chechnya**.

# 1995

## JANUARY

**1** Austria, Sweden and Finland join the **European Union**, bringing the number of member states up to 15.

**Fred West**, accused of 10 murders and sexual abuse in Gloucester, England, hangs himself in prison.

**17** Over 6,000 people are killed and 100,000 buildings destroyed when an earthquake hits **Kobe**, Japan.

## FEBRUARY

**27** The 200-year-old London-based **Barings Bank** collapses as a result of a $930 million debt accumulated by a rogue trader in Singapore.

## MARCH

**3** Members of the **Aum Shinrikyo cult** in Japan release the deadly nerve gas sarin in the Tokyo underground, killing 12 and injuring 5,500.

**CHANNEL LINK** A set of postage stamps is issued in France and the UK to celebrate the completion of the Channel Tunnel.

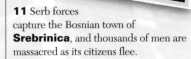

**3** In Operation *United Shield* UN troops pull out of **Somalia**, having failed to resolve the civilian distress caused by warring factions.

## APRIL

**19** The Alfred P. Murrah Federal Building in **Oklahoma City** is bombed, killing 168 people, apparently in revenge for federal action against the Waco ranch two years previously.

## MAY

**26** In Pale, Bosnia, local Serb troops take **UN soldiers** hostage to use as "human shields" against threatened bombing by NATO aircraft.

## JUNE

**24** The **rugby union World Cup** is won by the home nation, South Africa.

**25** The Bulgarian-American artist Christo wraps the **Reichstag** parliament building, Berlin, in fabric.

## JULY

**10** In Burma, the opposition leader **Aung San Suu Kyi** is released from house arrest, after six years.

**11** Serb forces capture the Bosnian town of **Srebrinica**, and thousands of men are massacred as its citizens flee.

## AUGUST

**25** At the world's largest **mass wedding,** 35,000 couples belonging to the Unification Church of World Christianity are married by Sun Myung Moon at the Olympic Stadium in Seoul.

## SEPTEMBER

**5** France begins a series of **atomic tests** on Mururoa in the South Pacific.

**10** The hanging of writer and human rights activist **Ken Saro-Wiwa** in Nigeria brings international condemnation.

## NOVEMBER

**4 Yitzhak Rabin**, Israel's prime minister, is shot dead by a young Jewish radical opposed to the peace settlements with the Palestinians.

**28** The Turner Prize for contemporary art is won by **Damien Hirst**, famous for his glass cases containing animals preserved in formaldehyde.

**30** President Bill Clinton makes the first visit by a U.S. president to **Northern Ireland**.

## DECEMBER

**14** The **Dayton Accords** for peace in Bosnia are signed in Paris. Bosnia becomes a federation of carefully mapped Muslim-Croat and Serb lands.

Quentin Tarantino's ***Pulp Fiction*** brings a new director-led edge to Hollywood movies.

**SOUTH AFRICA TRIUMPHANT** Nelson Mandela congratulates François Pienaar on leading South Africa to victory in the Rugby World Cup final.

# 1996

## JANUARY

**7** Over 100 die in the northeast U.S. in the worst **blizzards** in 70 years.

**21 Yasser Arafat** is elected president of Palestine.

**30** A bomb planted by **Tamil Tigers** kills 75 in Colombo.

## FEBRUARY

**9** The IRA signals the end of their 17 month ceasefire by detonating a huge bomb in the **Canary Wharf** area of London, killing two.

## MARCH

**2** The Liberal-National Coalition wins a landslide victory in Australia and **John Howard** becomes prime minister.

**13** A gunman kills 16 children and a teacher at an elementary school in **Dunblane**, Scotland.

**20** The **BSE crisis** erupts in Britain when the government announces that the fatal Creutzfeldt-Jakob disease may be connected to brain disease in cattle.

## APRIL

**13** The Israeli bombing of Palestinians in **southern Lebanon** intensifies, and 400,000 refugees flee the area.

**29** A gunman in **Hobart**, Tasmania, kills 35 people.

## MAY

**4** The European Space Agency's **Ariane-5** rocket is aborted shortly after takeoff from Kourou in French Guiana.

**16** The BJP Hindu-nationalist party forms a coalition government in India under the leadership of **Atal Behari Vajpayee**.

**31** Right-winger **Benjamin Netanyahu**, of the Likud Party, is elected prime minister of Israel, raising doubts about the progress of the peace initiative.

## JUNE

**15** A massive IRA bomb devastates the center of **Manchester**.

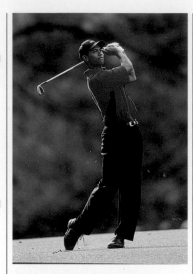

**NEW FACE IN GOLF** Age 21, Eldrick "Tiger" Woods wins the Masters golf tournament by the highest-ever margin of 12 strokes.
Background: For 40 years the royal yacht *Britannia* served as a symbol of British prestige.

## JULY

**18** A **TWA jet** explodes in midair off New York, killing all 228 on board.

**27** A **nail bomb** planted at the Olympic Games in Atlanta, Georgia, kills two.

## AUGUST

**28** Prince Charles and Princess Diana **divorce**.

## SEPTEMBER

**13 Gangsta rap** star Tupac Shakur dies, age 24, after a shooting incident, a victim of the kind of urban violence that was the focus of his music.

## OCTOBER

**13** The British driver **Damon Hill** wins the Formula One world championship.

**28** In Afghanistan, the **Taliban** (Sunni fundamentalists) take control of the capital, Kabul. The former president, Muhammad Najibullah, is executed in public.

## NOVEMBER

**5 Bill Clinton** is re-elected as president, but the Republicans retain majorities in both Houses of Congress and in the governorships.

## DECEMBER

**3** A rush-hour bomb in the **Paris Métro** kills two; Algerian Islamic fundamentalists are suspected.

# 1997

## JANUARY

**1 Kofi Annan** of Ghana becomes secretary-general of the UN.

## FEBRUARY

**22** A bio-technology laboratory in Scotland announces that it has produced a clone of a sheep, named **Dolly**.

## MARCH

**9** The British all-girl pop group, the **Spice Girls**, becomes the first to achieve four number one hits with their first four singles.

**11** Crisis erupts in **Albania** as rebel forces from the south close in on the capital, Tirana; refugees flood into Italy.

## APRIL

**13** Twenty-one-year-old **Eldrick "Tiger" Woods** becomes the youngest player ever to win the Masters golf tournament.

**23** Some 42 villagers are massacred as the confrontation between Islamists and the government in **Algeria** becomes ever more brutal and bloody.

## MAY

**2** In Britain, the Labor Party scores a resounding election victory over the Conservative government, and **Tony Blair** becomes prime minister.

In Zaire, opposition forces oust the despotic regime of President Mobutu, and their leader **Laurent Kabila** becomes president. Zaire is renamed the Democratic Republic of Congo.

## JUNE

**29** The disgraced boxer **Mike Tyson**, attempting a comeback, bites off part of the ear of his opponent, Evander Holyfield.

**30 Hong Kong** is formally handed back by Britain to China.

## JULY

**4** The U.S. probe Pathfinder lands on **Mars** to analyze the composition of rocks using a remote-controlled vehicle.

**18** Hungary, the Czech Republic and Poland are admitted into **NATO**.

Thailand's **economy** falters, the first signs of a slump that engulfs the Tiger economies over the next 18 months.

## AUGUST

**15 Timothy McVeigh** is sentenced to death for carrying out the Oklahoma bombing in 1995.

**31 Princess Diana**, former wife of Prince Charles and mother of his two sons, dies in a car crash in Paris.

## SEPTEMBER

**5 Mother Teresa of Calcutta** dies at 87.

## OCTOBER

**1** A ceasefire is called in **Algeria** but is ignored; some 65,000 have died in political savagery since 1992.

## NOVEMBER

**17** Islamic terrorists kill 58 foreign tourists in a **machine-gun attack** near Luxor in southern Egypt.

**25** The **royal yacht** *Britannia* is decommissioned on grounds of cost.

## DECEMBER

**12** South Korea, with the 11th largest economy in the world, receives a **$57 billion rescue package** from the IMF to save its ailing economy.

**LIVING SAINT** Mother Teresa devoted her life to the poor and dying in India. Her death was overshadowed by that of Princess Diana a few days before.

# 1998

## JANUARY

**17** President Clinton denies that he had an affair with 21-year-old White House intern **Monica Lewinsky** in 1995.

## FEBRUARY

**1** The first visit by the Pope to communist **Cuba** comes to a close.

## MARCH

**10** An exodus begins in **Kosovo**, Yugoslavia, as action by the Kosovo Liberation Army provokes retaliation by Serb forces.

## APRIL

**6** Britain and France ratify the **Comprehensive Test Ban Treaty**.

**10** The **Good Friday Agreement** lays the foundations for a democratic power-sharing assembly and a lasting peace in Northern Ireland.

**15 Pol Pot**, the former Khmer Rouge leader, dies at 73.

## MAY

**5** In the U.S., the **Unabomber**, Theodore Kaczynski, is given four life terms in prison for killing and injuring 29 people between 1978 and 1995.

**11** The ruling Hindu-nationalist coalition in India orders the **testing of five atomic bombs** in north-western India.

**29** Pakistan responds to India's **atomic tests** by carrying out its own series of tests.

## JUNE

**9 General Sani Abacha**, military dictator and president of Nigeria since 1993, dies at 54.

**18** Figures for the Japanese economy show that it is in **recession** for the first time since the 1974 oil crisis.

**FRANCE TRIUMPHANT** France wins the soccer World Cup with a 3-0 victory over Brazil in the final.

## JULY

**12** The home team, France, wins the **World Cup** soccer competition.

**17** The remains of **Tsar Nicholas II** and his wife and three daughters are reburied in St. Petersburg.

## AUGUST

**2** The **Tour de France** cycling race ends in fiasco amid accusations of the use of performance-enhancing drugs.

**14 Terrorist bombs** explode near the U.S. embassies in Nairobi and Dar es Salaam, killing over 200.

**15** A bomb is detonated in **Omagh**, Northern Ireland, by a breakaway republican group calling themselves the Real IRA, killing 28 people.

**27** President Clinton orders **cruise missile attacks** on targets in Sudan and Afghanistan in retaliation for the Nairobi and Dar es Salaam bombs.

## SEPTEMBER

**27** Helmut Kohl, for 16 years the chancellor of Germany, is defeated in an election by the Social Democrat candidate, **Gerhard Schröder**, in coalition with the Green Party.

## OCTOBER

**15** David Trimble and John Hume receive the **Nobel peace prize** for their efforts to resolve the conflict in Northern Ireland.

**16 General Pinochet**, former dictator of Chile, is detained in London pending extradition hearings demanded by Spain.

**29 John Glenn**, age 77, the first astronaut to make an orbit of the Earth in 1962, returns to space on board the Shuttle *Discovery*.

**29** South Africa's **Truth and Reconciliation Commission** delivers its report, and accuses both the apartheid regime and the ANC of crimes and human rights abuses.

## NOVEMBER

**1 Hurricane Mitch** causes massive inundation and mudslides in Honduras, Guatemala and Nicaragua, claiming over 10,000 lives.

**24** The World Health Organization announces that 33 million people in the world are living with **HIV**.

## DECEMBER

**17** U.S. and British forces begin a four-day **aerial bombardment** of Iraq's military facilities in response to Saddam Hussein's repeated obstruction of UN arms inspectors.

**19** Congress approves two counts of **impeachment** against President Clinton arising over the Monica Lewinsky affair. The case passes to the Senate for trial.

# 1999

## JANUARY

**1** The European single currency, the **euro**, is launched. Participating countries are Austria, Belgium, Germany, Finland, France, Ireland, Italy, Luxembourg, the Netherlands, Portugal and Spain.

## FEBRUARY

**7 King Hussein** of Jordan dies after a 47 year reign, and is succeeded by his son, Prince Abdullah.

**12** President Clinton is **acquitted** by the Senate of perjury and obstruction of justice, evading impeachment.

## MARCH

**12** Poland, Hungary and the Czech Republic officially become full members of **NATO**.

**15** Jacques Santer and the EU commissioners **resign en masse** over a report on fraud and incompetence.

**24 NATO launches airstrikes** against Serbian military targets in support of the Kosovo Albanians.

## JUNE

**20 NATO calls off** its air campaign against Serbia, after assurances that all Serbian troops have left Kosovo.

**JORDAN MOURNS** King Hussein of Jordan, a force for stability and dignity in the Middle East, is mourned throughout his country.

# INDEX

# ACKNOWLEDGMENTS

Abbreviations:
T=top; M= middle; B= bottom;
L= left; R= right.

3 Allsport, L; Ronald Grant Archive, LM; Corbis/Everett, RM; Sygma/Franken, R. 6 Topham Picturepoint, TR; David King Collection, BL. 7 CORBIS/Bettmann, TR; Corbis/Bettmann/UPI, BR. 8 Hulton Getty, TL; John Walmsley, BL; Sygma/Stuart Franklin, BR. 9 Kobal Collection, TR. 10 Ronald Grant Archive, TL. 10-11 Science Photo Library. 11 Tony Stone, TR. 12 Popperfoto, TL. 13 Magnum Photos, TR; Popperfoto, B. 14 Topham Picturepoint, T; Sygma, MR. 15 Popperfoto; Magnum Photos/Gilles Peress, L; Rex Features, LM; Topham Picturepoint, RM; Magnum Photos/Philip Jones Griffiths, R. 16 Magnum Photos/James Nachtwey, BL. 17 Popperfoto, TL; Magnum Photos/Marc Riboud, BR. 18 Sally and Richard Greenhill, TL; Sygma, MR, Magnum Photos, B. 19 Popperfoto, TR; Magnum Photos, BR. 20 Sygma, T; Sally and Richard Greenhill, ML. 21 Magnum Photos/Gilles Peress, BL; Suddeutscher Verlag, M. 22 Sygma, TL, TM; Topham Picturepoint, BR. 22-23 Sygma. 23 Sygma, TL. 24 Magnum Photos, MR, B. 25 Magnum Photos, TL; Rex Features, T. 26 Topham Picturepoint, TL; Popperfoto, M. 27 Magnum Photos/Raymond Depardon, T; AKG, BR; Rex Features, BL. 28 Suddeutscher Verlag, TR; AKG, BL; Topham Picturepoint, M. 29 Sygma, ML; Magnum Photos, BR. 30 Topham Picturepoint, BL; Rex Features, TR. 30-31 Rex Features. 32 Network/Judah Passow, TR; Sygma, MR; Popperfoto, BL. 33 Suddeutscher Verlag, TL; Popperfoto, TR; Rex Features, B. 34 Rex Features, R. 35 Popperfoto, BR; Suddeutscher Verlag, MR. 36 Rex Features, ML. 36-37 Popperfoto; Hulton Getty, TR. 38 Rex Features, TM; AKG, M. 39 Popperfoto, TR; Rex Features, BM; Sygma, B. 40 © H. David Seawell/CORBIS, TL; Hulton Getty, TR; Network/Judah Passow, B. 41 Magnum Photos, TR; Network, B. 42 Sygma, TR, MR. 43 Action Images; Pictorial Press Images/J. Mayer, L; Saatchi Gallery, London, LM; Topham Picturepoint, RM; Sygma/R.Bossu, R. 44 Mirror Syndication International, R. 45 Hulton Getty, R; Topham Picturepoint, M. 46 Popperfoto, TL; Sally and Richard Greenhill, B. 47 Magnum Photos/Chris Steele-Perkins, TL; Magnum Photos/Eli Reed, R. 48 Sygma/R. Bossu, TR; Sally and Richard Greenhill, BL. 49 Magnum Photos/Alex Webb, TL; Amnesty International, BR. 50 © Bob Witkowski/CORBIS TR; © Peter Turnley/CORBIS, BL.

51 Rex Features, TR, BL. 52 Still Pictures/Nigel Dickinson, M; Topham Picturepoint, BL. 53 Format/Jacky Chapman, TL; Magnum Photos/Rene Burri, BR. 54 Format, TR; Sally and Richard Greenhill, BL. 55 Magnum Photos/Steve McCurry, TL, MR. 56 Hulton Getty, BR. 57 Rex Features, TR; Sygma, MR. 58 Pictorial Press/Jeffrey Mayer, TR; Format/Val Wilmer, BL; Hulton Getty, BM; Redferns/Elliott Landy, BR. 59 Corbis/Steve Jennings, TM; Sygma, MR; Redferns, BM; Pictorial Press, BL. 60 Robert Opie, TL; Pictorial Press, MR, BL. 61 Pictorial Press, B. 62 Redferns, TR; Cameron Macintosh/DeWynters, MR; Corbis/UPI, BL. 63 Topham Picturepoint, BR, ML. 64 Corbis/David Allen, TL; Corbis/Bettmann, BM; Sygma/R. Hartog, BR. 65 Sygma, TL; Topham Picturepoint, BR. 66 Topham Picturepoint, ML; Popperfoto, TM; Corbis/Everett, BR. 67 Sygma, TL; Kobal Collection, ML, MR. 68 Sygma, BL; Popperfoto, M. 69 Corbis/Reuter, MR; Saatchi Gallery, London, BL. 70 Bite Communications, BL, B. 71 Sally and Richard Greenhill, BL, BR; Magnum Photos/Stuart Franklin, MR. 72 Sally and Richard Greenhill, TR; © Todd Gipstein/CORBIS, BL. 73 Sygma, BR. 74 E.T. Archive, MR; Corbis/UPI, B. 75 Magnum Photos, T; Still Pictures/Dylan Garcia, BL; Ajax News and Feature Service, BR. 76 Still Pictures/Hartmut Schwarzbach, BL. 77 Allsport, TR; Colorsport, ML; Sygma/Jean-Pierre Laffont, B. 78 Colorsport, TL; Allsport, BR. 79 Allsport, TM; Corbis/Bettmann/ UPI, BR. 80 Corbis/UPI, ML; Allsport, R. 81 Colorsport, TL; Allsport, BR. 82 © Adam Woolfitt/CORBIS, BR; © Bettmann/CORBIS, TL. 83 Sygma/Stuart Isett; SPL/Tom Myers, L; Magnum/Abbas, LM; John Frost Newpapers, RM; Popperfoto, R. 84 Advertising Archives, TR; Still Pictures/Mark Edwards, BL. 85 Popperfoto, TR; © Bettmann/CORBIS, BL. 86 Advertising Archives, TR; Sygma, BL; Format/Raissa Page, BR. 87 © Morton Beebe, S.F./CORBIS, TL; © Fotografia, Inc./CORBIS, BR. 88 Magnum Photos, BL; Popperfoto, ML. 89 Format/Sheila Gray, ML; © Bettmann/CORBIS, TR; Sygma/O. Franken, BR. 90 Magnum Photos, BL; Still Pictures, MR. 91 Magnum,TL; Popperfoto, ML; Still Pictures, BR. 92 Still Pictures, TL; Popperfoto, B. 92-93 Magnum Photos/Paul Lowe, B. 93 Magnum/Paul Lowe. 94 Magnum Photos/Stuart Franklin, TL. 94-95 Sygma/Patrick Robert, B. 95 Sygma, ML; Sygma/Les Stone, TR; Format/Brenda Prince, BR. 96 Magnum Photos/Ian Berry, TR; Sygma, B. 97 Magnum Photos/

Marilyn Silverstone, BL; Magnum Photos/Abbas, BR. 98 Corbis/Bettmann/UPI, TL, M; Sygma/J. Latlan, BR. 99 Sygma/Moshen Shandiz, TL; Magnum Photos, B. 100 Sygma/Peter Marlow, ML; Popperfoto, B; Sygma, TR. 101 © Peter Turnley/CORBIS,L, R. 102 Magnum Photos/Steve McCurry, ML, BR. 103 Sygma/Robert King, TR; Magnum/Steve McCurry, B. 104 Sygma, ML, TR. 104-5 Hulton Getty, B. 105 Hulton Getty, BR. 106 Sygma, TL; Corbis/Bettmann/Reuter, BL; John Frost Newspapers, MR. 107 Corbis/Bettmann, BR. 108 Hulton Getty, TR; Corbis, BR. 108-9 AKG, B. 109 Popperfoto, TR. 110 Magnum Photos/Ian Berry, T; Topham Picturepoint, BR. 111 Sygma, ML; Topham Picturepoint, BR. 112 Sygma/R. Bossu, T. Bradbury and Williams, BR. 113 Topham Picturepoint, TR; Magnum Photos/Paul Lowe, BL. 114 Bradbury and Williams, TR; Popperfoto/AFP, B. 115 Sygma/Patrick Chauvel, TL; Popperfoto, BR. 116 Topham Picturepoint/The Image Works, TR; Sygma, B. 117 Popperfoto, TM; Topham Picturepoint, MR; Sygma, BR. 118 Bradbury and Williams, TR; Topham Picturepoint, BL. 119 Sygma/Raymond Reuter, BR; Popperfoto, Background. 120 Science Photo Library/Tom Myers. 121 Rex Features/Simon Walker, TL; Sygma/Jacques Langevin, BR. 122 Still Pictures, B. 123 Sygma/Arnie Sachs, TR; Magnum/Abbas, BL. 124 Corbis/Bettmann/Agence France Presse, TR; Sygma/Jacques Langevin, ML. 124-5 AKG/AP Background. 126 Network/Peter Jordan, BL. 127 Still Pictures, TL; Magnum Photos/Gilles Peress, BR. 128 Corbis/Bettman/UPI, TM; Magnum Photos/Philip Jones Griffiths, BL. 129 Network/Roger Hutchings, MR; Magnum Photos, Raghu Rai, BL. 130 Corbis, BL; Magnum Photos/Raghu Rai, TR. 131 Popperfoto, B. 132 Sygma/Reza, T. 133 Corbis/Bettmann, T; Magnum Photos/G. Mendel, BR. 134 Sygma, TR, BM. 135 Joel Robine, B; © AFP/CORBIS, T. 136 Popperfoto/Reuters, BL; Ronald Grant Archive, MR. 137 Sygma/Jacques Langevin, BL; Popperfoto, MR. 138 Rex Features/Tim Rooke, TL; Corbis/Bettmann, BM; Sygma/Vladimir Velengurin, TR. 139 Popperfoto, T; Corbis/AFP, BR. 140 Science Photo Library, TL, BR. 141 Magnum Photos, M; Popperfoto, Background. 142 Popperfoto, ML. 142-3 Magnum Photos/Gilles Peress, Background. 143 Sygma, TR; John Meek, M. 144 Redferns, ML; Roger-Viollet, TR. 144-5 Hulton Getty Background. 145 Magnum Photos/Peter Marlow, TL; Topham Picturepoint, BR. 146 Rex Features, ML. 146-7 Popperfoto, Background.

147 Colorsport, TR; Topham Picturepoint/Press Association, ML. 148 Allsport, ML. 148-9 Colorsport, Background. 149 Magnum/Fred Mayer, TM; Popperfoto, MR; Topham Picturepoint, BL. 150 Rex Features, TM, BR. 150-1 Corbis/Bettmann, Background. 151 Corbis/Bettmann, ML; Popperfoto/Reuters, BM; Popperfoto/AFP, TR. 152 Corbis/Bettmann/Reuters, BL; Popperfoto, TR. 152-3 Rex Features, Background. 153 Popperfoto, BR. 154 Allsport/David Cannon, TL; Topham Picturepoint, BR. 154-5 Topham Picturepoint, Background. 155 Colorsport/Andrew Cowie, TL; Rex Features, BR.

Front cover: Sygma, top; Magnum Photos, middle; Allsport, bottom.

Back cover: Corbis/Bettmann, top; Popperfoto, middle; Pictorial Press, bottom.

The editors are grateful to the following individuals and publishers for their kind permission to quote passages from the publications below:

The Long Bow Group, taken from the film *The Gate of Heavenly Peace*, 1995, interviews by Carma Hinton, extract from account by Zhao Hongliang (a worker).
National Geographic, 1982, article by Allen A. Boraiko.
Andreas Ramos from *Personal Account of the Fall of the Berlin Wall: the 11th and 12th of November*, 1989 (Http://www.andreas.com/berlin.html).
The Spectator, August, 1979, article by Alistair Horne.
Vintage, an imprint of The Random House Group Ltd, from *An Evil Cradling* by Brian Keenan, 1992.